THE FUNAMBULISTS

Gender, Culture, and Politics in the Middle East
miriam cooke, Simona Sharoni, and Suad Joseph, *Series Editors*

For a full list of titles in this series,
visit https://press.syr.edu/supressbook-series
/gender-culture-and-politics-in-the-middle-east/.

THE
FUNAMBULISTS

Women Poets of the Arab Diaspora

LISA MARCHI

Syracuse University Press

First Edition 2022

22 23 24 25 26 27   6 5 4 3 2 1

∞ The paper used in this publication meets the minimum requirements
of the American National Standard for Information Sciences—Permanence
of Paper for Printed Library Materials, ANSI Z39.48-1992.

For a listing of books published and distributed by Syracuse University Press,
visit https://press.syr.edu/.

ISBN: 978-0-8156-3755-4 (hardcover)
       978-0-8156-3752-3 (paperback)
       978-0-8156-5547-3 (e-book)

Library of Congress Cataloging-in-Publication Data

Names: Marchi, Lisa, author.
Title: The funambulists : women poets of the Arab diaspora / Lisa Marchi.
Description: First edition. | Syracuse, New York : Syracuse University Press, 2022. |
    Series: Gender, culture, and politics in the Middle East | Includes bibliographical
    references and index.
Identifiers: LCCN 2022012340 (print) | LCCN 2022012341 (ebook) |
    ISBN 9780815637554 (hardcover ; alk. paper) | ISBN 9780815637523
    (paperback ; alk. paper) | ISBN 9780815655473 (ebook)
Subjects: LCSH: Poetry, Modern—Women authors—History and criticism. |
    Poetry, Modern—Arab authors—History and criticism. | Women and literature. |
    LCGFT: Literary criticism.
Classification: LCC PN1091 .M37 2022 (print) | LCC PN1091 (ebook) |
    DDC 809.1/99287089927—dc23/eng/20220509
LC record available at https://lccn.loc.gov/2022012340
LC ebook record available at https://lccn.loc.gov/2022012341

Manufactured in the United States of America

To Beirut and its worldly-wise people,
for granting me each time
the beauty of a new beginning

ففي السفر الحر بين الثقافات
قد يجد الباحثون عن الجوهر البشريّ
مقاعدَ كافية للجميع . . .
هنا هامش يتقدَّم. أو مركاز يتراجع
لا الشرقُ شرقٌ تماماً
ولا الغربُ غربٌ تماماً
لأن الهويَّة مفتوحة للتعدُّد
لا قلعة أو خنادقَ/
محمود درويش، طباق [إلى إدوارد سعيد]

By travelling freely across cultures
those in search of the human essence
may find a space for all to sit. . . .
Here a margin advances. Or a center
retreats. Where East is not strictly east,
and West is not strictly west,
where identity is open onto plurality,
not a fort or a trench/

Mahmoud Darwish, "Edward Said:
A Contrapuntual Reading"

Contents

Acknowledgments

This book benefited from the knowledge, support, and encouragement of many colleagues and friends. My greatest debt goes to Giovanna Covi for years of friendship, guidance, and close collaboration. I wish to acknowledge the University of Trento, Department of Humanities, for providing funding and support services for the development of this book, and the permanent poetry seminar SEMPER directed by Pietro Taravacci and Francesco Zambon for being a stimulating arena for discussion. The JFK Institute at the Free University in Berlin offered a research grant that proved invaluable for the realization of this project, while the Center for Transdisciplinary Gender Studies at the Humboldt University granted time and space to develop this study. I thank both institutions for their support.

Many of the questions explored in this book have been inspired by the colloquia and seminars organized by Giorgio Mariani and Donatella Izzo at the OASIS Summer School (University of Naples, L'Orientale) on the Island of Procida. My participation to the international research groups Behind the Looking Glass: Other-Cultures-Within Translating Cultures and Out of the Ordinary: Challenging Commonplace in Anglophone Literature offered inspiring insights and exchanges. I am grateful to Joan Anim-Addo (Goldsmiths, University of London) and Joel Kuortti (Turku University, Finland) for inviting me to join these groups.

This project would not have been possible without the support and generosity of friends and colleagues in Beirut and abroad. I wish to thank the staff at the AUB (in particular Carla Chalhoub) and at the OIB for facilitating my library access during the days of the revolution. My warmest gratitude to Rula Jurdi Abisaab, Gerardo Acerenza, Pirjo Ahokas, Hazim Alabdullah, Elisabetta Benigni, Andrea Carosso, Tamara T. Chin, Cristina

Dozio, Ira Dworkin, Amina Elhalawani, Leela Gandhi, Nathalie Handal, Sirène H. Harb, Michelle Hartman, Rana Issa, Mina Karavanta, Musa Khamushi, William G. Martin, Henry Matthews, Samuela Pagani, Rajagopalan Radhakrishnan, Fatima Sai, Cinzia Schiavini, and Mirella Vallone for their encouragement and support. I owe special thanks to Georges Abou-Hsab and Prashant Keshavmurthy for their enduring friendship, generous reading, and insightful comments on earlier drafts of some of the chapters included in this book. I also would like to acknowledge the colleagues of the Italian Association for American Studies (AISNA) and the Italian Society for the Study of the Middle East (SeSaMO) for sharing thoughts and critiques.

Sections of this volume have been presented at conferences in Washington, DC, at Cairo University, El Jadida University in Morocco, the AUB, the University of Catania, and the University Eastern Finland. I wish to thank the organizers and participants of the AGYA conference Destruction/(Re)construction: Interdisciplinary Perspectives on Cultural Heritage in Conflict, particularly Julia Hauser, Konstantin Klein, Lena-Maria Möller, Mohammad Alwahaib, Bilal Orfali and Stefan Tobias Maneval for rich conversations and exchanges. I am grateful to the organizers and participants of the Conceptions and Configurations of the Arabic Literary Canon workshop organized at the Columbia Global Center in Paris for providing meaningful feedback. My heartfelt appreciation to Muhsin al-Musawi, Claire Gallien, Sara R. bin Tyeer, Abdelfattah Kilito, Marina Warner, Omnia El Shakry, Lara Harb, and Marwa Elshakry for their enthusiasm, advice, and support.

I owe the editorial team at Syracuse University Press, especially Acquisition Editor Margaret Solic and the anonymous reviewers, my thanks for careful reading and essential suggestions.

Last but not least, I wish to thank my family and close friends for their unfaltering love and trust.

Parts of this book have appeared previously in print. I am grateful for the permission to reprint this material here.

A section of chapter 1 first appeared in Italian as "Dis/Equilibri: Districare il nodo genere e potere nella poesia araba diasporica," in *Districare il nodo genere-potere: sguardi interdisciplinari su politica, lavoro, sessualità e cultura*, ed. Elisa Bellè, Barbara Poggio, Giulia Selmi (Trento: Università degli Studi di Trento, 2015), 313–330. Reprinted with permission by the editors.

An earlier, shorter version of chapter 3 was published as "Emerging from the Darkness: Mina Boulhanna's 'Immigrata' and 'Africa,'" in *Cultures and Languages in Contact IV*, ed. Reddad Erguig, Abdelaziz Boudlal, Abdelkader Sabil, and Mohamed Yeou (Rabat: Editions Bouregreg, 2017), 269–76. Reprinted with permission by Faculté des Lettres et des Sciences Humaines, Chouaib Doukkali University, El Jadida.

Excerpts of chapter 6 first appeared as "Radical Others in the New 'Contact Zone': Tensions, Breaks, Relations," ed. Joan Anim–Addo, Giovanna Covi, and Lisa Marchi, *Synthesis* 7 (2015): 27–32. Reprinted with permission by the editor of *Synthesis*.

Another section of chapter 6 was previously published in Italian as "Frammenti di interfede nella poesia arabo-americana contemporanea: Una lettura contrappuntistica," in *Faith in Literature: religione, cultura e identità negli Stati Uniti d'America*, ed. Mirella Vallone (Perugia: Morlacchi Editore, 2017), 131–44. Reprinted with permission by Morlacchi Editore.

———

Permission has been granted to reproduce poems and translations of poems, or portions of poems or texts in and by the following:

Quotations from the collection *Tender Spot: Selected Poems* by Naomi Shihab Nye are reprinted with the permission of the author, text copyright © 2015 Naomi Shihab Nye.

Excerpts from "Daily," "Yellow Glove," "Kansas," and "Going for Peaches, Fredericksburg, Texas" from *Words under the Words: Selected Poems* by Naomi Shihab Nye, copyright © 1995. Used with permission of Far Corner Books.

Excerpts from "The Attic and its Nails" and "Valentine for Ernest Mann" from *Red Suitcase* by Naomi Shihab Nye, copyright © 1994. Reprinted with the permission of The Permissions Company, LLC on behalf of BOA Editions, Ltd., www.boaeditions.org.

Quotations from the collection *These Are Not Oranges, My Love* by Iman Mersal are reprinted with the permission of the author and editor, text copyright © 2008 Iman Mersal and Khaled Mattawa, Sheep Meadow Press.

Quotations in Arabic from the collections *Mamarr mu'tim yaşluh lita'llum al-raqs* by Iman Mersal are reprinted with the permission of the author, text copyright © 1995 Dār Sharqiyāt.

Quotations in Arabic from the collection *Jughrāfiyā badīla* by Iman Mersal are reprinted with the permission of the author, text copyright © 2006 Dār Sharqiyāt.

Quotations from "Immgrata" and "Africa" by Mina Boulhanna from *Nuovo Planetario Italiano* are reprinted with the permission of the editor, copyright © 2006 Città Aperta Edizioni.

Quotations from "Piove" by Gëzim Hajdari from *Ombra di cane / Hije qeni* are reprinted with the permission of the author, copyright © 1993 Gëzim Hajdari.

Quotations from the collection *Ce que vous ne lirez pas* by Nadine Ltaif are reprinted with the permission of the author and the editorial press, copyright © 2010 Le Noroît.

Maram al-Massri, selections in the original Arabic and translated by Khaled Mattawa, from *A Red Cherry on a White-Tiled Floor: Selected Poems*, copyright © 1997, 2000, 2004, 2007 by Maram al-Massri. Translation copyright © 2004, 2007 by Khaled Mattawa (Bloodaxe Books, 2004). Reprinted with the permission of The Permissions Company, LLC on behalf of Copper Canyon Press, coppercanyonpress.org and Bloodaxe Books, www.bloodaxebooks.com.

Quotations from the collections *breaking poems* (2008) and *ZaatarDiva* (2005) by Suheir Hammad are reprinted with the permission of the editorial press, text copyright © Suheir Hammad.

Quotations from "Moving towards Home" by June Jordan are reprinted with the permission of the editor, copyright © 2021 June M. Jordan Literary Estate from *The Essential June Jordan*, edited by Jan Heller Levi and Christoph Keller, Copper Canyon Press.

Quotations from the original Arabic version (Tibāq) and English translation of "Edward Said: A Contrapuntual Reading" by Mona Anis are reprinted with the permission of the Darwish Foundation and Minnesota University Press, text copyright © Darwish Foundation and Minnesota University Press.

Translated and paraphrased quotations from passages of *Ballando con Averroé* by Toni Maraini are reprinted with the permission of the editor, text copyright © Giuseppe Goffredo on behalf of Poiesis Editrice.

Note on Transliteration and Spelling

For the sake of consistency and accessibility, I have followed the conventions established by the International Journal of Middle Eastern Studies (IJMES).

THE FUNAMBULISTS

Introduction

Literary and Worldly Tensions

The Funambulists: Women Poets of the Arab Diaspora brings together and compares a selected group of poetry collections written by women poets who have lived part of their life either in an Arab country or in a first-generation Arab immigrants' family. Poets Naomi Shihab Nye, Iman Mersal, Mina Boulhanna, Nadine Ltaif, Maram al-Massri, and Suheir Hammad are contemporaries, yet, so far, they have never been considered together. All of them are positioned on a precarious edge and share the challenging experience of "living and writing on the threshold," as poet Mersal puts it.[1] They walk on a rope stretched taut above the globe to connect languages, cultures, and faiths in a time dramatically marked by physical distancing, divisions, and tensions of all sorts. Despite their distinctive places of origin, their different linguistic choices, and their unique life and work trajectories, the poets included in this book participate in a joint project of aesthetic re-vision aimed at poetically reimagining the ways in which we see ourselves, others, and the world.

While the book covers a good number of poets and texts, it does not aspire to be an anthology; it wishes instead to be recognized as a work of literary criticism, in which close readings of poetic texts act as a springboard for addressing broad literary matters—namely, the ancillary role (if compared to the novel) accorded to poetry, particularly to poems written by women and issuing from experiences of migration and diaspora; the aesthetic, social, and political significance of the chosen texts for different audiences (local, regional, global); and the impact of artworks created in the diaspora on how we regard, study, circulate, and critically evaluate

1

literary works, especially those that transcend the borders of the nation. Closely related to this final aspect are the effects produced by these texts on canon formations, on the organization of departments, and on current conceptualizations of world literature.[2]

In his introduction to the 2001 special PMLA issue on "Globalizing Literary Studies," Giles Gunn reflects on the changes introduced by global flows and networks in different fields of knowledge and provocatively asks: "What influence have such globalizing tendencies had on revising inherited notions not only of the literary and the aesthetic but also of the cultural and the historical? . . . In what specific way has this new sensitivity to the interconnections among discursive fields and expressive practices, in and across cultures and in and across periods, changed the object of knowledge in literary studies?"[3] This volume attempts precisely to find an initial and partial answer to these complex questions, by closely examining literary works that came into being in the Arab diaspora.

Unlike most studies that deal with the Arab diaspora more generally,[4] and with Arab American and Arab Anglophone literatures more particularly, this book follows a transnational and multilingual approach comparing texts written in English, Arabic, French, and Italian, with the aim of exposing their peculiarities, while also acknowledging potential points of contact.[5] Where available, I have used existing translations; in the case of untranslated texts, I have included my own English translations.[6] Again, the selection of poets writing in English, French, Arabic, and Italian makes no pretense of being exhaustive or particularly original. One should note, however, that I have purposefully not included texts written in the languages of the two major nations within Europe, France and Germany, opting instead to analyze the poetry of Ltaif, who lives in Québec and writes in what is considered to be a minority language within North America. Likewise, my reading of Boulhanna's two poems written in Italian—a minor language within Europe—is meant to shift the readers' attention from Europe's center to its often despised southern periphery.

In line with Edward Said's idea of the "contrapuntal," I have congregated in this book different poetic voices with no intention of harmonization but rather in an attempt to emphasize the uniqueness of each single voice.[7] The wider, underlying scope of this project is to avoid using circumscribed national and linguistic categories to identify the selected writers and to refrain from confining their literary works within imprisoning compartments, such as "migrant writing" or "ethnic literature." The study further wishes to challenge conventional readings of national literatures, histories, and languages as complete in themselves and standing happily on their own, with the label "migrant writing" being employed reluctantly by some critics to refer, at the most, to an annoying appendix they would gladly do without. This is why I have selected poets and texts that defy easy classifications and that metaphorically refuse to "stand still."

Together with Jahan Ramazani, I share the conviction that an analysis of poetry aspiring to be truly transnational must take into consideration the macroscopic as well as microscopic dimensions, addressing both "circuits of poetic connection and dialogue across political and geographic borders,"[8] as well as "aesthetic particulars without which the poetry of poetry would be lost."[9] I will embrace this bifocal approach throughout this book.

"Diaspora" as a theoretical term that resists qualification and refuses to be pinned down is at the core of this project.[10] Texts issuing from the diaspora oscillate between the local and the global, the here and the elsewhere, contesting fixed origins, a univocal sense of belonging, and monolithic identities. Yet, as the book's subtitle suggests, this study performs a rather unusual shift from identity to space. This is in line with the book's content, particularly with its detailed and reiterated discussion of the theme of im/mobility, with its attempts to fashion an alternative, subjective and poetic, revision of geography, and with its bottom-up and creative reconfigurations of atlases and collective imaginaries.[11] For a long time, diaspora has been considered an exclusive, even if dolorous, condition of a specific group, the Jewish one. By defining diaspora also as "Arab," my aim has been to underline the fact that innumerable individuals and groups today have to endure forced removal, displacement, and dispersal across the globe. Undoubtedly, these experiences leave devastating marks on the psychological, material, and affective level; from an aesthetic perspective, however, they can also be extremely fruitful. In the next section, I will explore further the tension between rupture and creation.

Tension

The book is built on the concept of "tension," recently theorized by Cristoph F. E. Holzhey as "an unstable equilibrium on the verge of transformation, providing the condition, energy, and direction for processes that can be productive as well as destructive."[12] A concept borrowed from physics and theorized, among others, by scientist and historical of science Thomas S. Kuhn, "tension" is a key term also for Islamologist Mohammed Arkoun and for philosopher Jacques Derrida. I build my own critical work on their theories and employ the concept of tension to illuminate both the breaking points and the creative energies that traverse the poetic production under examination. The concept is deployed likewise to regard the contemporary world fraught with tensions. I see both the texts and the planet as being traversed by potentially productive yet also destructive tensions, urgently demanding that we take charge of them.

In *The Essential Tension* (1977), Kuhn argues that tension—and, more specifically, the tension between convergent and divergent thinking, tradition and innovation—represents an essential force propelling the advancement of scientific thought. To quote Kuhn: "Only investigations firmly rooted in the contemporary scientific tradition are likely to break the tradition and give rise to a new one. That is why I speak of an 'essential tension' implicit in scientific research."[13] Moving from the sciences to the humanities, Arkoun employs tension both as a method of analysis and as an object of study in itself to rethink Islamic Studies in more dynamic terms. In his foreword to the English translation of Arkoun's work *Ouvertures sur l'Islam* (1992), Robert D. Lee underlines Arkoun's revolutionary look, by explaining: "For Arkoun, the history of Islamic society is inextricably linked with that of the West: There is no dichotomy between Western reason and Islamic reason. The two have fed upon each other."[14] Rather than conceiving faith and reason, divine Revelation and its human enactments, Islam, Judaism, and Christianity, Shi'ism and Sunnism, West and East in opposition, Arkoun tirelessly foregrounds in his works the vital exchanges, historical entanglements, and modern ruptures characterizing the relation between the two.

An uncompromising thinker, working constantly on the edge of a variety of languages, cultures, and disciplines, Arkoun, in *Essays sur la Pensée Islamique* (1973), considers Islamic thought as being inextricably bound to rather than in conflict with other cultural and religious movements and develops the notion of *"tradition vivante"* (living tradition) to foreground the creative, animated, and dynamic character of Islamic studies as a discipline filled with its own inconsistencies, contradictions, and paradoxical elements.[15] A visionary in his own way, Arkoun foresees in the lively and dialectical character of Islamic societies the seeds of a potentially revolutionary effervescence, which we witnessed during the first (2010–11) and second wave of protests (2019) that have stormed the Arab region. As Arkoun writes in his 1973 work: "Contemporary Muslim society is in its full revolutionary effervescence. To approach and understand it, it is important to situate oneself within its own perspective which is socio-dynamic and dialectical."[16]

The poetic collections analyzed in these pages are also traversed by a similar revolutionary effervescence. While partaking in a common and well-established poetic tradition—that of the lyric—the poets included in this book twist to their own purposes easily recognizable literary, linguistic, and stylistic conventions, while at the same time eroding classical literary genres and canonical forms, thus introducing not only formal but more substantial changes both in literature and in society. As we will see, a sense of deep indebtedness as well as a "filial lack of piety," to borrow Derrida's poignant expression, mark their writing indelibly.[17] This is why I employ the concept of "tension" to explore and illuminate the different pressures that traverse their texts. The figure of the funambulist personifies these tensions.

The Funambulists

The book revolves around seven poets-funambulists, who use their art of balance and flexibility together with a good portion of courage and transgression to walk a tightrope stretched out across continents, cultures, and faiths. These funambulists train patiently and make constant adjustments

to find a precarious balance in a world dangerously and increasingly lean-
ing toward extremism; they make incessant attempts to connect what from
below may appear simply as unreachable ends.

Since they are aware of at least two cultures, settings, and homes as
well as the gender differences that mark humanity, these poets embody a
Saidian "plurality of vision" that enables them to fruitfully contrast essen-
tialist and extremist claims.[18] These funambulists are indeed acquainted
with the danger of living one's specificity as a nonnegotiable difference
and of the subsequent rejection of the very idea of a common ground.
Hence, the everyday—as a simultaneously shared yet highly heterogeneous site of dwelling—becomes for them a sort of new canvas on which
to redraw with significant and at times surprising brushstrokes the bright,
connecting details of daily life that bind together individuals, collectivi-
ties, and histories.

Despite their different sociopolitical and geographical locations, their
distinctive stylistic choices, and multifarious imaginations, the poets
addressed in this book are pushed toward writing by a set of common
preoccupations, which are not only locally or regionally significant but
also globally relevant. In singular and complex ways, these poets address
issues of public concern by examining sentiments and affects. Opposition
against gender oppression and authoritarianism, historical depredation
and memory effacement, problems of religious practice and spirituality,
matters of race, class, gender and sexuality as well as the horrors of war,
colonialism, and ethnic cleansing resonate across their writings.

By developing a lucid and well-balanced poetics that is inclined,
responsive, and polyphonic, these poets-funambulists cannot but stand
out from a whole mass of stiff sovranists, religious fanatics, impassive autocrats, and dull technocrats. Far from cultivating the Andalusian myth of
communal life as happy *convivencia*, these poets put readers on guard
against the tensions and divisions that threaten our living together, showing, for instance, that the violent manifestations of the present may have
roots that extend into a widely forgotten yet still burning past. Through
an intricate and defamiliarizing poetics and the activation of unattractive affects, such as boredom, frustration, resentment, and nervousness,
these funambulists detect and intensify social and political ills that have

generally come to be accepted as normal. From the heights of their wire, readers clearly spot authoritarian drives and democracies in crisis, resurgent forms of obscurantism and fanaticism one thought buried forever, the danger posed by mythic origins and entrenched states as devilish "engines" producing harmful divisions, fatal exclusions, and devastating wars. Their funambolic art accords stunning vistas, yet each one of them performs a tightrope walk that is unique: either hesitant, audacious, or poised.

The Choice of Women

The book's exclusive focus on women poets and the poetic genre has been motivated by the need to delimit the territory of my analysis but also as an attempt to redress the gender imbalance and double invisibility that mark the condition of migrant women and their representation in the arts. This asymmetry and double invisibility has been lamented, among others, by scholars working in the social sciences such as Rutvica Andrijasevic and Monica Boyd.[19]

In migration and diaspora studies, women are generally underrepresented as agents and almost absent as poets; in diasporic literature, the novel is considered to be the diasporic genre par excellence. It follows that women and diasporic poetry are two emerging fields of interest that tend to remain separate; in this book, an attempt has been made to bridge this gap together with suggesting that the feminist claims uttered by the chosen poets offer the possibility to redefine politics in terms that are necessary and urgent for everybody.

As I am writing this book, I myself occupy the position of a precarious female scholar who feels rooted in one place but has been on the move for quite a while, both as a matter of choice but also out of necessity, and whose position within the academy is inflected by economic insecurity and by the act of juggling multiple jobs. This project was initially triggered by my particular interest in finding out the ways in which these poets managed to balance their life and work, endured everyday frustrations, and reacted to critical moments. "Dark times," as Hannah Arendt rightly notes in her 1968 collection of essays, *Men in Dark Times*, "are not only not new, they are no rarity in history."[20] I share with Arendt the conviction

that "even in the darkest of times we have the right to expect some illumination, and that such illumination may well come less from theories and
concepts than from the uncertain, flickering, and often weak light that
some men and women, in their lives and their works, will kindle under
almost all circumstances and shed over the time span that was given them
on earth."[21] I see the women included in this book as shedding that kind
of light.

To what extent, I ask in this book, do the selected poets help readers see
and grasp the dramatic transformations, structural problems, and numerous crises that we are currently witnessing? What is their contribution to
ongoing debates about politics and the political, migration and belonging,
gender and sexuality, individual and collective agency, violence and commemoration, the limits of policy choices and the potential of the imagination to cast better futures in terms of dignity, justice, and sustainability?
Finally, which kind of affects do these writers mobilize and why?

Let me forewarn readers that they will not find in this book prophetic
figures predicting cataclysmic events nor subversive intellectuals invoking
armed revolt. The poets at the center of this book are first and foremost
ordinary women, whose discreet poetic voices are often in conflict with
the rhetorical bombast of certain political pronouncements and, quoting Arendt again, the "'mere talk' that irresistibly arises out of the public realm."[22] Moreover, the affects they mobilize (i.e., tedium, weariness,
frustration) do not excite powerful sentiments nor inspire extraordinary
deeds. The events and people they describe are most of the time extremely
common and apparently unimpressive. Still, the feminist revision of the
everyday they stimulate in readers is radical and bound to last.

A Feminist Analysis of the Everyday

In her original reading of the works of the Beirut Decentrists—a group
of women writing in and about the Lebanese Civil War in the 1980s
and 1990s—Miriam Cooke argues that their decentered position within
the Lebanese nation together with their feminist analysis of the everyday allowed these writers to develop representations of the war that were
radically different from the ones produced by men, which accentuated

violence, chaos, and nonsense.[23] As Cooke writes in *War's Other Voices*: "Only women's literature which focuses on the dailiness of survival can capture and develop the subtleness of an irrationality that becomes categorized as madness if it is presented in black and white. Only feminine literature documents details that seem too trivial and personal to note. Yet these same details suggest transformations of feeling that finally weave, for each individual, the fabric of war experience."[24]

Thanks to their liminal position as insiders/outsiders and the female invocation of the intimate details of the everyday, the poets included in this book subtly disclose literary, social, and political aspects that would otherwise go unnoticed. By effect of a creative re-vision deeply rooted in the quotidian, these poets bring to light everyday injustices and inequalities, material devastations and human atrocities, thus stimulating in readers the desire for things to happen in a different way. Through an unusual, intricate and disorienting, aesthetics that assembles antithetical elements, demands active engagement on the part of readers, and often disrupts their expectations, these poets intervene rather than stay away from politics and the political.

In opposition to the media's largely spectacular and sensationalist coverage of global wars, refugee crises, natural disasters, and health emergencies, the poets considered in these pages favor a shrinking, less imposing approach. Some of them, for instance, write in fragments or opt for a minimalist form, while others describe "ambivalent situations of suspended agency" and mobilize affects such as boredom, delusion, and frustration in opposition to more excitable passions such as anger and terror.[25] Their minor, yet extremely incisive, responses to forms of denigration, marginalization, and institutional effacement produce an aesthetic change in the "regime of the visible" that stimulates an ethical rebellion and together with it the desire for a radical political change.[26] Their poetic reconfiguration is indeed not an automatic reaction to a given situation but rather a creative retelling that contributes to expose as well as shift the power dynamics that are at play. For example, by composing a poetry of testimony and memory that refuses to condone violence and avoids the danger of being manipulative or divisive, poets such as Ltaif and Hammad promote a hard labor of excavation, analysis, and ultimately reflection aimed at promoting a prise de conscience and an assumption of responsibility, which all together represent, according to Marianne Hirsch, "the first anti-war act."[27]

In the current political scenario marked by the COVID-19 pandemic, acclaimed negationist and sovranist leaders, global environmental risks, and the military confrontation of rival superpowers, the poets discussed in this book turn simultaneously inward and outward, writing with discretion not only about the widespread material devastations and the human desperation that follow war but also about the hushed desolation of a daughter sitting at her father's hospital bed and the imperceptible sense of abandonment experienced by a yellow glove, which a neglectful child lost on her way home. In sum, they patiently compose a polyphony out of soloist voices, by according full dignity to minor events and neglected places, people, and objects on earth.

Their invitation to zoom in and look more closely at the mechanisms that construct Others as threatening and out of reach comes together with an invitation to zoom out and extend one's horizon and hopes with the intention of finding alternatives to the spreading imperative of keeping Others at arm's length. In opposition to political discourses that circulate fear and predicate the benefits of social isolation, the poets considered here make endless attempts to heal divisions and bridge gaps, while also mobilizing affects such as mutual care and trust in place of the mounting consternation and distrust. In doing so, they produce a shift in perspective, urging readers to take on responsibility and collaborate through the performance of considerate and solicitous acts toward the construction of a more just, livable, and nonviolent community of planetary size.

The Redefinition of "Politics" and "the Political"

In open contrast to a plethora of political leaders who are self-absorbed if not self-interested, have lost touch with society at large, and are therefore unable to hear and respond to the disappointment, irritation, and exasperation that individuals and groups articulate at various levels, the funambulists included in this book bend down toward their public. In so doing, they show what politics is mostly lacking in its current manifestation:

inclination toward others, recognition, and concrete actions directed to assure a dignifying and flourishing life for all. These poets, in particular, demonstrate in different ways that a meaningful politics should work toward the common good and not be divisive. It should be capable of responding to the material and affective demands that arise in times of crisis and be able to discern what can be monetized and what cannot (e.g., public health and education, access to public spaces and services, the preservation of cultural heritages and natural resources, civil and political rights, the right to work and have a life worth of this name). To truly matter, in other words, politics should resituate human dignity, social justice, individual and collective well-being at the center of its agenda and outline a set of clear actions aimed at redressing the economic inequalities, violent exclusions, and human violations that the citizens bemoan. This is, at least, one of the lessons that the popular uprisings in Tunisia, Egypt, Algeria, and Lebanon—to name just a few examples of protests and movements that have involved the Arab region—should have taught us. And this, I argue in this book, is the perspective embraced and lyrically articulated by the poets addressed.

Because of the spreading disappointment with traditional politics, it is not surprising to find in this book individuals and groups who structurally lack institutional power or act outside contentious politics and formal institutional channels while carrying out micropolicies that are performed in the everyday.[28] The book shows that these individuals and coalitions are not passive and feeble but politically interested and mobilized actors, who have certain principles and solidarities, are capable of acting on their own behalf, and pursue a future of freedom, equality, dignity, and justice for all.

Having lost not only its purpose, but also its credibility and legitimacy, the agonizing political power embodied by frugal technocrats, irresponsible sovranists, and bloody autocrats appears in this book as a mere abstraction, a specter (sometimes benign, most of the time terrifying and despised) haunting with its ghostly presence the local and global community. Intrigued by the unusual perspectives granted by the impressive walks performed by these poets-funambulists, I suggest that a politics reduced to mere bureaucracy, economic rationality, and securitization or conceived and practiced in authoritarian ways can only produce more damages and harm; it can only incite fright, dismay, and rage in the people it rules. To thrive again, the political must put human dignity, equal opportunities, and economic well-being at the center of its agenda and work closely with its citizens to reduce the inequalities and injustices that make the life of so many people unbearable. This is the larger, overarching narrative to which the single analyses and chapters tie in.

Methodology

Since political claims are tightly enmeshed in the texts with intricate poetics, I employ in this study an interdisciplinary approach that spans from the humanities to the social sciences and includes, among others, the fields of literary theory and criticism, Arab and Islamic studies, philosophy, gender studies, sociology, and history. I further make use of a hybrid methodology that combines theoretical tools drawn from deconstruction, gender/sexuality studies, postcolonial studies, and the theories of the everyday. All these theories have indeed strived to spotlight and break down artificial boundaries and conceptual oppositions, such as writing vs. orality, man vs. woman, rationality vs. affects, the colonial metropolis vs. the colony, the extraordinary vs. the ordinary, inaugurating radical theoretical shifts and paradigmatic revisions that echo the aesthetic innovations and epistemic revolutions invoked and performed by the selected authors.

Readers will find throughout the book references to what are usually considered "big" names in critical theory, such as Jacques Derrida, Erich Auerbach, Edward Said, and Ngũgĩ wa Thiong'o. Through my textually engaged practice of critical analysis, my historically situated and contrapuntal reading of the poetic texts, and my genuine interest in the global dynamics through which texts and knowledges travel, get translated, and transform global imaginaries, I hope to prove that I do not merely invoke such big names but rather concretely engage with their theories. Within the field of gender and sexuality studies, I found both inspiration and method in the works of Black feminist writers and theorists such as June Jordan, Toni Morrison, and Audre Lorde, who have taught me to think across the intersecting axes of race, gender, sexuality, ethnicity, and class.

The writing of younger scholars of color, such as Daphne A. Brooks and Therí A. Pickens, who have explored corporeality, performativity, and bodily fragility, as well as the social and political outreach of dissenting corporeal practices, has also been incredibly stimulating. Judith Butler's groundbreaking work on sexuality and subversion, gender performativity, agency, and intentionality together with her more recent publications on individual and state violence, war, precariousness, and the difficulty (perhaps impossibility) of making sense of loss have deeply influenced the ways in which I approach and critically read the poetic collections included in this book. This is why I pay particular attention to performing acts of both discursive and embodied insurgency and interpret vulnerability as a resource—rather than an impediment—that enables new modes of personal connection.

Equally important is the affective and queer "turn" that has shaped gender studies in the past recent years. This study naturally takes up and continues a conversation first begun by feminist thinkers such as Lauren Berlant, Sara Ahmed, Heather Love, Judith Halberstam, Kathleen Stewart, and Jane Bennett, who have placed affects, ethics, and queerness at the center of their inquiry. I use the theoretical term "queer" in this book not to refer to actual forms of sexuality but to highlight the aesthetic deviations and political disruptions performed by the chosen poets in their collections. Given my double interest in the quotidian and the material, the theories of the everyday both from their early origins (with the Dada movement and the Surrealists) to their latest developments (with the Marxist thinkers Henry Lefebvre and Michel de Certeau, to name just a few representatives) occupy a crucial position in this book. Throughout, I have privileged affective, materialistic, and political readings of the selected texts inspired by postcolonial, feminist, and Marxist theories concerned mainly with the implications and complications of (neo)colonialism, patriarchy, and finance capitalism. I have avoided, on the contrary, psychoanalytical analyses that would be less in tune with the book's overall spirit.

Since this is first and foremost a book of literary criticism, it differentiates itself from existing anthologies on Arab-American poetry.[29] Its unique focus on the poetic genre and its transnational approach further distinguishes it from more recent critical works on Arab-American fiction, aesthetics, and the Arab Anglophone novel.[30] While my work relies on endeavors of all these studies, its inclusion of poetic texts in multiple languages, its bifocal (both micro- and macroscopic) approach, and its deployment of gender, affect, and especially queer theories distance it from the critical approaches of these other works. Among others, Nathalie Handal's transnational anthology *The Poetry of Arab Women* (2001) has provided a crucial reference, given its focus on women poets writing in multiple languages and living both in the Arab region and in the diaspora. Still, while her anthology introduces readers to the poetry written by women from across North Africa, the Middle East, and the diaspora, my study is geographically more circumscribed and analytically more deeply focused, as it considers not only the aesthetic particulars but also the political impact of the works under examination, relating literature to wider cultural and sociopolitical concerns and debates.

Encounters / Crossings / Breaks

The Funambulists is divided into six chapters grouped into three thematic parts of two chapters each: part 1 focuses on chance meetings taking place either in an enchanting (Nye) or in a stagnant (Mersal) everyday; part 2 takes into consideration maritime and oceanic crossings in Boulhanna's and Ltaif's poetry; part 3 emphasizes both aesthetic ruptures and radical political outlooks in al-Massri's and Hammad's poetry. The three parts—titled "Encounters," "Crossings," and "Breaks"—are not meant as divides between the authors but rather as keywords that resonate across the whole book and characterize, in different degrees, each single collection.

Part 1, "Encounters," opens with a critical reading of a selection of Nye's poems included in the collection *Tender Spot* (2008). I suggest that Nye's emphasis on small, ordinary objects and on everyday, domestic practices operates as a form of micropolitics that has powerful ethical and political implications, since it contributes to a reevaluation of "things" (human and nonhuman alike) that normally pass as lives that do not count. Nye's Palestinian heritage with its legacy of struggle that is carried out steadily on the ground through concrete daily actions and the use of material, quotidian objects is at the core of her aesthetic and political gesture, which is firmly rooted in the ordinary. Nye's supreme art of balance and extreme resourcefulness together with the far-reaching and simultaneously grounded perspective she offers to readers have pushed me to include her among the finest funambulists.

Chapter 2 closely reads and critically discusses a group of poems originally written in Arabic by Mersal and included in the collection *These Are Not Oranges, My Love* (2008) translated by Khaled Mattawa. A strong-willed funambulist, Mersal struggles to find a precarious balance on a rope stretched taut between genders, generations, and worldviews. As the poet narrates the considerable obstacles and challenges encountered by her female speaker in the here, she further captures the trials and tribulations that she faces and endures as a migrant in the elsewhere. The chapter moves from the personal to the political, sparking a discussion on the apathy and vexations caused by an obstructive political, while at the same time putting readers on guard against the all too pleased and self-congratulatory attitudes engendered by multicultural policies.

Part 2, "Crossings," opens with an analysis of two poems originally written in Italian by Mina Boulhanna and dating back to the 1990s. This backward look enables my reading of the two poems as paradigmatic of the slow yet powerful arrival of the migrant woman (as a yet-to-be poet) on the "scene" of writing. The chapter is built on the tension between invisibility and visibility, submersion and emergence, darkness and light. My intention in this chapter is to show what readers can gain when they accept to abandon the security and comfort of their habitual standpoint and follow Boulhanna on a tightrope stretched taut across the Mediterranean. As I celebrate Boulhanna's first, hesitant steps into the world of writing, I further call attention to the feelings of inadequacy, abandonment, and failure that may seize a funambulist like her.

The chapter dedicated to Boulhanna may look particularly "eccentric," since she is rather an obscure poet, if compared to the other more popular chosen writers. Still, Boulhanna is relevant to this book, since she is one of the first writers in the Italian context to have turned the reader's gaze toward "Africa" and to have challenged the historical construction of Italian literature, using Caterina Romeo's apt formulation, "as a white space."[31] Inspired by her daring act, I take the risk of juxtaposing

Boulhanna's neglected voice with that of a "world classic": T. S. Eliot's canonical poetic voice. The attempt aims to reveal unforeseen literary affinities between two poets that traditional reading practices would either mutually ignore or locate at the antipodes. Moreover, the irreverent act of placing an internationally acclaimed poet and a Nobel laureate along-side a little-known writer raises a set of thorny questions concerning not only Eliot and Boulhanna's distinctive positions within their respective national canons but also their role in the now à la mode category of world literature. Let me ask provocatively: Since Eliot chose to live almost his entire life abroad and drew from a variety of literary sources and languages to compose *The Waste Land*, how does his experience of expatriation and his practice of borrowing from multiple sources alter his iconic image as a premier US poet? Conversely, to what extent has Boulhanna's status as a migrant woman caught up in material challenges and with no multiethnic literary tradition to rely upon impacted negatively on her career as a poet?

These questions lead us to the digressions also included in Chapter 3 on two premodern notables: al-Idrisi and Ibn Rushd. The anecdote refer-ring to Ibn Rushd's burial, in particular, which Toni Maraini narrates in *Ballando con Averroè* (*Dancing with Ibn Rushd*) (2015), has no pretense of absolute veridicity yet is essential for propelling a rethinking of the Mediterranean Sea, and the Mediterranean basin more in general, from a battlefield and a graveyard to a vital site of bodily crossings and cultural cross-breedings. The fact that we may find this dynamic and interactive history strange and "embarrassing" says a lot about the need to change old paradigms. In opposition to the rather widespread belief, that sees Europe as wrapped up in itself and standing happily on its feet, the digressions on al-Idrisi and Ibn Rushd show that there are contagions—in the cultural field, for instance—that are not pestilential but beneficial and have histori-cally contributed to the circulation, increase, and advancement of human knowledge.

Chapter 4 focuses again on the present, by shifting the attention from Mediterranean to oceanic crossings, as performed in Ltaif's 2010 collec-tion *Ce que vous ne lirez pas* (*What You Will Not Read*). Far from idealiz-ing a mythic past and reinforcing existing divisions, Ltaif takes courageous steps forward on a global tightrope stretched taut above the Atlantic and

Indian Oceans with the aim to build networks of relations and convergences that promise to destabilize fixed and therefore potentially deadly identities and categories. In her search for poise, lightness, and grace, she proves to be an impeccable funambulist.

Al-Massri's poems, included in the bilingual Arabic-English collection *A Red Cherry on a White-Tiled Floor* (2004) translated by Khaled Mattawa, open part 3, "Breaks." A bold funambulist, al-Massri audaciously walks on the tightrope of love, training hard to find a precarious balance between two opposite poles: the pursuit of her speaker's physical pleasure and the standards of morality that regulate gender relations in conservative societies or deregulate them in neoliberal societies. Al-Massri's original combination of images and rhetorical expressions drawn from Islamic sources together with a lexicon of bodily parts and the activation of mutually exclusive affects, such as euphoria and delusion, make her sexual revolt unique, if compared to that of her literary predecessors and even contemporaries. Her immaculate yet abortive lyrics, which call to mind Sappho's censored compositions, further call attention to the unfortunate communality that monotheistic religions share with ancient Greek and Roman cultures, namely the attempt to put women under the control and custody of men.

As discussed in chapter 6, Hammad simultaneously pays tribute to and breaks down the iconic image of the Palestinian refugee, by creatively entwining her personal story of forced uprooting, displacement, and relocation with other traumatic experiences of violence and community dissolution. A fierce funambulist, Hammad takes intrepid steps on the global tightrope in the attempt to help readers see the destructive consequences of global violence but also the mobilizing force of poetry and its capacity to build networks of solidarity across racial, cultural, and religious divides. Chapter 6 closes with a discussion of the remarkable ways in which the funambulist Hammad breaks religion in the name of interfaith through the simultaneously disruptive and binding force of the poetic word.

The book ends with a reflection on the stunning vistas enabled by the art of these poets-funambulists, as a point of entry to discuss issues pertaining to the literary and the political dimensions, to our dark times and their representation in the arts, to the role of poetry in shaping a less catastrophic vision of our time. Throughout, the book endorses a far-flung though grounded practice of reading literary texts that intersects temporal plans and geographic areas usually seen as separate. In Wai Chee Dimock's apt formulation: "Literary space and time are conditional and elastic; their distances can vary, can lengthen or contract, depending on who is reading and what is being read. No mileage can tell us how far one author is from another; no dates can tell us who is close to whom."[32] Accordingly, some readers may be struck to find in chapter 2 the "degenerate" paintings and caricatures produced by the members of the Art et Liberté Group (*jamā'at al-fann wa al-ḥurriyya*), who were active in Egypt in the 1930s, juxtaposed with Mersal's often crude and bizarre poems composed at the dawn of the new millennium. Her mostly uneven and puzzling poetics evoke the rough and outlandish aesthetics of the so-called Egyptian Surrealists as well as their dream for a political comradeship that would be internationalist, anticolonial, and democratic in spirit.

After a long reflection, I have decided to eliminate national and linguistic labels (one exception being "Palestinian," for evident reasons) to pin down the artists and intellectuals included in this book. I find these categories limited, misleading, and incapable of communicating the complexity and intricacy of their life and work trajectories. Instead of confining the poets discussed in imprisoning categories, I invite readers to gradually retrace the fascinating web of intertextual connections, elective affinities, and political alliances that the individuals mentioned in this book have fashioned in the course of their life. For example, the fact that Derrida was born in Algeria as a member of a Jewish minority and is internationally recognized as a French intellectual—a labeling that renders his Algerianness, let alone his Arabness invisible—is relevant to this study, which favors complexity over simplification, self-crafted and adaptable forms of identification over clear-cut and imposed categories. Derrida's liminal position within Algeria and France, his geographical and disciplinary crossovers, and the dizzying vertigoes produced by his writing mirror to a certain extent the edgy positions, poetic innovations, and epistemic shifts occupied and performed by the chosen poets. I suggest that all the artists mentioned in this book belong to a loose grouping and are kept together not by the narrow nationalism of a flag or the fervent devotion to a religious creed, but by a shared aesthetic and political project based on experimentation and radicalism. Their suspicion of synthesis and reconciliation, for instance, together with their genuine interest for what is foreign and unfamiliar, contributes to tie these apparently unrelated artists and thinkers together.

Before embarking upon our walk on the global tightrope, however, a final word on the term "funambulists" is necessary. I have used this word in the title and will continue using it throughout the book, not to denote erudition or to catch the reader's attention with an outdated Latinate term. Rather, the Latin roots of the word "funambulist" extend far beyond the contemporary period and our contingent geographical location catapulting us into that mixed and dynamic literary space—the Mediterranean region in premodern times, as described by Karla Mallette—that saw Latin coexisting along Arabic, Hebrew, and the local vernaculars and that ideally represents the book's core. Instead of domesticating a foreign word and substituting it with a more familiar English term (such as "tightrope walker" or "wire walker"), I have preferred to stick to the word "funambulist," with the intention to pay homage to the multilayered and dynamic history this word hides in itself as well as to underscore its threatened presence due to the monolingual ideal to conform and standardize. Needless to say, this is precisely what the author of this book along the lines of the chosen poets has attempted to do throughout—namely, to show the beauty of what is generally perceived as unfamiliar/strange and to exalt the uniqueness of what is in danger of being assimilated and disappearing, since difference is often considered in our speedy globalized world as a mere nuisance and a burdensome inconvenience. On a more poetic level, "funambulist" in the English context resonates with the verb "to fumble," thus indirectly communicating an idea of "maladroitness" and "awkwardness," which well describes the initial feelings experienced by the poets—and perhaps by the author of this book and its readers, too—as they take their first steps on the global tightrope.

PART 1

ENCOUNTERS

1

The Everyday as Protean and Enchanting

Naomi Shihab Nye's Tender Spot

Born in Missouri in 1952, Naomi Shihab Nye grew up between the United States and the Middle East, moving from St. Louis to Jerusalem and from there to St. Antonio, Texas, where she currently resides. An errant poet, Nye has traveled across North, Central, and South America; Europe; and Asia, condensing in her poems her most intimate impressions and touching memories of her travels around the world. Besides being a poet, Nye is also an essayist and a short-story writer and has experimented with a variety of literary genres, always with the aim of fostering intercultural exchange and understanding.

Whether she writes about small-scale scenes of daily life in Palestine or praises the wide, breathtaking views of US rural landscapes, Nye accentuates often unnoticed, neglected aspects of the everyday that have revealed themselves to her in bright clarity thanks to occasional encounters with fellow travelers or improvised road trips to unfamiliar places. As she herself admits, "The primary source of poetry has always been local life, random characters met on the streets, our own ancestry sifting down to us through small essential daily tasks."[1] I argue in this chapter that it is precisely this careful attention to the overlooked, the marginal, and the unnoticed that opens her poetry to a much wider, almost philosophical investigation of worldly concerns such as, among others, the painful experience of racism and social exclusion in the United States and abroad, violence as a vicious cycle, the fragility of human life and of affective bonds more generally, and the difficulty of finding one's way, particularly in a new country.

The chapter opens with an analysis of what I call, together with Robert Bonazzi, Nye's "domestic poems," which have so far received little critical attention. I suggest that the poet makes readers reencounter the everyday in unusual ways, prompting a re-vision of it as highly heterogeneous, intricate, and enchanting. The second part of the chapter is devoted to what I call Nye's poems "on the road," a group of compositions in which the speaker abandons the circumscribed space of her home and travels on board of a bus or a private car across the US landscape, making occasional encounters and crisscrossing unbounded flatlands.

Although utterly unpretentious, Nye's poems foreground the vibrant and vital character of the everyday, thus promoting a reconsideration of this usually underappreciated site as charming, animated, and therefore worth engaging with. Rita Felski, among others, has underlined the transformative potential of accentuating the extraordinary within the everyday through defamiliarizing aesthetic strategies. As she writes, "The everyday must be rescued from oblivion by being transformed; the all too prosaic must be made to reveal its hidden subversive poetry. The name for this form of aesthetic distancing is of course defamiliarization."[2]

Nye's Palestinian background, with its legacy of struggle conducted steadily on the ground through concrete daily actions and quotidian items, is at the core of this subversive aesthetics firmly rooted in the everyday. Among others, poets Fadwa Tuqan and Mahmoud Darwish together with visual artists Mona Hatoum and Khalil Rabah have employed ordinary objects (i.e., suitcases, pieces of furniture, shoes, soap bars, olives, spools of thread, candles, nails) in their poems and installations to set readers and viewers at odds with their familiar milieu and shake them out of their habitual comfort zone.[3]

Similarly destabilizing, Nye's poetic art is precariously located on a tightrope stretched out between the United States and Palestine, the domestic and the planetary, the intimate and the public. As a skilled funambulist, the poet moves with agility back and forth between these two opposite poles, connecting them in unexpected ways.

Lovable Skunks and Tender Seeds:
The Everyday as a Utopic Common Ground

Nye's interest in the everyday and her attempt to awaken readers to the wonders but also iniquities it hides under its surface are evident in "Valentine
for Ernest Mann." The poem opens with the speaker's disclosing a secret
to the reader: that poems are elusive, bewitching, and furtive "things" that
hide in the most unexpected places and elude our capacity to take hold of
them. Finding a poem thus requires a special disposition, an "acuity of perception," as Felski would say, which allows one to perceive the everyday as
enchanting.[4] This is how the speaker shares this confidence with the reader:

> You can't order a poem like you order a taco.
> Walk up to the counter, say, "I'll take two"
> and expect it to be handed back to you
> on a shiny plate.
>
> Still, I like your spirit.
> Anyone who says, "Here's my address,
> write me a poem," deserves something in reply.
> So I'll tell a secret instead:
> poems hide. In the bottoms of our shoes,
> they are sleeping. They are the shadows
> drifting across our ceilings the moment
> before we wake up. What we have to do
> is live in a way that lets us find them.[5]

Poems are reconfigured here as animated, slippery entities that sleep in
shoes, drift across ceilings, and nestle in unlooked-for places the moment
one wakes up. By accentuating their marvelous animation, anthropomor-
phic vitality, and cheeky playfulness, Nye changes the reader's perception
and orientation toward them from indifference to recognition.

The speaker's secret confidence is followed by a bizarre anecdote concerning an earnest man with a terrible fascination for skunks:

> Once I knew a man who gave his wife
> two skunks for a valentine.

He couldn't understand why she was crying.
"I thought they had such beautiful eyes."
And he was serious. He was a serious man
who lived in a serious way. Nothing was ugly
just because the world said so. He really
liked those skunks. So, he re-invented them
as valentines and they became beautiful.
At least, to him. And the poems that had been hiding
in the eyes of skunks for centuries
crawled out and curled up at his feet.[6]

Intrigued by the beauty of the skunks' eyes, the "serious man" at the center of this poem reinvents as a valentine an animal that is commonly despised. Nye's poem praises the man's capacity to see the beautiful in what is normally constructed as menacing and ugly, his ability to disrupt common sense and subvert ingrained beliefs through sincere affection. From a personal anecdote about the negative consequences of narrow-mindedness, Nye sparks a reflection on the ways in which hatred against Others is deeply embedded in our society and leads to nefarious consequences.

In order to alert readers to the damages produced by stigma and blame, Nye uses the creative force of poetry to expose and criticize the construction of Others as ontologically different and therefore as intolerable within the contours of one's worldview.

The serious man portrayed in this poem appears as a rather eccentric subject. He indeed has the "spunk" to resist common sense and think in nonconformist ways; his "queer"—that is to say nonnormative and nonaligned—attachment to the skunks is subversive, since it muddles strictly defined categories such as human/animal, beautiful/ugly, lovable/dreadful, and the hierarchies attached to them.

Like the "serious man," who reinvented the skunks as valentines, so the poet (and, more in general, each ordinary person,) should think, Nye seems to suggest here, outside the box and liberate the everyday from its harmful stereotypes, mistaken beliefs, and biased views.

Edward Said, among others, has explored the many ways in which Arabs (especially Muslims) have been historically the object of a denigrating and vilifying gaze.[7] More recently still, Alfred Hornung and Martina Kohl have shown that, with the rise of Islamophobia and the implementation of racist policies following the 9/11 attacks, Arabs and Muslims have been "lumped together in first reactions" and constructed homogeneously as enemies of the nation.[8] "Valentine for Ernest Mann" subtly anticipates these sociopolitical tensions.

In the closing lines, the speaker openly invites readers to perform, in Michel de Certeau's own words, acts of "clandestine creativity, evasion of the law, inventive ruses and subterranean refusals" to liberate Others and ourselves from the oppressive, invalidating perspectives that imprison us all.[9]

Perception in this context becomes a performative action; seeing Others as lovable and charming rather than threatening and nasty may indeed change one's orientation and attitude toward them while also promoting the desire for things to be different. As the speaker suggests in the closing lines:

> Maybe if we re-invent whatever our lives give us
> we find poems. Check your garage, the odd sock
> in your drawer, the person you almost like, but not quite.
> And let me know.[10]

Nye's re-vision of the everyday as a common ground and a fertile terrain to introduce change in one's orientation and attitudes is particularly evident in "Daily."[11] This time, Nye magnifies minuscule acts of survival and elevates shared, domestic activities to the status of sacred rituals, capable of reconstructing a sense of community among subjectivities who, at first glance, may appear to be poles apart:

> These shriveled seeds we plant
> corn kernel   dried bean
> poke into loosened soil
> cover over with measured fingertips
>
> These T-shirts we fold into
> perfect white squares

These tortillas we slice and fry to crisp strips
This rich egg scrambled in a gray clay bowl

. . .

The days are nouns: touch them
The hands are churches that worship the world[12]

Ordinary, domestic activities, such as folding a T-shirt, slicing a tortilla, and scrambling an egg, are elevated here to dignified, almost sacred, yet in the end extremely profane because totally mundane, acts. By sprinkling smoothly flowing lines with minuscule entities ("corn kernel"; "dried bean"; "measured fingertips"), Nye emphasizes how light touches enable even tiny grains to reach full growth. The poet connects the microscopic and the macroscopic, the intimate and the cosmic, the personal and the political, particularly when the speaker mentions the repetitive act of washing and hanging clothes, as a shared activity that gives birth to a common "we": "This bundle of clothes I wash and hang and wash again / like flags we share, a country so close / no one needs to name it."[13]

Simple, poor objects, such as an egg or a T-shirt, and quotidian rituals, such as slicing a tortilla, are represented here as the kernel around which a flourishing collectivity germinates—not one that finds its foundation in the narrow nationalism expressed by the flag, but one that performs a core of shared human activities that are considerate, careful, and nourishing.

I claim that Nye sees in the secular/sacred everyday extraordinary political potentialities, since this is a dimension that holds together utterly heterogeneous elements in a setting that is perceived as common. Still, one should not forget that the everyday and the domestic space, celebrated by Nye as the site of sheer variety and concerted action, has historically been and still is for many women horizon-less and burdensome. In Alice Kaplan and Krish Ross's words: "Everyday life has always weighed heavily on the shoulders of women."[14] Not only imposed repetitions but also desolate confinement and violent abuse can transform the home into a nightmare.

Nye's interest in the everyday—at least as I see it—does not open the way to a forgetful and superficial naivete, one that neglects gendered forms of inequality and oppression or economic disparities, nor to an idealist or elitist form of escapism that eschews the political. Rather, the poet's emphasis on collectivity and her desire to accord full dignity to ordinary individuals who cultivate care, sustainability, and ultimately hope for the future represent a form of counterpolitics that is action-oriented and generative, one that gives prominence to those strata of the population—the common everyday men and women—that politics in its current formulation tend to neglect or dismiss as unimportant. Nye's crucial shift from aesthetic to politics will become clearer in the next section, as I retrace Nye's gradual yet decisive transition from private feelings to public affects.

Touching Nails and Stranded Gloves: The Everyday as an Intricate Bundle

In "The Attic and Its Nails," Nye shares with the reader the widespread experience of going up in the attic to look for a much-needed thing. Without warning, readers find themselves involved with the speaker in a feverish search for a thing that is nowhere to be found:

> It's hard up there. You dig in a box for whatever the moment requires: sweater, wreath, the other half of the walkie-talkie, and find twelve things you forgot about which delay the original search, since now that you found them you have to think about them.[15]

The unexpected encounter of the speaker with a group of forgotten things stored away in the attic functions as a kind of shock; the material, concrete presence of the things and their proximity to the speaker make a claim on her and require that she takes responsibility for them, now that they are in front of her. The proximity of the speaker to the things found in the attic, in other words, changes the ways in which she perceives them; now that they are close, she feels almost compelled to reconsider her relation to them in more attentive ways.

In *Queer Phenomenology* (2006), Sara Ahmed draws a connection between location, perception, and orientation, arguing that our location vis-à-vis a thing influences the ways in which we perceive and orient ourselves toward it. To quote Ahmed: "We are turned toward things. Such things make an impression upon us. We perceive them as things insofar as they are near to us, insofar as we share a residence with them. Perception hence involves orientation; what is perceived depends on where we are located, which gives us a certain take on things."[16]

What had previously been considered by the speaker as useless, superfluous things are now perceived as worthy of attention. The white ceramic cup, in particular, refuses to be dismissed as junk and makes a claim on the speaker; its singularity emerges out of the casual assemblage of things and demands to be taken in charge.

The world of the attic gradually emerges as an "interworld," to use Rosalyn Diprose's term, an "open circuit" where human and nonhuman entities—the speaker, the box with the twelve things, and the glazed ceramic cup—share the same space on equal grounds and have an enhanced sense of their mutual connection and implication.[17] Things, in this particular case, appear to be vital, willful, and insubordinate agents that exert a certain power on the speaker. The latter is indeed outlined as an affective subject in Kathleen Stewart's sense of the term, a receptacle of intensities, a "thing" herself drenched in the everyday and enchanted, affected—moved by the things she encounters and the sensations they trigger in her. Accordingly, in the following lines, the speaker appears to be following a capricious and urgent drive, which is released by the things themselves:

> Your search takes on an urgent ratlike quality as you rip paper out of boxes, shredding and piling it. Probably by now you've stood up too fast and speared your head on one of the nails that holds the roof shingles down. They're lined up all along the rafters, poking through, aimed. Now you have to think about tetanus, rusty nails, the hearty human skull. A little dizzy for awhile, you're too occupied to remember what sent you up into the dark.[18]

A banal, everyday activity, such as looking for a thing stored in the attic, becomes the occasion for Nye to open up a much wider scenario, which extends from the circumscribed space of the home to include the planet at large.

In opposition to the media's often shocking coverage of the so-called *event*[19]—a sublime, overwhelming accident or a prepackaged, catastrophic scene—Nye accords central stage to a series of "non-events," small-scale scenes of daily life and to quotidian incidents that can happen to anyone.[20] By recounting a fact of life that both the speaker and the reader share, Nye involves the latter into a microcosm of fluid affects and powerful things, in which the boundaries between human and nonhuman, animated and inanimated things appear to be blurred and the human is decentered and returned to the world of material existence. Nothing is heroic or sublime here; the poem indeed centers on a rather commonplace search, which happens in the attic and ends with the speaker being hurt by the strange touch of the nails hanging from the roof. It is precisely this painful and uncanny encounter with the nails (things that had so far passed unnoticed) that functions as a kind of revelation, contributing to bring them back to life. As Ahmed explains: "To re-encounter objects as strange things is hence not to lose sight of their history but to refuse to make them history by losing sight. Such wonder directed at the objects that we face, as well as those that are behind us, does not involve bracketing out the familiar but rather allows the familiar to dance again with life."[21]

The transition from the private to the public sphere is best exemplified in "Yellow Glove."[22] Once again, in this poem, Nye delves into a shared human experience—childhood, with its little joys and big dramas—to weave a larger meditation on today's dramatic political situation. The poem opens with an enigmatic question, "What can a yellow glove mean in a world of motorcars and governments?," to which the speaker answers by narrating an episode that goes back to her childhood years.[23] The whole poem is structured on the dichotomy between a private, intimate world, which gravitates around a yellow glove and is identified, at least initially, as being typically feminine, and an external, public world of cars and governments, identified as typically masculine. These two apparently distant spheres will later overlap, promoting what Samina Najmi has called a "countersublime of benevolence and global connectivity," in which affects such as care, mourning, and responsibility break out of the intimate and circulate on a global scale to change an affective and political atmosphere dominated by clamor, terror, and mutual distrust.[24]

This is how the speaker recalls and narrates the precise moment in which she first encountered the yellow gloves:

> I was small, like everyone. Life was a string of precautions: Don't kiss the squirrel before you bury him, don't suck candy, pop balloons, drop watermelons, watch TV. When the new gloves appeared one Christmas, tucked in soft tissue, I heard it trailing me: Don't lose the yellow gloves.[25]

By recovering a childhood memory, with its innumerable prohibitions and warnings, Nye brings readers in close proximity to the speaker and implicates them within a world they recognize as their own. Childhood is a crucial point of reference for Nye for another reason, too. As Judith Halberstam notes, childhood represents a queer—in the sense of nonnormative—universe, which follows a set of values and priorities that deviate most of the times from the ones that govern the world of adults.[26] This is why in "Yellow Glove" the loss of a small, apparently meaningless thing provokes in the child a deep sense of turmoil and is experienced by her as a real catastrophe:

> I walked home on a desperate road. Gloves cost money. We didn't have much. I would tell no one. I would wear the yellow glove that was left and keep the other hand in a pocket. I knew my mother's eyes had tears they had not cried yet, I didn't want to be the one to make them flow.[27]

The loss of the glove triggers in the child the awareness of her own and her mother's vulnerability. Theorizing matter as being animated by a certain force, Jane Bennett writes, "The relevant point for thinking about thing-power is this: a material body always resides within some assemblage or others, and its thing-power *is a function of that grouping*. A thing has power by virtue of its operating *in conjunction* with other things."[28] The child-glove bond is powerful yet unusual, since it transgresses the classical distinctions human/nonhuman, animate/inanimate matter, foregrounding an affinity between two entities that seem to have little in common. Yet the glove in this poem appears to have power precisely by virtue of this weird connection to the child, the mother, and the other glove, which is referred to as "its sister." Once again, Nye returns readers to the material, everyday dimension to foreground a world in which all things, regardless of their status, are inextricably bound to each other and feel the power of this entanglement.

The girl's grief suddenly dissolves in a summer afternoon, when she sees her yellow glove reemerge from the river near her house: "The yellow glove draped on a twig. A muddy survivor. A quiet flag."[29] The apparition of the stranded glove fills the child with wonder. The little girl now in her adulthood and in a much different context, dominated by uproar and bank rates, interrogates herself on the meaning of that bond, on the significance of that loss, and on the unexpected joy that followed the glove's unexpected "return." From an exquisitely personal and intimate recollection, from a reflection turned both inward and backward, the poet now moves forward and reflects on the present situation:

> Where had it been in the three gone months? I could wash it, fold it in my winter drawer with its sister, no one in that world would ever know. There were miracles on Harvey Street. Children walked home in yellow light. Trees were reborn and gloves traveled far, but returned. A thousand miles later, what can a yellow glove mean in a world of bankbooks and stereos?
>
> Part of the difference between floating and going down.[30]

"Yellow Glove," as it appears clear now, is only apparently a childish and naive poem; its candid style hides in fact a serious and timely meditation on deep-seated problems regarding material and human precariousness, the force of relationality and interdependence, individual and collective mourning, the difficulty (perhaps impossibility) of making sense of loss. By setting the speaker's intimate and hushed inner world in contrast to the unemotional, profit-oriented, and cacophonous world governed by banks and stereos, Nye poetically replaces a world that follows the logic of self-interest with one in which the dignity and value of even the smallest thing is acknowledged and protected. By narrating an episode belonging to her childhood and by circulating private affects that reveal themselves inexorably as public, Nye alerts readers to notice and take actions to counter the spreading disaffection, devaluation, and political disinvestment.

From marginal, liminal spaces—such as childhood and the attic—Nye succeeds in short-circuiting official narratives, which most of the time are disenchanting, terrifying, and hopeless. Nye supplants the current downhearted, atomized, and death-driven political with one that is effervescent, vital, and sustainable, since it is based on beneficial affects, such as recognition, care, and mutual responsibility. This political yet-to-come finds its force in and resides on unorthodox forms of connection, coalition, and mobilization that do not follow the usual patterns.

In Nye's domestic poems, the everyday emerges in all its ambiguity, with its coercive routines and unexpected wonders, its platitude and transformative potential.[31] By highlighting the polydimensionality of the everyday, Nye poetically reconfigures it as a messy, intricate bundle, where interspecies crossings and atypical collective formations take place. Nye does not only awaken readers to the intermittently beneficial and harmful aspects that the everyday hides under its surface; she further calls attention to those small, ordinary things and lives that may be worthy of respect, yet commonly pass as lives that do not count.

Moments of defamiliarization and shock open the way to powerful re-visions that enable readers to reencounter things and humans as significant and enchanting again. This complex aesthetics, which breaks expectations, triggers wonderment in the reader, and has the ability to "move the soul" and render the familiar strange, has a long tradition. Its ramifications stretch from the twentieth-century avant-garde movements such as Dadaism and Surrealism, whose members used art to modify perception with the aim to shock, amuse, and revolutionize conventional views and behaviors, to premodern popular and anecdotal literatures as well as to the "wonder-evoking" poeticity (shi'riyya) of Arab poets emerging around the turn of the eleventh century, as Lara Harb fascinatingly argues in Arab Poetics.[32]

A "true poet" in André Breton's sense of the term, Nye manages to transform through her poetic art "the mediocrities of daily life into a zone of illumination and poetic infusion."[33] In line with her Surrealist predecessors, she employs the everyday life paradigm "to relate the particular to the general, locate the concrete in the universal, and to grasp the wider socio-historical context within which everyday practices are necessarily inscribed."[34] Nye further weaves in her poems stories-inside-stories, populating them with animated, marvelous things that leave the reader spellbound.[35] In their capacity to clear human fear, anger, and hatred through enchantment, Nye's poems represent-like Scheherazade's tales— some sort of white magic simply because, as Naguib Mahfouz writes with reference to the *Nights*, "they open up worlds that invite reflection" and, in doing so, momentarily suspend and infinitely postpone the calamity of violence, oppression, and loss.[36]

Road Trips and Treasure Hunts: The Everyday as a Workshop for Learning Larger Truths

Nye's representation of the everyday as a utopic common ground and an intricate tangle is not limited to her domestic poems but extends to include what I call her poems "on the road." Supplementing the compositions analyzed so far, the ones included in this final section focus on outdoor rather than indoor activities and present a woman traveler who leaves the circumscribed space of her home to embark on road trips.

"Flinn, on the Bus"—the first poem in this category—is effervescent enough to suggest an idea of inauguration, adventure, exploration.[37] The Irish name of the protagonist, Flinn, meaning "son of a man with red hair," indeed conveys stereotypically an idea of innocent wrongdoing, innocuous mischievousness, and joyous escape.[38] Readers thus expect to encounter in this poem a cheerful local boy, riding a bus for the first time and roaming freely across the country.

The opening lines, however, bend the initial euphoria and dramatically divert the readers' expectations. The first line, in particular, which mentions the collapse of some familiar buildings, opens a crack in the poem; it sends shivers of fear and troubles the readers' first positive assumptions. A liminal figure, half-boy and half-grown-up, Flinn's representation in the poem shifts unevenly between that of a gentle-eyed man and that of a renegade.

Written in the form of a spontaneous conversation that rises impromptu between two occasional travelers, "Flinn, on the Bus" rewrites, by following an aesthetic strategy we have now grown familiar with, Flinn's personal story within a larger sociohistorical and political framework. It is precisely through a minor event—the speaker's occasional encounter with Flinn—that Nye chooses to illuminate the wider catastrophe of 9/11, as the date written in italics at the end of the poem clearly suggests.

Writing on Paul Celan's simultaneously luminous and obscure poetic art, Jacques Derrida describes the date he includes in his poems as a "noch" or an "incision that the poem carries in its body, like a memory";[39] he further compares it to a "singular wound."[40] Derrida's figuration has led me to read as a scar Nye's inscription of the date—*September 11, 2001*—at the end of the poem. At the same time particular and universal, the date incised in the poem points to a very specific, national trauma. This scar, however, is also losing its singularity and extending its meaning to signify human vulnerability to violence and suffering on a global scale. To borrow Derrida's own words: "Once [the date] is read, whether it makes reference to the calendar or not, it is immediately repeated and, consequently, in this iterability that makes it readable, it loses the singularity that it keeps. It burns what it wants to save."[41] Likewise, the date inscribed at the end of the poem is both saving a traumatic memory yet also burning its exceptionality.

The chance encounter between Flinn and the speaker on a bus that crisscrosses the green fields of Oklahoma thus becomes the occasion for Nye to discuss pressing issues, including life's precariousness, rebirth from cinders, the difficulty to preserve peace and cultivate hope for the future in a present plagued by violence, which have a planetary resonance. It follows that the reference to Oklahoma is not casual. As we all know, Oklahoma City was in 1995 the setting of one of the greatest domestic terrorist attacks to hit the United States; the media had initially hypothesized that the bombing had been undertaken by Islamist terrorists, so attacks to Muslims and people of Arab descent were reported in the aftermath of that event.[42]

Despite its fresh tone and crystalline style, "Flinn, on the Bus" thus points to a cluster of dark themes such as homegrown violence, inter/

national terrorism, the deleterious effects of prejudice and racism, which are both locally and globally relevant. By alluding to the story of a young man who has been in troubled waters, has lost his way, and has ended up in prison, the poet further challenges the promise of the American dream and the myth of the United States as a safe haven.

The encounter between Flinn and the speaker is at the same time fortuitous and miraculous: Flinn's naive enthusiasm, exemplified by the young man looking in wonder "at his free hands," touches the interlocutor with intensity, healing in a certain sense the desperation and hopelessness that had overwhelmed her after she had heard the news.[43]

At first glance then, "Flinn, on the Bus" describes a chance meeting between two strangers who entertain themselves with small talk; after a more careful analysis, however, we soon realize that the poem actually opens up a completely different, much wider scenario. Nothing seems to happen on this bus, the fulcrum of the poem being apparently a simple, broken, and spontaneous conversation between two travelers. It is precisely around this nonevent, I claim, that Nye weaves a splendid, evocative tapestry in which the life stories of these two strangers meet and get entangled. As in Scheherazade's famous cycle, there is a story beneath the story that hides under the apparently transparent and clear surface of the poem. Flinn's story, in other words, refracts and diffracts the larger history of the US nation and of the contemporary world more generally, that we perceive perhaps for the first time in all its tragedy and dissonance. The image of the bending trees, which the poet describes as a light deflection, suggests that something is out of joint, that the time in which we live, as Derrida once wrote with regard to the legacy of Marx in a neoliberal age, "is disarticulated, dislocated, dislodged, time is run down, on the run and run down [*traqué et detraqué*], *deranged*, both out of order and mad. Time is off its hinges, time is off course, beside itself, disadjusted."[44]

One of Nye's greatest gifts then, is precisely her capacity to help readers see more clearly amid the general turmoil, to extract little drops of wisdom out of this disjointedness. Affects such as sorrow, caution, and apprehension surface the poem together with the luminous surprise of a fissure that cracks the darkness open, the promise of a possible way out despite the traumatism.

The idea that the road—and, in particular, the occasional encounter with unknown strangers—may provide travelers with some kind of revelation is further developed in the poem "Going for Peaches, Fredericksburg, Texas."[45] This time, the atmosphere is much more encouraging and rosy. The poem describes an almost idyllic situation in which a heterogeneous group of people (the speaker, a young boy, two old relatives) drive across the Texas countryside to buy peaches. As it will soon become clear, this leisurely activity becomes for the travelers an occasion to express and exchange divergent ideas on the fragility of human life, the circulation of prejudice and stereotypes, and the facility through which animosity lurks in apparently innocuous everyday conversations:

> Those with experience look for a special kind.
> *Red Globe*, the skin slips off like a fine silk camisole.
> Boy breaks one open with his hands. Yes, it's good,
> my old relatives say, but we'll look around.
> They want me to stop at every peach stand
> between Stonewell and Fredericksburg,
> leave the air conditioner running,
> jump out and ask the price.
>   . . .
> In Fredericksburg the houses are stone,
> they remind me of wristwatches, glass polished,
> years ticking by in each wall.
> I don't like stone, says one. What if it fell?
> I don't like Fredericksburg, says the other.
> Too many Germans driving too slow.
> She herself is German as Stuttgart.
> The day presses forward wearing complaints,
> charms on its bony wrist.[46]

Idiosyncratic personalities and oppositional ideas converge in this poem around a shared, common goal. The concerted action of finding the best peaches unites the car's passengers despite their distinctive traits. The activity of going for peaches thus turns out to be a kind of ritual, in which knowledge is passed down from generation to generation and a novel sense of community arises, as the result of shared actions performed with the intention to reach a wider, common scope.

In an interview with Phebe Davidson, Nye confirms that for her small daily activities and minute details "have always been the doorway by which we approach and apprehend the larger things of the world, the larger truths, whatever they might be."[47] It follows that by buying peaches from "a scarfed woman," who has ironically given up "teachin' for peachin'," one learns that "nature isn't perfect," that peaches can have slight bruises, that hands can be spotted too.[48]

The whole poem is traversed by an incredible vitality, a latent sense of wonder, a lightness of the heart that animate all the people involved in this unusual quest; their patience, their capacity to accept the slight flaws of nature, and their perseverance really strike readers, who sense that this rather frivolous activity hides in fact a political quality. The image of the old aunts, selecting peaches as if they were precious stones, loading and reloading their baskets, and exchanging views on the best way to preserve their treasured fruits, conveys an idea of dignity, gravity, dedication to a common cause, and, ultimately, steadfastness. In response to the claim that her poetry is not political, Nye explains that even dignity can be political, and that it is "a political act to do something with firmness."[49] "Going for Peaches," in my opinion, is exemplary of such politics.

One cannot but evoke here Nye's Palestinian heritage, particularly the countless hindrances that Palestinians experience daily in terms of restrictions to travel, to access their farmland, and to import certain goods.[50] In an interview with Ken Kurson, Nye remembers laconically "a very big thing about whether a particular fruit could travel between Gaza and the West Bank"; this painful reminiscence sheds a different, darker light on this apparently airy and untroubled poem.[51]

Nye's emphasis on collaboration within tension and on coalition within antithesis is further addressed in the third and last poem I analyze in this chapter, which takes us back to the United States, as the title "Kansas" clearly suggests.[52] This time the speaker is traveling together with an unknown person, possibly her partner, across the plains of Kansas at midnight; they are having a conversation about regrets, lost occasions, and failed expectations. All of a sudden, the driver takes "the wrong road," and without being aware of it, both travelers find themselves in the middle of an unknown territory, in an uncanny place that fills them with disorientation and fear:

> Signposts appear and vanish, ghostly,
> ALTERNATE 74.
> I'm not aware it's the wrong road,
> I don't live here,
> this is the flattest night in the world
> and I just arrived.
> Grain elevators startle us,
> dark monuments
> rimmed by light.[53]

In the absence of recognizable landmarks to be used as a point of reference, both travelers in this poem feel vulnerable and lost. The darkness and remoteness of the place, its absolute flatness and monotony, its silence and total emptiness, are at the same time spectacular and spectral. When a wave of exhaustion and discouragement unexpectedly overwhelms the driver, his desperation seems to have reached a point of no return:

> Later you pull over
> and put your head on the wheel.
> I'm lost, you moan. I have no idea where we are.
> I pat your arm.
> It's alright, I say.
> Surely there's a turn-off up here somewhere.
> My voice amazes me,
> coming out of the silence,
> a lit spoon,
> here,
> swallow this.[54]

Reacting to the hopelessness and despair of her traveling companion with an unhoped-for act of faith, the speaker in this poem touches his arm tenderly and reaffirms her comforting presence by uttering a few gleaming words. Her voice communicates hope, the strength of regained confidence, and unconditional trust; her words function as "a lit spoon," a curative potion and a luminous presence, one that offers warmth and consolation but also guidance and direction.

In her original reading of the elegy "Counterpoint: For Edward Said," which Mahmoud Darwish dedicated to Said right after his death, Judith Butler notices that there is a strange, even surprising, reaffirmation of hope that Darwish makes Said pronounce toward the end of the poem. Words such as "Invent a hope for speech, / invent a direction, a mirage to extend hope. / And sing, for the aesthetic is freedom" sound so incredible to the reader's ears, especially because they are pronounced by a dead person whose dreams and hopes have remained largely unfulfilled.[55] As Butler indicates, the words pronounced by Said are simultaneously unimaginable and radically imaginative since they represent "a declaration of hope, but also of unfathomable confidence, given the threats to life, the slow sporadic, yet systematic erosion of everyday life under occupation."[56] In a similar vein, I suggest, the reassuring words uttered by the speaker in "Kansas" sound difficult to imagine yet extremely efficacious, since they succeed in lifting the driver's mood, dissolving his desperation, and transmuting his weariness into hope. Her words invent a new possibility, a road to follow, and an illusion that serves precisely to extend hope.

Funambolic Vertigoes: Throwing the "I" Out of Balance

First published in 1957, Jack Kerouac's milestone novel *On the Road* narrated the restlessness, sense of disorientation, lack of goals, alienation, and ultimately dissatisfaction of a whole generation of postwar young people in the United States.[57] One of the defining works of contemporary US fiction, the book chronicles the story of a series of cross-country road trips made by Sal Paradise between 1948 and 1950. In it, Kerouac counterpoints a rather brutal and unforgiving urban environment with a scenic, almost idyllic countryside; he further celebrates youth, deviation, freedom, and self-determination and clings to the belief that it is possible to experience moments of authentic affective connection, however fleeting, however incautious, with some of the people encountered on the road.[58]

Both inheriting and departing from the tradition of US travel writing, Nye keeps the memory of this literary past alive, while at the same time abandoning the beaten track and inaugurating something altogether new. She indeed directs her compass not toward the south or the west, as was usually the case, but toward the east—toward Palestine, more specifically—following a personal desire line, a trajectory that is unique in US travel writing, since it brings the United States in close proximity to the Middle East and throws the (American) self out of balance, moving it away from his fundamental cardinal point—the mythic West—and therefore from his center of gravity. By effect of this physical redirection and affective reorientation, the supposedly upright and self-sufficient (American) self is replaced with one who is inclined, dangerously pushed eastward, toward the outside and away from himself.

Developing a captivating feminist critique of rectitude across the disciplines of philosophy, the arts, and religion, in *Inclinations* (2016), Adriana Cavarero draws on Virginia Woolf's critique of the English pronoun "I" as "straight, lone, self-sufficient, independent, domineering, deadly, and prevaricating" to celebrate instead a subjectivity that is "inclined, unbalanced, and pendent"—in one word, responsive.[59] I see Nye's poetics as cultivating a similar idea of the self as precariously inclined, relational, and receptive.

Whether retrieving a childhood memory or narrating an exciting road trip to buy peaches in the Texan countryside, Nye constantly solicits readers to lean forward, to abandon their solipsistic "I" and move past self-centeredness and insularity. When asked during an interview what poetry can do in the wake of catastrophe and death, Nye firmly responds: "Well, we need to keep extending imaginations, pressing, repeating, invoking, suggesting that other realities may exist, instead of the nightmares of war and hatred and conflict."[60] Nye's poetry, although not providing readers with the comfort of a landing place, may nonetheless function as a guiding light, that fortifies our spirits with its intermittent light and indicates a new direction to follow amid total darkness. I believe that only by learning from Nye the fine art of inclined balance and the resourcefulness of a well-trained funambulist, we may be able to walk the tightrope of global despair and make it to the other side, toward hope.

2

The Everyday as Claustrophobic and Stale

Iman Mersal's These Are Not Oranges, My Love

Born in 1966 in Mit 'Adlan in the northern Egyptian Delta, Iman Mersal begins to write poetry early in her life, during her high school years. She soon adheres to the independent feminist group *Bint al-Arḍ* (Daughter of the Earth), a collective that had provincial origins and organized periodic meetings in private homes and local cultural centers in Lower Egypt to discuss dissenting books and articles relating to gender and class equality.[1] Starting in 1985, and during a period of seven years, Mersal is coeditor of the independent feminist magazine *Bint al-Arḍ* (Daughter of the Earth), which published works by young female writers and essays on feminism and Islam.[2]

A member of the so-called 1990s generation, Mersal starts to write poetry in free verse (*shi'r ḥurr*) and to experiment with the form of the prose poem (*qaṣīdat al-nathr*) early in her career, thus openly deviating from the strict rhyme schemes and metrical measures of classical Arabic poetry as well as from the vernacular poetry of the 1960s and 1970s.[3] As Huda Fakhreddine writes, prose poetry had been "launched in Arabic with the founding of *Shi'r* magazine by two poets and theorizers of Arab modernism, Yusuf al-Khal and Adunis, under two major influences: Baudelaire's *poèmes-en-prose* and Jubran Khalil Jubran's experimental compositions, which blurred the boundary between poetry and prose."[4]

Still, in opposition to the "hyperbolic valorization of the individual" that, as Robyn Creswell has recently shown,[5] marks the poetry of the *Shi'r* group, Mersal's poetry manages, in Khaled Mattawa's own words, "to preserve the integrity of individual experience while keeping an eye on their turbulent surroundings."[6] Like other rebel poets of the 1990s, such as Ahmad Taha, Mohamed Metwalli, and Osama El-Dinassouri, who were initially rejected by the literary establishment and had to publish their experimental poems in personally founded magazines, Mersal employs a plain and simple language, avoids sentimentalism, and writes about the prosaic details of everyday life.[7] Together with them, she develops a gritty and convoluted poetics, stimulating the emergence of what writer and critic Edwar El-Kharrat has called "a new sensitivity" (al-ḥasāsiyya al-jadīda), forcing readers to find new ways to engage with, decipher, and interpret the poetic text.[8]

These poets, who combined a variety of influences ranging from classical Arabic poets to bohemian modernist forerunners à la Baudelaire, appropriated a derogatory term, Locusts (al-Jarād), that had been used to scorn them in a way similar to the members of the Art et Liberté Group (jamā'at al-fann wa al-ḥurriyya), who had turned the degrading label "degenerate art" on its head. As Marina Warner notes, these artists, who came from different cultural and religious backgrounds, employed an international artistic language—that of Surrealism—to address local issues.[9] As expressed in their manifesto "Vive l'art dégénéré!," these artists countered the rise of fascism and British colonialism, rejected ethnic and religious labels, and cultivated the dream of a global camaraderie. Pioneering female painters such as Inji Aflatoun, Amy Nimr, and Natalija Tile together with photographer Étienne Sved, cartoonist Kimon Evan Marengo, and caricaturist Kamel El Telmissany are among the members of this group, founded by Georges Henein in 1938. Mersal's poetry, which expresses a biting yet covert social critique and presses, although cryptically, for political change through the elaboration of a poetics that is rough, obscure, and most of the time unpalatable, bears among other influences that of this long-neglected artist collective of the 1930s and 1940s that was based in Egypt, addressed local concerns, yet was internationalist and cosmopolitan in spirit.[10]

A cosmopolite herself deeply rooted in the local, Mersal operates a re-vision of the nostalgic and sentimental paradigm traditionally employed by exilic poets to describe their homeland, while at the same time avoiding any celebratory representation of the host country. Her speaker feels out of place both in the busy streets of Cairo as well as in the quiet suburban alleys of a North American metropolis. These two apparently distant spaces—Egypt/Canada, homeland/host country, here/elsewhere—converge most of the time in her poems, destabilizing neatly compartmentalized spatial and temporal divisions and showing that these supposedly antithetical geographical places are in fact not fixed and isolated, but rather shifting and overlapping.

The exhibition "Here and Elsewhere" (*Hunā wa Hunāka*), opened in 2014 at the New Museum in New York City and displaying artworks from the Arab world, had a similar scope: to destabilize familiar outlooks and conventional angles, call attention to multiple places and perspectives simultaneously, while also inviting visitors "to look 'elsewhere' to understand our 'here.'"[11] I contend that a similar heterogeneous treatment of space and alteration of given confines is also at play in Mersal's poetry.

Life Here: Encountering Tribulation, Deception, and Obstruction

One of the most distinctive voices in the current Arab (diasporic) literary panorama, Mersal's poetry is frequently obscure and puzzling. As Stanley Moss rightly notes, "the beauty of her poetry is often in shadow, often hidden from the reader, suddenly revealed in bright Egyptian sunlight that hurts the eye and challenges the mind."[12]

Like Egyptian melodramas, Mersal's poetry is concerned with the minutiae of everyday life and features common characters that are neither heroic nor "universally known."[13] In contrast to Egyptian serials, however, which are generally imbued with clear moral codes and very sentimental, Mersal's poetry utterly refuses to morally educate and mobilize readers both sentimentally as well politically along conventional lines. As Mattawa observes: "Mersal shows the failure of ideologies—Marxism, Islamism, and Nasserism and other forms of Arab nationalism—as she refuses to buy into the vagaries of liberal democracy. We see the serious, heroic, fake, tiresome, and ineffectual attempts to overcome such pressures."[14]

The tension between individual integrity and the pressure exerted by
an oppressive sociopolitical environment is crucial to understand Mersal's
often dissonant and recalcitrant poetics. In her poetry, short-lived moments
of gaiety and elation interrupt an otherwise desolate and claustrophobic
everyday, while creativity and the imagination are the only available tools
to counter situations of crisis that erupt in the everyday. I suggest that her
poems are very personal and at the same time obliquely political, since
the malaise to which the speaker alludes is both existential and sociopolitical. The environment in which she operates is indeed uncooperative and
therefore draining, as the poem "Not Likely" makes patently clear:

قد لا يحدُث

قد لا يحدُث
أن آخذ أبي في آخر العام إلى البحر
لهذا
سأعلِّق في مقابل سريرِه
صورةَ مصطافين،
وشطوطاً ممتدّة لجهاتٍ لا أعلمها.
قد لا يحدُث أن يراها
لهذا
سأكتُم صوت تنفُّسي
وأنا -أبلِّل- أطرافَ أصابعه بمياهٍ مالحة،
سأُصدِّق بعد سنواتٍ
أنني سمعتُهُ يقول:
"أشمُّ رائحةَ اليود"[15]

Not Likely

It is not likely
that I will take my father to the sea at year's end.
So
I will hang in front of his bed
a poster of beach-goers
and beaches that stretch to places I do not know.
He may not see it at all.
This is why

I will silence the sound of my breathing
as I wet his fingertips with salt water.
And I will believe years later
that I heard him say:
"I smell iodine."[16]

Through the use of plain language, disturbing repetitions, and a slowly paced rhythm, Mersal expresses the misery and lack of prospects experienced by the speaker at her father's hospital bed. The poet addresses here both personal and universal themes relating to filial love, human precariousness, and mortality. What is unique in this poem is therefore not the theme per se but rather the strange atmosphere—simultaneously frantic and paralyzed—that surrounds the father-daughter duo and the disconcerting impression that what readers witness here is a deceitful pantomime, in the tradition of the shadow play theatre (*khayāl al-ẓill*).[17] In particular, the poet's emphasis on physical sensations (*yarāhā, samiʿtuhu, ashummu*) as well as her insistence on the unreliability and illusory nature of these impressions qualify the actions as senseless and the two performers as delusional. The dissonance between the speaker's inventive tricks to extend her father's claustrophobic room and her father's actual confinement to bed is accentuated formally by the disproportionate relationship between the long, mellifluous verses and the brusque turning points produced by the isolated expression "so" (*lihādhā*) as well as by the use of three different verb tenses intricately entwined in the final lines (*saʾuṣaddiqu, samiʿtuhu, ashummu*). Accordingly, the poem appears to be disharmonious and disrupted, reinforcing feelings of confusion and estrangement in its readers.

Feelings of disorientation and dissimulation can also be found in "House of Mirrors."[18] Here, the speaker retracts from a painful reality marked by privation and loss and finds a temporary relief from a bothersome everyday, by escaping into a house of mirrors, where reality is distorted, thus rendering it more bearable. The hilarity expressed in the first lines, however, lasts only briefly and is soon replaced by a deep sense of disillusion and discouragement:

بيت المرايا

سنذهب معاً إلى مدينة الملاهي
وندخلُ بيتَ المرايا
لترى نفسَكَ أطولَ من نخلة أبيك
وتراني بجانبك قصيرةً ومحدَّبة.
سنضحك كثيراً بلا شك
وستمتدُ الرحمةُ بيننا
وسيعرف كُلٌّ منا،
أن الآخر يحمل فوق ظهرِه
طفولةً حُرِمتْ من الذهاب
إلى مدينة الملاهي. [19]

House of Mirrors

We will go together
to the amusement park
and enter the house of mirrors.
You will see yourself taller
than your father's date palm
and I will stand beside you
misshapen and dwarfed.
No doubt, we'll laugh a lot
and mercy will spread between us.
Each of us will realize
that we carry on our backs
a childhood without
amusement parks. [20]

The speaker and her friend enter the house of mirrors together, thus coming in touch with a world of happy deformations and dispro-portions that is absurd yet soothing. In this poem, Mersal once again creepily introduces incongruity, dissonance, and rupture, where one would expect symmetry and wholeness, thus making readers experience firsthand the bitterness and burden of a childhood marked by depriva-tion and interdiction. The conflicting division of the poem into two parts suggests that reality is two-faced, while the disjointed syntax and a lexicon emphasizing opposition and otherness (*al-marāyā, aṭwal, qaṣīra,* al-ākhar) reinforce feelings of estrangement and unease. The harsh tone of the closing lines and the strange pair (ṭufūla ḥurimat) leaves no space for innocence.

In *Life as Politics* (1995), Asef Bayat explores Islamism and its struggle over fun, noting the following: "Sorrow, sadness, a somber mood, and dark, austere colors defined the Islamist public space, media, and religious rituals. In such a state of virtue, the shape and color of clothing, the movement of the body, the sound of one's voice, the level of laughter, and the intensity of looks all become matters of intense control and discipline."[21] The initial excitement and genuine hilarity expressed by the speaker in "House of Mirrors" is clearly at odds with a public mood afflicted by economic hardship and social interdictions.

One encounters again the everyday as a site of weariness, tribulation, and discomfort in "Wards." The whole composition reads like a detached inventory of the habitual objects and people one can find in hospitals. Despite the familiarity of the scene, however, the reader senses that behind this façade of apparent normality hides in fact a worrisome reality. The anaphora that opens each stanza (ʿādatan) and the repetitive parallel structure of the poem rather than being reassuring are perturbing:

خانات

عادةً ما تكون النوافذُ رماديَّةً،
وجليلةً في اتساعها،
بما يسمح للموجودين داخل الأَسِرَّة
بتأمُّل سير المرور،
وأحوالِ الطقس خارجَ المبنى.

عادةً ما يكون للأطبّاء أنوفٌ حادّةٌ،
ونظاراتٌ زجاجيَّةٌ،
تُثَبِّتُ المسافةَ بينهم و بين الألم.[22]

Wards

Usually the windows are gray
and splendid in their width
allowing the bed-ridden

to view the traffic below
and the weather outside.

Usually the doctors have sharp noses
and eyeglasses
that secure the distance between them and pain.[23]

The detailed description provided by the speaker is sound and realistic, yet what reveals the sordid character and double nature of the whole scene are imperceptible bodily signs and well-camouflaged subterfuges, such as the clutching of X-ray sheets in the fourth stanza and the doctors' use of eyeglasses as immunization against pain. In "Wards," mourning and loss have become habitual and recurrent events, with new bodies simply replacing previous ones. Mersal's surgical description contrasted with a lexicon that is generalized (al-*khānāt*, al-*nawāfidh*, al-*mawjūdīn*) contributes to desentimentalize the scene, showing that the public specters of privation, immunization to pain, and falsification under authoritarian rule have grown intimate. What readers witness here is indeed a slow agony from which there is no escape, as the tension between inside and outside (*dākhil* vs. *khārij*) that pervades the poem implies.

The political character of Mersal's poetry, so far largely implied in her compositions, becomes more explicit in the poems she published in 2006, after her relocation from Egypt to the United States first and to Canada next. In "The State" (*al-dawla*), for instance, the poet condenses, in one single sentence made up of nine lines with no punctuation, the sense of nausea and disgust that overwhelms the speaker, as she watches a military parade from the window of an anonymous building. The poem opens with the reference to "one head" (*ra's wāḥida*), orchestrating a series of spasmodic actions involving an army of mutilated soldiers, which the speaker can only see as "hearts, limbs, and genitalia."[24] This obscene army, which calls to mind the crude bodies of *Coups de batons* (1937), painted by Mayo, one of the most prominent members of the Art et Liberté Group, is juxtaposed to a hopeless "generation that no one needs."[25] Both are represented against a deafening and repellent background, in which nationalist songs flow out from public bathrooms into public squares uncontrolled as diarrhea.

The speaker observes the scene while biting her nails, a bodily action that clearly communicates her nervousness. Her affective misrecognition of the monstrous head that monopolizes the scene and darkens the street is evident, and so is her affective dissonance with the (fake) public mood of national unity and the ear-splitting noise produced by the bombastic ceremony. Mersal's insistence on the speaker's disgust, expressed through a convoluted syntax, obscene words, and repellent images, leaves the reader unsettled. The frustration they both experience—note the use of the pronoun "you" that may refer either to the speaker or, alternatively, to the reader—interferes with the public mood of unity and festivity. The domineering "one head" portrayed in this poem is neither a beneficial nor an amiable political creature; rather, it is a disgrace for the people it rules. Accordingly, the "you" in this poem is not a cheerful participant but a distant and disgusted observer, not yet crushed but nonetheless "curved" (munḥan) by the burden this one head represents.

Mersal's critique becomes even stronger in "The War" (al-ḥarb), a poem that opens in medias res with the speaker confessing: "As for me, I have been standing on tiptoe for years behind his window spying on him. But I cannot see the screen he's pegged in front of."[26] In this strange game of mirrors, the "fat creature" (al-kā'in al-samīn) mentioned in this poem appears to be closely surveilled by the speaker, whose torment is once again expressed through an uncomfortable bodily posture. The speaker observes the creature and explains that he "chews [French fries] slowly" while sitting comfortably on his sofa, watching the show, and commanding to a heedless pilot to detonate his bombs. The sarcasm hidden between the lines communicates the speaker's unwillingness to allow the fat creature, with its greed, immovability, and disregard, to go unnoticed. As the speaker explains, "he has not left the sofa for years" and has consumed French fries in great quantity.[27]

Although written before the Egyptian Revolution of 2011, "The War" undeniably captures and finely reproduces the tense atmosphere, growing sense of frustration, and repressed anger that led to the uprising in Tahrir Square. As Farida Makar rightly notes, humor and the use of caricatures were among the instruments that the protesters used to affectively belittle the power of someone who was in fact very difficult to physically remove. Among the many jokes through which the protesters expressed their exhaustion with the state of things, the ones they cracked about the immovability of their political leader clearly stand out. "Irhal!" (Leave!), for example, was one of the most repeated slogans that people cried out during those days, of which the demonstrators offered translations into many languages and even a reverse version "Lahri!" ("Evael!") in the hope that the addressee would finally understand and depart.[28] As we all know, the state media slandered the protesters in the square as Western puppets fueled by dollars and American fast food, which is highly ironic if we consider Mersal's description of the fat creature in this poem, who is voraciously eating French fries and being fed by a worldly "substance most delicious and beyond compare."[29]

In Mersal's poetry then, the here emerges as a site of tribulation, deception, and paralysis. Quite surprisingly, perhaps, Mersal's depiction of the elsewhere is equally bleak and dismaying.

Life Elsewhere: Encountering Public Scrutiny, Prescription, and Conformity

Mersal refuses to rewrite the Arab homeland within a nostalgic framework, while also avoiding to market the multicultural nation as a purely "happy object."[30] Her representation of the life of the migrant as sorrowful, for instance, breaks the myth of the arrival in the so-called New World as necessarily good and thriving.

The sense of loss, disorientation, and estrangement that overwhelms the speaker in the new homeland and her failed attempts to fit are expressed emblematically in "Why Did She Come?" The poem is built on a series of tiny accounts, each one disclosing one facet of the migrant's dim life abroad. As Youseff Rakha rightly notes, these vignettes read as "humorous and wrapped up miniatures epic of the self," since they condense in a thumbnail sketch the (mis)fortunes of a single migrant, who becomes representative of an entire national community condemned to expatriation.[31]

In opposition to the classical heroes of both ancient and medieval epics, such as Odysseus and Antar, who traveled widely, fought valiantly, and were often received as revered guests, the traveler this time is a woman, who cannot count either on the benevolence of the Gods or on the hospitality of the people she encounters. The opening lines of the poem in particular recreate the distrust and open hostility that the speaker faces once she embarks on her *hijra* to the West and lands in an unfamiliar place, where she finds only suspicion and resentment: "Why did she come to the New World, this mummy, this subject of spectacle / sleeping in her full ornament of gray gauze, / an imaginary life in a museum display case?"[32] As in an ancient Greek tragedy, a chorus of people comments on the deeds of the heroine, yet the aim is not celebratory, and the tone is neither benevolent nor compassionate. Mersal subtly derails the use of Pharaonic mythology by the Egyptian state's propaganda, with its tendency to resurrect ancient symbols to celebrate the grandeur of the Egyptian nation.[33] Under the scrutinizing gaze of a collectivity that disapproves of her arrival, the Egyptianness of the speaker is reduced to an unattractive vestige and, ultimately, to a corpse. Her mummified body is equated to a kind of Oriental mirabilia, whose life is preserved and exposed publicly as if it were an object of curiosity, an extravaganza to be exhibited "in a museum display case."[34]

Mersal develops here a queer epic that does not follow the norms of the genre but openly deviates from its normative system. The speaker has indeed no quest to accomplish or any heroic exploits to boast. On the contrary, she is in a state of inertia and apathy, limiting herself to coldly register the differences between the here and the elsewhere:

هنا أيضاً أشجارٌ خضراء تقف تحت ضغط الثلج، وأنهارٌ لا يتعانق
بجانبها عشاقٌ خلسة، بل يجري بموازاتها رياضيون مع كلابهم
في صباح الأحد، دون أن ينتبهوا للمياه التي تجمدت من الوحدة.
ومهاجرون لم يتدربوا على محبة الطبيعة ولكنهم يصدّقون أن
نسبةَ التلوث أقل، وأن بإمكانهم إطالة أعمارهم بمضغ الأوكسجين
قبل النوم عبر كبسولاتٍ هوائية.[35]

There are trees here too, standing under the weight of snow, and rivers where lovers do not sneak an embrace. Instead, there are joggers who run along the banks with their dogs on Sunday mornings not noticing the waters that froze from solitude. There are immigrants who were not trained in loving nature, but who believe there is less pollution here, and that they can prolong their lives by chewing on oxygen capsules before going to bed.[36]

The female speaker in this scene coldly registers both similarities and differences between the old and the new country; her list is scrupulous yet disheartening because, although things may on the surface appear similar, as the expression "here too" (hunā ayḍan) suggests, they are in fact awkwardly different. In particular, the trees that hardly bear the "weight of snow" convey a sense of fatigue, while the representation of the self-absorbed joggers replacing the clandestine lovers back home communicate feelings of human neglect and emotional detachment. Despite the invigorating cold and salubriousness of the air, readers are pushed to think that life in the new country is reduced to a prolonged agony. The image of the immigrants "chewing on oxygen capsules before going to bed" suggests feelings of claustrophobia, artificiality, and existential anguish.[37] Rather than listing the wonders (ʿajāʾib) of the New World, as was often the case in medieval travel accounts, the speaker compiles here a stock of apparently familiar yet in fact totally foreign/strange (gharīb) images that inspire in the reader desolation rather than astonishment.

The speaker's contemplative attitude and her being oriented toward the past, her being turned both inward and backward are clearly in contrast to the neoliberal imperative to be "healthy" and "fit," which the above-mentioned joggers clearly embody, as well as to the "happiness duty" that the multicultural nation expects the migrant to perform.[38] A veritable misfit, the speaker not only refuses to follow the prescriptions imposed by the neoliberal health, food, and fitness industries; she also reveals what is not good in the multicultural nation, thus cracking the myth that depicts it as purely benevolent and well-disposed toward outsiders:

يجب شراء organic food ولكني منذ ساعة أتأمل صورة أمي
جالسة على عتبة دار أبيها التي لم تعد هناك؛ أقصد العتبة،
رغم أن أمي نفسها لم تعد هناك.
لا أحد يمرّ في الشارع لأن العربات تدخل وتخرج بالريموت
كنترول. كنتُ قد اشتريتُ هذا البيت الذي لا يمكنني الجلوس على

عتبته من أرملة نحاتٍ أسبانيّ, كان قد بناه على أرضٍ تؤول إلى
مهاجر أوكرانيّ أعطتها له الحكومة الكنديّة بعد نزعها من الهنود
الحُمرِ؛ لكي تقيم مدينةً فيها عدة جامعات وعشرات من الشوبنج
مول وآلاف مثلي يعرفون الفوائدَ الصحيةَ للأورجانيك فوود
ويمتلكون عربات تدخل وتخرج بالريموت كنترول.³⁹

One must buy organic food, but for an hour I have been
      contemplating a photo of my mother
sitting on the doorstep of her father's house which is no
      longer there. I mean the doorstep,
even though my mother too is no longer there.
No one passes by on this street because the cars enter and
      leave by remote control.

I bought this house on whose doorstep I cannot sit, from the widow
of a Spanish sculptor who built it on land that belonged to a Ukrai-
nian immigrant given to him by the Canadian government after it was
filched from the Indians to build a city with several universities and
tens of shopping malls and to house thousands like me who know the
health benefits of organic food and who own cars that enter and leave
by remote control.[40]

The speaker's meditative mood and static posture reveal a lifestyle that
is at odds with the dynamic and goal-oriented logic that governs neoliberal societies such as the one portrayed here. The verb "must" (*yajib*),
in particular, suggests an idea of prescription and obligation, while the
reference to the remote control, wittily transliterated into *rīmūt kuntrūl*,
expresses a subtle critique of an automatized way of life, where humanity
has been replaced by technology. Furthermore, by retracing the genealogy
of her house, the speaker indirectly discloses Canada's colonial crimes,
thus raising serious doubts about the construction of Canada as a purely
benign and hospitable nation-state moved by multicultural love. Through
speculation and innuendo, the speaker reveals another threat lurking in
neoliberal societies: the risk of conformity.

The elsewhere in Mersal's poetry is not, as readers may expect, an
idyllic place providing the migrant with comfort and protection. There is

yet another danger concealed in the apparently pristine character of the elsewhere: slumbering peacefully into political atrophy and complacency. As the speaker explains: "What you learn here is not different from what you learned there: / You read to absent reality."[41] The poem ends with the following words:

> Nothing here deserves your rebellion.
> You are content and dead
> and life around you appears like a merciful hand
> that lit up a blind old man's room
> so that he can read the past.[42]

The interchangeable use of *hunā* and *hunāka* and the blurring of the traditional boundaries separating poetry from prose contribute to increase the reader's disorientation, a bewilderment that is addressed not only lexically and formally but also visually. On the front cover of the Arabic edition of *Alternative Geography* (*jughrāfiyā badīla*), Egypt and Alberta are indeed split from existing maps and juxtaposed; on the back cover, the African continent and the Canadian nation are outlined as missing those two fragments. The map as a whole appears to be defective, distorted, and partly defamiliarizing, in that Africa and Canada are adjacent yet flipped.

Ostracized by the community that is supposed to "liberate" her and disaffected from the hasty world that surrounds her, the migrant speaker in Mersal's poetry appears to be estranged, bored, and politically unmoved. Whereas in the here the speaker's individuality was marked by a "damaged . . . agency," in the elsewhere the speaker willfully refuses agency as prescription and emerges as a "diasporic misfit," to use Heather Love's apt formulation.[43] Both in the here and in the elsewhere, the speaker appears to be an "affect alien," in Ahmed's sense of the term, a subjectivity experiencing alien affect and being "out of line with the public mood."[44] I suggest that the underlying pain, which the speaker constantly evokes yet refuses to share, functions as a powerful call for a more sympathetic, humane, and welcoming way of life. To the demand for this different kind of inhabitance we will now turn.

Tense Microcosms: "Frankfurt Airport" and "Map Store"

In *Walled States, Waning Sovereignty*, Wendy Brown unveils a set of economic and political asymmetries that traverse today's globalized world generating tension. As she writes: "What we have come to call a globalized world harbors fundamental tensions between opening and barricading, fusion and partition, erasure and reinscription."[45]

Mersal's "Frankfurt Airport" addresses these multiple pressures poetically, by condensing in one tiny scene two intersecting and colliding mobilities—that of the intellectual expatriate and of the refugee—together with two conflicting identity categories: the privileged and the needy.

في مطار فرانكفورت

خمسةُ أطفال تائهين بين قدميّ أُمٍّ محجبةٍ وأبٍ يرتعش
ينتظرون الرجلَ الآمن خلف جدارٍ من الزجاج،
الرجلَ الذي سيحدّد لهم بأيّةِ أرضٍ سيموتون.
خبّأتُ جوازَ سفري في جيبي وأنا أمرُّ
هكذا لا يكلّفُ ادعاءُ الإنسانية أكثرَ من تذكّر الطفولة
"لا يجب أن يأكلَ الواحدُ حلوى أمام محرومين"[46]

Five children lost between the feet of a veiled woman
        and a trembling father.
They are waiting for the official, safe behind the glass wall,
        the man
who will decide in which land they will die.
I hide my passport in my pocket as I walk past.
This way claiming humanity costs no more than remembering
        childhood:
"One should not eat sweets in front of the needy."[47]

In this poem, the speaker seems to move at a different speed with respect to the family: she moves fast, while the others are stuck. The contrast is expressed, formally, through the division of the poem into two incongruous parts and, stylistically, through the use of a swiftly flowing line to describe the speaker's quick and unproblematic passage across the security check opposed to three dense and burdensome lines to describe the family's halt.

Feelings of impotence and shame surface this poem, raising uncomfortable questions regarding the different distributions of power and the asymmetrical allocation of the right to move that characterize the contemporary age. By carefully selecting her words, particularly "veiled" (*muḥajjaba*) and "deprived, needy" (*maḥrūmīn*), Mersal lays bare the two predominant qualities that, according to Brown, activate aversion in neoliberal states: Islam constructed as a foreign and inassimilable presence and destitution as a personal sin rather than a structural form of inequality. By effect of this careful selection, the family appears to embody, in Brown's own words, "two disparate images that are currently merged to produce a single figure of danger justifying exclusion and closure: the hungry masses, on the one hand, and cultural religious aggression towards Western values, on the other."[48] The poet, however, skillfully bends these stereotypical constructions, by signaling that this is not a threatening mass but just a family and by exposing the father's own vulnerability through his trembling. The poet, moreover, blocks the activation of strong feelings in favor of more imperceptible affects, such as shame, frustration, and resignation. The speaker's antipathy and contempt toward the border agent and the blockade he officially puts in place is expressed subtly by the poet through the use of the generic term "the man" (*al-rajul*), a move that indicates that the officer has lost all credibility and authority in the eyes of the speaker.

Here, Mersal clearly writes back to the postmodern fantasies that celebrate nomadism and cultivate the illusion of fluidity and speed as universal markers of global mobility. The first-person speaker is in fact an impotent spectator in the face of the negative mobility of the family and feels in part complicit in the situation; the rule of law in this scene appears to be suspended and responsibility to be replaced by nonaccountability. The speaker's final withdrawal rather than overt action, her restraint, silence, and sense of guilt subvert ostentatious displays of wealth and privilege as well as self-centered fantasies of universal mobility, while at the same time calling into question her unwillingness (or, perhaps more realistically, her inability) to intervene. Rather than actively engaging in, Mersal's speaker appears to publicly disengage; her impotence and shame raise uncomfortable questions regarding the political disempowerment of subjectivities in today's neoliberal democracies, particularly the real capacity of common citizens to make a difference and have a say in the decisions that different political actors—in this specific case, the European Union—take.

The absurdity of the scene witnessed by the speaker and its Kafkaesque quality propels the metamorphosis of the airport, originally conceived as a site of "progressive thinking and utopian planning," into a penal colony or a penitentiary.[49] Following the transformation of the airport into a high-security prison, Alastair Gordon forcefully notes:

> Antiterrorism measures turned the airport into an electronically controlled environment rivaled only by the maximum security prison. It was more than mere coincidence that the architects responsible for some of these fortified terminals had also designed penitentiaries. Both the airport and the cell block used similar kinds of logic. Interior and exterior spaces were under 24h surveillance from electronic eyes, motion detectors, and video cameras. Both inmates and passengers moved through a similar series of sealed passageways, automatic doors, and narrow checkpoints, where personal screenings were administered with metal detectors and body searches. Only the duration of incarceration differed.[50]

The transformation of the airport from a site of progress and radical imagination to a maximum security prison goes hand in hand with the metamorphosis of the European Union from a free union of states, antagonistic to tyranny, social injustice, and war into a fortress. The state confederation imagined by Altiero Spinelli and Ernesto Rossi in their draft manifesto compiled during their political confinement on the island of Ventotene during World War II is far apart from today's Schengen Area with its hardened and militarized external borders as well as its "policies of containment that treat migrants as undesirables."[51]

Unable to govern the many contradictions, asymmetries, and tensions exerted by globalization—this, at least, is Brown's argument—states have resorted to a policy of blockading and to the construction of walls, whose function is, however, mainly theatrical, as they project a power that they cannot and do not actually exercise.[52] The global proliferation of security procedures mirrors the dissemination of walls, security fences, and barriers in many states that, as Brown rightly notes, "cannot block out without shutting in, cannot secure without making securization a way of life, cannot define an external 'they' without producing a reactionary 'we.'"[53] As Mersal suggests in this poem, in a highly securitized political, the erosion of democratic principles and values is a real risk. The political conceived as a military outpost watched over by a high-tech surveillance system and patrolled by guards and warships can only fail.

In "Map Store," Mersal provides readers with an alternative conceptualization of the political, one in which exterior walls, sealed passageways, and narrow checkpoints have been replaced by confluence, mutual recognition, and the right to self-determination. Before getting to that point, however, let's first follow Mersal as she retraces the strange genealogy of that curious shop:

دكّانُ خرائط

بإمكانَك تخيله عائداً من الحرب
تلك الحروب التي تنمو في مكان آخر
ليعود بعضُ أفرادِها بذكرياتٍ قَّد تبدو كافية
لصناعةِ فيلم شبه واقعي
المُهم، أنه عاد من صحراء في شمال إفريقيا،
وبخبرةٍ في العطش افتتحَ دكاناً لبيع العصائر.[54]

You can imagine him returning from war,
one of those wars that broke somewhere else
and whose combatants return with enough memories
to make an almost realistic movie.
What is important is that he came back from the deserts of
        North Africa,
and with his expertise in thirst he opened a juice bar.[55]

Mersal's apparently dispassionate and objective reconstruction of the store's genealogy hides in fact a sharp critique, as expressed through lexical pairs that express alterity and absurdity (*makān ākhar; shibh wāqiʿiyy; khibra fī al-ʿatash*). With a note of sarcasm, Mersal obliquely addresses here crucial political issues, such as the controversial relation between war and profit, the mystifying construction of the elsewhere as a deserted place available for conquest and occupation, and mainstream representations of the war as a sublime, movie-like distraction or a formative experience that provides training and discipline. In particular, Mersal subtly criticizes America's "civilizing mission" of exporting justice and democracy to other, supposedly uncivilized countries; this is indeed a theory that has many leaks, as the image of the seeping water in the following lines clearly suggests:

كان يضعُ الثلجَ فوق المشروبات الصحية التي أصبحت في أواخر
الأربعينيات أمارةً على أمريكا في عهدها الجديد العادل
حين اكتشف مياهاً تنزُّ من الصناديق
فتهَيأ له بحر، يابسة، ثم جزيرة
من هنا تولّدت لديه فكرةٌ مشوشةٌ عن الجغرافيا
ثم جاء حفيدُهُ الذي لم يدهب أبداً إلى الحرب
فحوّل الدكانَ إلى مكان لبيع الخرائط.[56]

He was tossing ice in the healthy beverages that were, in the late
forties, a symbol of America and her new era of justice when he
discovered water seeping from a stack of boxes
and he imagined a sea, dry land, and an island.
From then on he developed a skewed notion of geography.
Then his grandson, who had never gone to war,
turned the shop into a map store.[57]

Mersal ingeniously reveals here with striking nonchalance how apparently innocuous items such as juices and maps and neutral disciplines such as cartography have been employed by colonial and imperial power to conquer foreign lands and subjugate foreign people. As David Atkinson notes with reference to European imperialism: "[It] had long used cartography and survey to transform *tarrae incognitae* into measured and knowable territory: rendering space governable in practical terms as well as capturing it symbolically."[58]

Conceived in modern times as tools at the service of colonial and imperial powers to separate, control, and discipline the indigenous population of distant lands, maps are creatively reconfigured in this poem as an instrument through which a variety of displaced people cope with their sense of loss and estrangement and maintain in creative ways their connection with the land they lost. A microcosm set in the heart of Manhattan, the map store evoked by Mersal appears as a place of confluence and collective gathering for a group of alienated strangers. In their hands, geography stops being the usual "totalizing stage" where big powers show off their force, and becomes an effective tool through which forcibly uprooted people reclaim, reconstruct, and make publicly known in very intimate ways their severed relationship to their original land:[59]

لو مررتَ من هنا يوماً،
في هذا الشارع الذي يشبه شرياناً مسدوداً في قلب مانهاتن
سترى أُناساً ليسوا من هنا
يدخلون ويخرجون ونادراً ما يشترون شيئاً
أنا مرةً رأيتُ امرأةً تمسحُ الترابَ عن جبلٍ
وبنتاً ترسلُ خصلةً من شَعْرها في بحيرةٍ
وسمعتُ آخر يحاولُ أن يصفَ لآخر معه
موقعَ بيته البعيدِ في قريته البعيدة بالقرب من مدينةٍ بعيدةٍ
تظهر مثل نقطةٍ في خريطة بلده البعيد.[60]

If you come here one day,
to this street that resembles a blocked vein in the heart of
        Manhattan,
you will see people not from here
who enter and leave, rarely buying anything.
I once saw a woman wipe the dust off a mountain
and a girl dipping a tress of her hair into a lake
and heard someone trying to explain to someone else
the location of his distant house in his distant village near
        a distant city
which appears like a dot on the map of his distant country.[61]

In this singular shop, where nobody seems to buy anything, maps are not reduced to consumer goods but reimagined as performative tools to exchange shared stories and experiences of loss, recall meaningful details, and pinpoint distant locations. Traditionally employed by colonial and imperial powers as an instrument to speed up the occupation of foreign lands and explain away the removal and dispossession of its native peoples, maps are reconfigured here as an empowering rather than coercive tool. They are the practical means through which ordinary men and women develop a sense of their own location and translate it to others with the help of narration. I argue that these oral tales do not simply contribute to locate a small village on the map; rather, they recompose it, refound it, publicly reclaim its importance, and thus authorize its existence despite its smallness. As Michel de Certeau claims: "The story's first function is to authorize, or more exactly, to *found*."[62]

In the final stanza, however, the speaker reveals to be irresistibly driven to this place also for another—this time more disquieting—reason:

انا أمرُّ من هنا

لا لأشارك هؤلاء الغرباءَ حسرتَهم

ولا لأضع الماءَ في النيل الذي يبدو مثل ثعبانٍ نائمٍ

في الرسم المعلق في مواجهة الباب

ولا حتى لأتأمل ذلك البهاء الذي لابد كان هناك

في أعلى الرّكبة اليمنى لصاحب الدُّكان الأصليّ

الذي أرى الآن صورتَه في زيّ الجنديّ ونيشانه

دون أيّ ذِكرٍ لرِجْله الخشبيّة

أو للماءِ الذي نَزَّ من الصناديق.

أنا لا أعرفُ لماذا أمرُّ من هنا حقيقةً

لكني الآنَ أشهدُ بعينيّ

بائعَ الخرائطِ

مرعوباً ربما للمرة الأولى

في حربٍ لم يجد وقتاً ليذهب إليها

الحرب، هذه المرة، جاءت إليه.[63]

I come here
not to share with these strangers their sorrow,
or to pour water into the Nile which appears like a sleeping
      snake
in the drawings hung facing the door,
not even to witness that glory that must have been there
above the right knee of the store's original owner
whom I see photographed in army uniform and medals
with no mention of his wooden leg
or the water that seeped from the boxes.

In truth, I don't know why I come here.
But I see now with my own eyes
the map seller
frightened, possibly for the first time,
in a war he had no time to go to,
a war, this time, that had come to him.[64]

In the closing lines, the speaker sees her own fear and puzzlement reflected in the eyes of the young owner, who cannot get used to the idea that the war is not happening this time in an elsewhere disconnected from the here, but has instead already moved to Manhattan and thus to the heart of the United States.

As in Mona Hatoum's installation *Hot Spot* (2009), the planet is outlined in the poem's closing lines as being in a permanent state of alertness, traversed by a red grid signaling the omnipresence of danger and pointing to hot spots of conflict everywhere. Placed against this tense global background, the map store functions as a space for hope, a gathering place, a stronghold against colonial/imperial violence and the loss produced by it. In this miniaturized world that contains multitudes, where the actual scale of "things" is distorted and the Nile has the size of a sleeping snake, everyday men and women engage in nonviolent, creative practices to reclaim, refound, and ultimately reauthorize the existence of small, neglected places and of their indigenous peoples that maps (and the imperial powers that commissioned their drawing) have erased from public imaginaries.

A Far-Reaching Wire: Walking the Heights
to Change Global Imaginaries

In line with the members of the Mahjar Group, such as Jibran Khalil Jibran and Amin Rihani, who arrived in North America at the end of the nineteenth century and articulated in their literary works their experience of dislocation and alienation, Mersal resorts to the prose poem to recount her own and her speaker's *hijra* to North America.[65] The poet's personal journey and poetic trajectory, however, is fundamentally different from that of her famous literary predecessors. Mersal clearly dissociates, for instance, from what she considers Jibran's tendency to respond to Orientalist expectations and transform his identity accordingly.[66] In opposition to Jibran's prophet, her speaker has no wisdom to share, keeps sentimentality at bay, and remains willfully a misfit, positioned on a precarious edge. To quote Mersal: "Diasporic misfits who avoid a kitschy position reside neither at the center nor at the margin as constructed by the center; they reside in a margin unrecognized by the center."[67]

Whether set in the obstructed streets of Cairo or in the uniform suburb of a Canadian metropolis, Mersal's poetry shifts unevenly between the here and the elsewhere, poetry and prose, individual experience and its turbulent social and political surroundings. The global in her poetry appears to be intricately bound together with the intimate. This is why the collection zooms in on intimate scenes of everyday life—at a hospital bed, in an amusement park, and on the steps of a family home—while at the same time offering broader shots of a high-security international airport, a strange map store located in the heart of Manhattan, and a monotonous suburbia where nothing happens except the opening and closing of automatic gates.

Distant geographical spaces such as Canada and Egypt, global metropolises such as Cairo and New York City, and minuscule places that maps have either promptly erased or cut off and isolated condemning them to a slow death are redrawn by Mersal's poetic imagination as contiguous places belonging to the same bizarre planetary map made of odd couplings—beachgoers and patients, dwarfs and palm trees, fat creatures and spying women standing on tiptoes—twisted geographical notions, and unexpected changes of scale. Egypt, in particular, is outlined in Mersal's poems as a place where the street is overshadowed by a domineering presence, a monstrous "single head" that scrutinizes everything; Canada, too, is Cyclopean in size, and the migrant, as a recalcitrant Ulysses, must ingeniously survive in order not to be devoured by the terrible creature with one eye that assimilates everything.

At times disturbing, the alien affects that Mersal mobilizes, such as frustration, aversion, nervousness, and impotence, force readers to take notice and to witness perhaps against their will things they were not supposed to see. This is why the poems become simultaneously intimate and creepy. Mersal, as we have seen, expresses her political discontent by mobilizing "ugly feelings" and by performing a politics of retreat, disengagement, and withdrawal, which is at odds with the political imperative of neoliberal democracies: engage, act, change.[68] This awkward political project, that dodges participation in the traditional sense, goes hand in hand with a defamiliarizing aesthetics, which privileges the use of dissonant tones, disturbing repetitions, unexpected changes of scale, and strange lexical pairs, which the reader experiences as disconcerting and disorienting.

Far from being showy, Mersal's art is obscure, introverted, and secretive. The poet introduces questions of embodiment into the analysis of politics and outlines modalities of action that deviate from the usual political vocabulary. Mersal's original conceptualization of political action is instead grounded in practices of negation, refused agency, and withdrawal. Since it has, politically speaking, the size of a Lilliput, Mersal's speaker is unable to fight back against the political perceived as Colossus; she can, nonetheless, make persistent, small breaches in the walls of this entrenched titan. As Mersal explains with reference to the political quality of her poetry: "You play and enjoy not just creating something, but deconstructing things and the rhetoric that surrounds them."[69]

To keep her individual integrity hale, Mersal's (anti)heroine continually opts out from existing systems and refuses to adopt stereotypical categories of womanhood. Hers is a feminist politics as defined in Judith Halberstam's words, one that "issues not from a doing or becoming woman but from a refusal to be or to become woman as she has been defined and imagined."[70] Accordingly, Mersal's speaker defies conventional representations of womanhood. She is neither virtuous and modest, as Islamic standards would dictate, nor sexually loose and socially defiant, as a stereotypical feminist line would prescribe.

Both in the here and in the elsewhere, the political in Mersal's poetry is revealed for what it really is: a space of atrophy, alienation, and oppression. Since it is intrinsically rotten, the speaker cannot but disengage from it. Faced with a crumbling political, the poet nonetheless cultivates the dream of an alternative, perhaps utopian, political as a space of genuine flourishing for all.

In opposition to her predecessors, particularly to the *nahḍa* intellectuals who were seduced by and rushed to adjust to Europe's ideas of progress and modernity, Mersal is not trapped by the lures of the elsewhere. She strongly criticizes, for instance, Rifa'a al-Tahtawi's "desire for modernizing and revolutionizing stagnant societies in the East by borrowing Western civilization."[71] Her uncompromising look dissects and disfigures both Egypt and Canada, the EU and North America, revealing their coimbrication and manifesting political stagnation as an endemic global problem, although with different degrees of gravity.

By powerfully detaching herself from the yoke of a politically engaged poetry that she perceives as having imprisoned Mahmoud Darwish, among other Arab poets and intellectuals of the 1960s and 1970s, Mersal develops what she herself calls an indirectly political poetry. Her art aims to pierce the darkness and let the truth emerge; its political force relies precisely in its capacity to illuminate what would otherwise remain in the dark. Terms such as "homeland," "belonging," and "citizenship," for instance, which have been coopted by the nationalistic authoritarian state and hollowed out of meaning, have been washed, in Mersal's own words, from "the rust of the dictatorship," finally acquiring a new shine.[72]

Because she alters given confines and overlaps places traditionally regarded as being at the antipodes, Mersal intervenes in what Edward Said once called the "struggle over geography."[73] This is not a neutral discipline but one complicit with power and imperial crimes, since, as he convincingly argues in *Culture and Imperialism*, "just as none of us is outside or beyond geography, none of us is completely free from the struggle over geography. The struggle is complex and interesting because it is not only about soldiers and cannons but also about ideas, about forms, about images and imaginings."[74]

Mersal draws an alternative, outlandish cartography of planetary size, where global metropolises and small villages are horizontally aligned; she further gives priority to oral narratives, indigenous knowledge, and the memory of ordinary men and women who repeatedly reclaim the existence and consequently refound and reauthorize the presence of places and people that official maps and imperial powers have wiped out from their land and the public imaginary. This is clearly a creative act of re-vision that has deeply political implications since it reinscribes, as in the case of Hatoum's *Routes* (2002), "new, imaginary cartographies upon and within those already established."[75] Undeniably, this is also an act of civil disobedience and a counterpolitics that, by granting recognition to all—even to the most neglected place or people on earth—makes an irrevocable step forward toward equality, recognition, and justice.

Mersal's poetry offers the gift of an alternative point of observation that is simultaneously rooted in the here and gliding over the elsewhere. In her altered, bottom-up geography remote, supposedly negligible, places and people are brought near and leave a lasting impression on us.

From the heights of her far-reaching wire, the funambulist Mersal shows readers that to imagine a planet liberated from the yoke of violence and war, dispossession and loss, one needs first to acknowledge, rejoice with, and honor a vanishing village that manages to strenuously survive, and only afterward marvel at the magnificence of the cosmos and eventually help the woman in the map store wipe off its dust.

PART 2

CROSSINGS

.

3

Maritime Crossings

Mina Boulhanna's "Immigrata" and "Africa"

In this chapter, I closely read two poems—"Immigrata" (Migrant Woman) and "Africa"—written in Italian by Mina Boulhanna. Both appeared for the first time in *Nuovo Planetario Italiano* (New Italian Planetarium), a volume edited by Armando Gnisci and published in 1996, when literary works by migrant writers living in Italy started to attract the attention of critics and the general public.[1] As Anika Kosic and Anna Triandafyllidou write with reference to the history of immigration to Italy, "Like other countries in Southern Europe, Italy has, in the course of less than two decades, rapidly and unexpectedly changed from a country of emigration to one of immigration."[2] Boulhanna's poems are emblematic of this change and clearly reflect Italy's discursive and political construction and widespread negative perception of migration as a "problem," "a threat to jobs," "a threat to cultural and religious identity," and, in its more recent formulations, "a security threat."[3]

After her first public appearance as a poet in 1996, Boulhanna's name has only been included in Paola Ceola's *Migrazioni narranti* (Migrant Narrations), an anthology collecting literary works written by migrants of African origin. Ceola, in particular, includes Boulhanna's name in a footnote of the section "Morocco," a subchapter of the anthology, which maps a wide galaxy of works written by African writers, coming to Italy from different areas of the continent.[4]

My intention in this chapter is to sketch an alternative geography— a *jughrāfiyā badīla*, in Mersal's sense of the term—in which Morocco, Boulhanna's country of origin, is not eclipsed by the blinding light of Italy and does not get lost in the galaxy of Africa. This is why I have included Boulhanna's two poems in this volume and placed them in close proximity to the works of the other women discussed in this book, so that a new sense of kinship may emerge.

Crossing the Borders of the Nation: Migration as *al-ghurba*

In "Immigrata," Boulhanna expresses the difficulties experienced by a migrant woman who has left her homeland and takes her first steps into a new country. The speaker compares her current life to a thick layer of fog, which renders her walking purposeless and uncertain, despite her great care and application: "Fog, this (life) of mine / It is random, my walk Even if I am very careful."[5] Boulhanna's poem emphasizes feelings of disorientation and alienation in ways comparable to the poet Gëzim Hajdari, winner of the prestigious Montale prize in 1997. To quote one of his poems: "Piove sempre / in questo / paese / forse perché sono / straniero" (It always rains / in this / country / maybe because I am / a stranger).[6] Besides communicating with efficacy a deep sense of discomfort and isolation, Boulhanna's "Immigrata" has the merit of introducing a gender dimension to migration, by placing at the center of the poem a migrant woman. Her rather conventional representation of the racialized and gendered immigrant body as coerced and victimized is, however, problematic. Boulhanna's sorrowful and lonesome newcomer, for instance, is quite distant from Mersal's resolute and single-minded (anti)heroine who makes fun of migrants belonging to earlier generations, still "dream[ing] of returning when they become corpses."[7] In opposition to Boulhanna's restless and destitute speaker, whose home is a tent and who keeps her treasures hidden in a suitcase, the woman portrayed in Mersal's "Why Did She Come?" owns a house and has exchanges with fellow newcomers, who have arrived on foreign soil before her. Not so, for Boulhanna, who was among the first migrants to reach Italy in the 1990s. Accordingly, not only practically as a newly arrived person but also aesthetically as an emerging poet, Boulhanna had no established multiethnic network to rely upon, since in Italy the "symbolic space in literature has historically been constructed as a white space" as Caterina Romeo explains.[8]

Despite the lack of established literary models, Boulhanna's bleak description of the condition of the migrant woman appears in fact to take up one of the most recurrent motifs in Arabic (particularly Maghrebi) literature: the topos of *al-ghurba*.[9]

According to sociologist Abdelmalek Sayad, the term *al-ghurba* concentrates three different, dark meanings in one word: first, the meaning "sunset," and attached to it the fear of losing one's way and getting lost amid total darkness; second, "exile," with the consequent sense of disorientation and isolation produced by the strangeness/foreignness of the place; and, third, a more generic sense of inner turmoil and loss that gives rise to feelings of misfortune and fright.[10] As Sayad observes, the idealized image associating migration with "a source of wealth and decisive act of emancipation" is to a certain extent neutralized by these other, more negative connotations, thus restoring *al-ghurba* to its original dark meaning.[11] Boulhanna's poem reinforces the negative qualities of migration, echoing Mersal's dark-humored description of the *hijra* as a grim condition. The urban landscape, in particular, both in Mersal and in Boulhanna is described as bare and unyielding. To quote Boulhanna: "My sky is gray Trees and branches bare Freezing air, humid."[12] These gaunt images juxtaposed with no interconnection call to mind T. S. Eliot's *The Waste Land*, where "the dead tree gives no shelter, the cricket / no relief, / and the dry stone no sound of water."[13] Both in Boulhanna and Eliot's poems the surrounding environment is experienced as barren and harsh.

Nomadism in Boulhanna's poem is not an abstract theoretical construct but a deeply concrete, quotidian experience marked by weariness and instability, as the two objective correlatives (a pair of worn-out shoes and a suitcase) suggest.[14] Accordingly, the conclusion cannot be but desolate and hopeless: "Saddening this life of mine / and the destiny that has chosen it for me."[15]

The urban space in Boulhanna's poem is outlined as anonymous and unavailable; it presents itself under a dark light, thus resonating with the following lines by Eliot: "Unreal City / under the brown fog of a winter dawn."[16] Far from being just a literary homage to Baudelaire's spectral city of Paris or a modern rendering of Dante's *Inferno*, as it happened in Eliot's poem, the urban landscape in Boulhanna's "Immigrata" stages and epitomizes the migrant's tangible and factual exclusion not only from the city she arduously traverses but also from the nation she spectrally inhabits. This eradication will become clearer in the next section.

Crossing a Patrolled Frontier:
The Mediterranean as Graveyard

Not only migration but also colonialism and racism have been largely removed from Italy's public consciousness. "As a crucial dimension of Italian colonialism in East and North Africa," Cristina Lombardi-Diop writes, "race has undergone a process of removal akin to the one described by Angelo Del Boca with regard to Italy's colonial crimes (and the memory of colonialism tout court) that he views as 'a product of the total denial of colonial atrocities, the lack of debate on colonialism, and the survival in the collective imaginary, of convictions and theories of justification.'"[17] In "Africa," Boulhanna forces readers to come to terms with this double denial by turning the reader's gaze toward Africa. The poem opens with a rather stereotypical representation of Africa as a bunch of sweet, warm, black grapes,[18] which revives to a certain extent bell hook's "over-riding fear . . . that cultural, ethnic, and racial differences will be continually commodified and offered up as new dishes to enhance the white palate— that the Other will be eaten, consumed, and forgotten."[19] Africa is further outlined as "simple and sincere Wild, spontaneous Victim of iniquity / Of torment and nature."[20] In the closing lines, the African continent is further reduced to an immense mourner dressed in black, whose embrace is full of warmth and generosity. The poem ends with the brutal question "And who understands you?" followed by the violent statement "You are black and ugly / You are poor foredoomed / You are the Africa that must remain in Africa."[21]

In *Playing in the Dark*, Toni Morrison urges both readers and writers to critically interrogate "the associative language of dread and love that accompanied blackness."[22] Solicited by Morrison's call, I wonder whether Boulhanna is really capable of disrupting the racist language that associates Africa with darkness, death, and poverty, employed by colonial powers to support and justify their *mission civilisatrice*,[23] a stereotypical representation that is still being used in the media up to this very day.[24] Has Boulhanna learned, I ask borrowing Morrison's question, "how to maneuver to free up the language from its sometimes sinister, frequently lazy, almost always predictable employment of racially informed and determined chains"?[25]

In "Africa," Boulhanna undoubtedly targets issues relating to vision and representation, which are crucial sites for intervention and change, particularly in postcolonial literature.[26] In particular, the poem exposes and denounces a certain European gaze, a *regard sur l'Afrique*, that Europe has cast upon Africa in colonial times and that disturbingly continues to circulate even today as, among others, the controversial book *Sexe, race, et colonies* proves.[27] Moreover, by mobilizing a group of images related to death and mourning, Boulhanna's "Africa" seems to anticipate not only the innumerable deaths of Black men, women, and children in the Mediterranean Sea; also and in retrospect, it revisits the old and repeatedly violent encounter between imperial Europe and Africa as its colony.[28] This is a topic that public opinion, at least in Italy, has to a great extent failed to address. As Ruth Ben-Ghiat and Mia Fuller write with reference to Italian colonialism: "In the Italian case, it is not only colonialism's many violences that were *rimosse*—to use the Italian word that means both removal and repression—but also the shame of its defeat."[29] Boulhanna, I suggest, forces her readers to reorient their looks toward Africa, thereby indirectly urging them to excavate Italy's obliterated history of colonial domination in the Horn of Africa and Libya, and ultimately to acknowledge together with the Italy that was and still is in Africa, the Africa that has historically been and currently is in Italy.[30]

Boulhanna's poems of the 1990s inaugurate a debate on colonialism and racism, which will be taken up in the new millennium by writers such as, among others, Gabriella Ghermandi, Kaha Mohammed Aden, Igiaba Scego, Ribka Sebhatu, and Cristina Ali Farah, who have contributed to unearth through their creative works Italy's colonial history and bring it back to public consciousness, while also shedding light on the durable impact of colonial and imperial histories on the present with their painful legacy of stereotyping, discriminating, and justifying racist and xenophobic violence.[31]

With their emphasis on violence, loss, and mourning, Boulhanna's poems function today—thirty years after their first publication—as a powerful reminder of the transformation that the Mediterranean has recently undergone, from "a varied yet also integrated space," to use Karla Mallette's apt formulation, to an entrenched and patrolled border.[32] No longer a highly heterogeneous and interconnected space, marked by mobility and interaction, the Mediterranean Sea with its overloaded boats and drowned Black bodies has become a huge graveyard, while Libya has basically turned into a market for human trafficking and a penal colony, as documented by the photographer Narciso Contreras in "Libya: A Human Marketplace."[33] Khaled Mattawa's recent poetry collections *Mare Nostrum* (2019) and *Fugitive Atlas* (2020) provide another poignant account of the ongoing refugee crisis in the Mediterranean and of the EU's failed military attempts to stem it. In the 2016 documentary *Fuocoammare* (Fire at Sea) by filmmaker Domenico Rosi, viewers see what the inhabitants of Lampedusa (in particular, its fishermen) have been witnessing for decades: the transformation of the Mediterranean Sea into the front line of an undeclared war and of Lampedusa as its military outpost. *Fuocoammare* proceeds with no commentary or soundtrack but with long silences, offering viewers disturbing glimpses of the strange immobility of everyday life on the island, with its regular rhythms and quotidian rituals, contrasted with the vortex of rescue operations happening offshore. These two universes, despite being so proximate, never in fact overlap.

Writing on the new migratory routes taken by migrants to reach Europe, Ali Bensaad underlines the central role played by the Sahara and the subsequent "inevitable drawing together of the Maghreb and black Africa."[34] To quote Bensaad: "If the Mediterranean is a line of demarcation between Europe and the South, the Sahara functions very much in the same way, an echo of the northern line, bringing Europe even further south."[35] This is why we can talk of the Mediterranean Sea as a desertsea, as Najet Adouani's poetry collection (*Ṣaḥrā'u al-baḥri / Meerwüste*) clearly suggests.[36] As Bensaad claims, North African countries have become the "sentinel outposts" of Fortress Europe, which imposes on them a repressive role rather than coresponsibility in the management of common concerns, jeopardizing these countries' slow transition toward democratic forms of government.[37] One of the most striking examples of this fatal venture being the memorandum of understanding signed by the Italian government and the Libyan Government of National Accord in 2017 and tacitly renewed in 2020, a deal that as Alessandra Generale notes has "provoked waves of indignation from the civil society, NGOs, and associations for human rights, who accused Italy and the European Union, to be guilty and co-responsible of violation of human rights (and consequently of duties coming from the International Conventions) which occurred in the African country."[38]

Historical Excavation and Revision:
The Mediterranean as Crossroads

In "Africa," Boulhanna represents Africa as a mourner. Is she mourning, I ask, the many deaths taking place in the Sahara and the Mediterranean Sea, as migrants attempt to reach Europe? Is she also mourning the radical effacement that migrants underwent in the mass media in the 1990s, where they were mostly represented as "non-persons"?[39] Finally, shouldn't we all mourn the failure of a Euro-Mediterranean partnership inaugurated twenty-five years ago and, more generally, the failure of Altiero Spinelli and Ernesto Rossi's idea of Europe?

Writing in the aftermath of the 9/11 attacks and in protest against US war campaigns and the increase of surveillance and securitization measures, in *Precarious Life* (2004), Judith Butler rejects the idea that security problems require and justify violent measures, arguing that attacks to first world privilege should be seen as a chance to reimagine global relations in more equal terms. To quote Butler: "The dislocation from first world privilege, however temporary, offers a chance to start to imagine a world in which that violence might be minimized, in which an inevitable interdependency becomes acknowledged as the basis for a global political community."[40] If the events of September 11 have displayed the vulnerability of the United States, the daily deaths in the Mediterranean Sea, and the terrorist attacks involving European capitals and cities are revealing Europe's extreme fragility. Following Butler, I suggest that these tragic occurrences should not reinforce existing divisions but rather prompt a conceptualization and realization of an alternative political, which does not content itself with providing trade concessions and financial forms of cooperation in exchange for migration control, particularly the surveillance of maritime borders and the detection of small vessels. Excavating and unearthing the history of the Mediterranean as a sea that binds rather than kills may be a good starting point to imagine and realize a more sustainable political.

In *The Kingdom of Sicily, 1100–1500*, Karla Mallette reconstructs the history of Sicily, and, more broadly, of the Mediterranean, as one made of "complex cultural affiliations," without forgetting the tensions, conflicts, and deportations that characterized centuries of strong interaction.[41] In particular, the *Kitāb al-Rujāri / Book of Roger*, commissioned by Roger II at the Norman Court of Palermo to the geographer al-Idrisi, is emblematic of this eclectic and multilayered history of intercultural and interfaith collaboration, as Malette argues. According to a tale told by al-Idrisi himself and reported by Malette, the Norman king had "required representatives from the merchant ships that called at Sicilian ports to state their accounts of all the lands they knew from personal experience."[42] It is important to note that al-Idrisi was born in *Sabtah* (now Ceuta) in 1099. A Spanish enclave on the Moroccan northern shore of the Mediterranean Sea, Ceuta is sadly known today as a patrolled patch of land surrounded by a double fence and barbed wire. I wonder what al-Idrisi, as a man who crossed the Mediterranean Sea many times, would think of the militarized transformation of his native town *Sabtah*/Ceuta and of the shutting down of ports periodically invoked by anti-immigration politicians in Italy. What kind of tales would he collect today from the fishermen's ships and inflated boats that call at the Lampedusa port? Finally, would his geographical treatise still carry on its cover the poetically far-flung title *Kitāb nuzhat al-mushtāq fī ikhtirāq al-āfāq* (Book of the Journey for One Who Longs to Pierce through the Horizons)? As Malette explains in *European Modernity*, al-Idrisi compiled his ambitious work of geography by listening carefully to the stories told by the travelers who had reached Sicily on board of their boats. From these narratives, he constructed "a silver globe" and compiled his geographical masterpiece "as a descriptive accompaniment to the globe."[43] The "Book of Roger," as Malette points out, was to become "one of the most ambitious and accurate geographies of the Middle Ages."[44]

Let me ask provocatively: What kind of geographic treatise are we compiling today? Are our government authorities still guided by the genuine curiosity and by the *stupor*/marvel that was moving Roger as he commissioned the work to al-Idrisi and contemplated the silver globe while listening to his stories? I think we are in great need today of subjective atlases similar to the ones conceptualized and designed by Annelys de Vet in partnership with local communities—atlases that "construct new narratives" capable of "distinguish[ing] and preserv[ing] the differences" and of "critically question[ing] the apparently objective."[45]

There is yet another story to be told as we proceed to the end of this chapter, involving multiple Mediterranean crossings and breakthroughs. It is a tale involving another prominent Andalusian notable: the famous Ibn Rushd/Averroes.[46] The story—half legend, half historical account—is narrated by Toni Maraini in *Ballando con Averroè* (Dancing with Averroes) and takes place after Ibn Rushd's death. It chronicles the strange ways in which his corpse crossed the Mediterranean Sea on board a mule from Marrakesh, where he had been buried, to Cordova, his native town.[47] Ibn 'Arabi, who was born in Al-Andalus like Ibn Rushd and was known in the Middle Ages as "Doctor Maximus," confirms the story, by declaring that the curious caravan had approached unexpectedly one day in front of his very eyes: a mule carrying on one side a breadbasket with Ibn Rushd's corpse and, on the other side, one containing his medical and astronomic treatises, the only ones that had not been burned by the religious zealots of the time, the Almohadi.[48] The two baskets functioned as a balance.[49]

Ibn Rushd was the illustrious descendant of a family of famous jurists who had worked at the service of the caliph in Cordova. Later, he had been appointed at the Almohadi court in Marrakesh as the personal doctor of the caliph Abu Ya'qub Yusuf and as the commentator of Aristotle's oeuvre.[50] Here, he had also discovered a luminous star—known today as Canopo—and had meditated on the rotation of the earth and its spherical form, thus preparing the ground for one of the major discoveries that would take place in Europe some centuries later, the "Copernican revolution."[51] At the court of Abu Ya'qub Yusuf in Marrakesh, Ibn Rushd had also met the renowned mathematician, doctor, astronomer, philosopher, and writer Ibn Tufayl, whose fame would cross the Mediterranean and reach Europe. According to Maraini, his groundbreaking work, known in its Latin translation as *Philosophus Autodidactus*, would inspire later generations of philosophers such as John Locke, Thomas Hobbes, Isaac Newton, Voltaire, and Jacques Rousseau.[52] The philosophical theories of Ibn Rushd, however, which supported the "equality of all human beings" and the possibility of a fruitful coexistence between the reason of philosophy and that of religion, did not win the sympathy of either the Almohadi rulers or his fellow compatriots. Accused of heterodoxy, Ibn Rushd was expelled from the Almohadi court and his philosophical books burned.[53] Confined in Lucena, an important Jewish center in the Andalusian province, his thought had a deep impact on medieval Jewish philosophers, which played a crucial role in circulating his knowledge.[54] Long after his death, as historian María Rosa Menocal writes, the Christian Inquisition joined the Islamic censors and banned his work in 1210.[55] The seed of his insurgent philosophy, however, did not die out and survived in underground currents contributing to keep alive the principle of equality and the belief that religion and reason may exist yet in separate spheres and thanks to a precarious balance. As Maraini claims, Ibn Rushd's audacious and pioneering thought in the field of philosophy would later inspire a long current of thought from the Renaissance to the Enlightenment.[56]

Malette and Maraini's recuperation of historical figures such as al-Idrisi and Ibn Rushd provide readers with an alternative atlas of the Mediterranean basin, as an intricate and dialectical network of both maritime and terrestrial crossings that favored intellectual exchanges, transmissions, and translations between the two shores. This is a complex web that counterpoints the usual description of the Mediterranean basin as the theater for holy wars, religious obscurantism, and piracy. I am not implying that religious fanaticism, cultural antagonism, and tyrannical power did not exist. Still, the anecdotes involving al-Idrisi and Ibn Rushd/Averroes prove that even in those dark times there were men and women who engaged in concrete actions to extend human knowledge and realize more equilibrated, discerning, and therefore nonviolent societies freed from the disasters provoked by dogma, ignorance, and hatred.

On Not Beginning Anew: Stalling the Walk of a Funambulist

Historical figures like al-Idrisi and Ibn Rushd/Averroes are rarely mentioned in our classrooms. This is also true for writers who breach the general agreement that the literary and national space—at least in the case of Italy—should be homogeneous and recognizably white. As Caterina Romeo writes in "Racial Evaporations":

> For more than twenty years, migrant and postcolonial writers in Italy have denounced racism as a pervasive element in Italian society, articulated through exoticism, patronizing attitudes, microscopic and macroscopic racist acts, systematic marginalization, and state racism. . . . They have represented Italian social space as diversified, a space in which the juxtaposition of terms such as "black" and "Italian" does not constitute an oxymoron."[57]

Examining the emergence of literary works produced by so-called migrants within their respective national literatures, in the introduction to *Migrant Cartographies* (2005), Daniela Merolla and Sandra Ponzanesi call into question the invisibility of these new voices within the Italian literary canon.[58] Boulhanna herself is a ghostly figure in the Italian literary panorama. What do we know about her life and work thirty years after she published her first two poems? As I see them, "Immigrata" and "Africa" represent a bare beginning; they bear witness to the immense effort that this woman, this yet-to-be poet made to describe things from the beginning, *in history*, as Edward Said would have it.[59] In Boulhanna's poems, readers do not only find the words of a newcomer giving an account of herself and of her painful experience of dislocation. Theoretically, she is not very different from those traveling merchants who would be invited at the Norman court in Palermo to recount what they had seen and witnessed during their journeys across the Mediterranean and well beyond it. Unfortunately, in her case, listeners were not as dedicated as al-Idrisi and Roger II.

Yet the account she gives is novel and engaging. In her beginning as a poet, Boulhanna returns to, repeats, and revises the classical image of the migrant as a displaced, marginalized subjectivity filled with nostalgia and loss. Her embodied representation of the migrant woman inaugurates a different production of meaning, one that bears the mark of her gendered body and deliberately produces an alternative sense of the migratory experience with respect to that produced by male writers. Through her writing, Boulhanna not only mobilizes and neutralizes, in Morrison's own words, the symbolic figuration of blackness with "delicious sensuality" that the initial metaphor of the black grapes repeats and revises.[60] By uttering clear audible words, she manifests racism as pervasive and widespread.

Since Boulhanna writes in Italian, she expects to be recognized as an insider; by appropriating the language of the supposed host, she refuses to be a guest. In *Je Parle Toutes les Langues Mais en Arabe*, Abdelfattah Kilito claims that one can never free herself completely from the familial, familiar language. To what extent, I ask, does Arabic make itself audible in Boulhanna's Italian? Does she somehow speak Italian with an Arabic accent? To my ears, Boulhanna's language is paradoxically monolingual. Readers do not encounter Arabic words or Arabic sounds and rhythms in her poems, not even hints of these. Similarly, there is no explicit sign of her Moroccan roots anywhere. It is as if these cultural traces had been willfully eradicated. And yet both poems seem to have been swallowed up by a typical Moroccan, Maghrebi preoccupation—*al-ghurba*. This is an aspect that should not go unnoticed.

Reflecting on the fragile nature of many new projects, Said explains: "It is, however, very difficult to begin with a wholly new start. Too many old habits, loyalties, and pressures inhibit the substitution of a novel enterprise for an established one."[61] What kind of pressures and old habits, I wonder, have contributed to stall Boulhanna's funambolic walk? Why has her writing after the first beginning not began again anew? What kind of obstacles—political, social, material—have emerged along the way to inhibit, mine, and ultimately block her writing process?

As Said makes patently clear, beginning to write always implies a good dose of optimism, since one usually finds numerous obstacles on her way; as Virginia Woolf convincingly argues, in order to write, a woman needs a room of her own.[62] What happened, then, to Boulhanna's initial optimism? Did she ever find that quiet room of hers?

As a female writer who has encountered discouragement many times, and whose writing has been stalled by obstacles of different sorts, I have looked with wonder at Boulhanna's first intrepid steps on the global rope; I have been intrigued by her timid beginning, by her radical starting point. Accordingly, I have also been deeply disappointed by the realization that her writing has stopped, that she may have lost sight of a direction, trust in continuity.

As I am confronted with Boulhanna's aborted beginning, I wonder if the ways in which we tend to study, organize, circulate, and evaluate literary works may have inexorably compromised the development of her talent and her confidence in continuity. Her silence, I believe, is eloquent on this regard and raises a set of uncomfortable questions relating to visibility, audibility, recognition, and inclusion.

My aim in this chapter then, has been precisely to pay tribute to Boulhanna's first steps as a promising poet, while also calling attention to the feelings of frustration, abandonment, and failure that may seize a funambulist like her.

4

Oceanic Crossings

Nadine Ltaif's Ce que vous ne lirez pas

Born in Cairo, Nadine Ltaif grew up in Lebanon and moved to Montreal, Québec, in 1980 during the Lebanese Civil War. Her work is located at the crossroads between the geography of the Middle East and that of North America, classical Greek and Roman mythology and the urgent problems of our time. I argue in this chapter that Ltaif's poetry participates in what Lise Gauvin has called, with reference to Québec's tense linguistic reality, les *"littératures de l'intranquillité"* (the *literatures of disquiet*).[1] She borrows this term from Ferdinand Pessoa, a writer who struggled incessantly to harmonize his multiple selves in *The Book of Disquiet* (1914), a kaleidoscopic work that Pessoa left unfinished. According to Gauvin, in a context such as that of Québec, language is never an object that the author possesses once and for all, but rather a constant challenge, a preoccupation, a matter causing permanent anxiety.[2] A polyglot and translator like Pessoa, Ltaif confirms this condition of linguistic irresolution in "Écrire ou vivre l'échange entre les langues" (Writing or living the exchange between languages) and explains: "Arabic remains the unconscious of my text: the rhythm that structures the sentence, the musical composition of the poem. It's like singing an Arabic language in French."[3]

Reflecting on the historically tense relationship between language, literature, and social change in Québec, Louise Dupré underlines that literary works in Québec have often mirrored, and at times even anticipated, societal change.[4] Poetry, in particular, has often been traversed by seismic shocks that have erupted in spectacular ways at precise historical moments producing social and political change. The 1960s and 1970s, in particular,

were a period of political turbulence and national literary revival for Québec, culminating with the 1970 October crisis and the proclamation by
the prime minister Pierre Eliot Trudeau of a state of emergency. Two years
earlier, in 1968, the poetic manifesto "Speak White" had been publicly
recited by Michèle Lalonde. This was a politically charged poem in which
the speaker sarcastically condemned the racist taunt "Speak White,"
which was hurled at people in Québec who chose to speak publicly in
French and who considered themselves "the white Negroes of America"
(Negrès Blancs d'Amérique).[5] As Smaro Kamboureli notes, the multicultural agenda followed by the Canadian government in the 1980s in reaction to these events favored the emergence of a body of texts written by
authors belonging to different Native and ethnic backgrounds.[6] This was
also the case of Québec. As Susan Ireland and Patrice J. Proulx observe,
"The 1980s and 1990s witnessed the explosion of Québécois literature
written in French by authors of immigrant origins."[7]

The beginning of Ltaif's work as a poet dates back precisely to those
tumultuous years. In 1987, Ltaif published her first poetry collection, *Les
Métamorphoses d'Ishtar*, later translated into English as *The Metamorphoses of Ishtar* by poet and translator John Mikhail Asfour (2011). In 1991,
Entre les fleuves, finalist for the Émile Nelligan prize, was released, followed four years later by *Élégies du Levant* (1995) and in 1999 by *Les livres
des dunes* (1999). Ten years later, Ltaif published *Ce que vous ne lirez pas*
(2010), a poetry collection that represents the fulcrum of this chapter.[8]

Ltaif's poetry, as I hope to show, is deeply lyrical and intimate; the
tone is mournful and the language evocative. This is in line with a more
general trend in the contemporary poetry of Québec written by women.
As Laurent Mailhot and Pierre Nepveu note, the 1980s witnessed a reorientation of women poets from the public toward the intimate sphere in
the attempt to offer "une expérience subjective du monde."[9] Ltaif's voice
is deeply humane and affected by loss; in that sense, it shares a strange
commonality with other contemporary poets in Québec such as, among
others, Monique Bosco (to which the collection is dedicated) and Mona
Latif Ghattas.[10]

Ltaif's artistic project stimulates a re-vision of traditional binaries, such
as Christianity and Islam, East and West, local and global, and a transition

from antithesis to entanglement. Her speaker is precariously located "dans l'entre-deux," within a temporal, geographical, and existential in-between condition.[11] It is precisely this condition of in-betweenness, I suggest, that grants her the experience of a "morte-vivante" (living dead) who is "en deuil perpetuel" (in perpetual mourning) but also capable of regeneration.[12] In her poetry, the painful memory of a violent and traumatic past still haunts the present, and the speaker-voyager takes on the role of seer, dissenter, admonisher. The journey in her case becomes a quest for truth and is strictly bound to an activity of self-reflection and self-questioning.

Far from idealizing the past and reinforcing existing divisions, Ltaif takes audacious steps on a tightrope stretched taut between continents, cultures, and faiths not only to raise awareness on intercultural relations and convergences but also on the horror of cultural and religious antagonism. In her search for poise, lightness, and sharpness, she proves to be a skilled funambulist.

At the Crossroads of Reality and Myth: Journey to Al-Andalus

Drawing on Pierre Nepveu's *L'Ecologie du Réel*, Elizabeth Dahab claims that within the poetry of Québec "the notions of exile/madness, alienation, and a sense of loss, as well as the feeling of an absent or incomplete country, were already quite prevalent."[13] Ltaif's collection revisits these themes, seeing them through the filter of her personal story. The memory of the Lebanese Civil War, in particular, is a ghostly presence that looms over the entire collection and haunts the speaker as she wanders through the streets of Seville, New Delhi, Montreal, and Beirut.

Ltaif favors a subjective and mournful view to conflicts rather than an objective, documentary approach, developing a narrative based on affects such as vulnerability and grief and on the regenerative force of memory. Historical excavation in her collection is blended with mythical and phantasmagorical elements, since the poet is well aware of the impossibility of reconstructing the events faithfully and of documenting what happened precisely.[14] There is no remedy to the material destructions and human devastations that took place in wartime. This is why the poet makes recourse to the imagination to fill in those gaps and lacunae.[15]

The collection *Ce que vous ne lirez pas* (What you will not read) is divided into six sections; three of them illustrate journeys that the poet made to Andalusia, India, and Lebanon.[16] The first poem that opens the section "Exil Andalous, Espagne Novembre 2006" (Andalusian Exile, Spain November 2006) is "Guernica." Here, the speaker reflects on the tangible traces left by the Spanish Civil War on the topography of Madrid, moving intermittently between past and present, the Spanish Civil War and her own tourist wanderings across the Spanish capital. The contemplation of Pablo Picasso's famous painting triggers in the speaker a process of self-reflection and in the urban landscape a metamorphosis from touristic hub to landing-place for refugees:

Guernica

Toutes les rues
où nous sommes passées
hier: Fuencarral Atocha
Anton Martin
près de laquelle nous logeons
avaient été bombardées.
Dans le musée Reina Sofia
la métamorphose du tabeleau
Guernica.
Là où la violence
espagnole
s'est étalée
dans son ultime cruauté.
Des rues de la capitale
des métros
remplis de réfugiés.[17]

All the streets
we walked down
yesterday: Fuencarral Atocha
Anton Martin
close to where we spend the night
had been bombed.

In the Reina Sofia Museum
the metamorphosis of the painting
Guernica.
There where Spanish violence
has unfolded
in its extreme brutality.
Streets of the capital
subways
filled with refugees.

Picasso's black-and-white mural-sized oil painting *Guernica*, representing the aerial bombardments carried out by the Italian Fascist Aviazione Legionari and the Nazi German Luftwaffe against the Basque town of Guernica during the Spanish Civil War, triggers the transformation of Madrid from holiday destination to devastated city. As Hisseine Faradj rightly notes, in Picasso's painting, symbols denoting beauty and survival—a hand holding a flower in the foreground and another clinging to a kerosene lamp—are represented in close proximity to a horse in agony and a group of dismembered corpses.[18] These incongruous juxtapositions bring the artistic practice of the Cubist painter in relation to Ltaif's poetic credo that "écrire c'est peindre la vie / dans sa laideur / et sa beauté" (writing means painting life / in all its ugliness / and beauty).[19]

The poet returns to the idea that history is a complex tangle of beauty and horror in "Giralda." As the speaker climbs to the top of the Cathedral's bell tower in Seville, she is pulled back in time and reflects on the hatred and vainglory that this religious building simultaneously displays and hides. Originally erected during the reign of the Almohad dynasty in the twelfth century as the minaret for the Great Mosque of Seville, the Giralda was later transformed into the bell tower of the Cathedral of Santa Maria after the expulsion of the Jews decreed by Ferdinand and Isabella de Castilla in 1492 and the subsequent eviction of the Moriscos signed by King Philip III of Spain in 1609.[20] As María Rosa Menocal notes, the politics of persecution, expulsion, and cultural epuration pursued by the new rulers happened in clear contrast to a long history of intercultural and interfaith coexistence marked by "flagrant contradictions" that had characterized the province of al-Andalus for over seven hundred years.[21] This was a time, as Menocal notes, "when Jews, Christians, Muslims lived side by side . . . despite their intractable differences and enduring hostilities."[22]

In "Giralda," Ltaif evokes the sectarian divisions and conflicts that left a visible mark on the urban landscape; in "Séville (Giralda 2)" she further reads the tower as the unequivocal symbol of the cultural purge that took place at the expenses of Muslims:

A tower
and some walls
that separate cultures
between the sumptuous cathedral
irremediably crashing
under the weight of its catholicity
and the Arab tower
with its wiped out script
in Old Seville
in Veracruz
—some crimes
could remain
unpunished.[23]

While not denying that the story of al-Andalus is also one of coexistence, survival, and exceptional cultural flourishing and mixture, Ltaif refuses here to reproduce the myth of a multifaith utopia, highlighting the religious antagonism and brutal violence that also marked that history.[24]

As Eric Calderwood has clearly shown, the periodical "re-discoveries" of al-Andalus are emblematic of the ways in which culture has operated in conjunction with colonial power and of the risks and dangers embedded in the political use of memory and the instrumental reappropriation of crucial historical moments by political forces. In the nineteenth century, for instance, Washington Irving joined other Romantic Orientalists and described the splendor of the ruins of the Alhambra, spreading a fascination for anything Oriental, which—as Calderwood claims—opened the way to the colonial conquest.[25] More than a century later, in the 1940s and 1950s, General Franco retrieved the memory of al-Andalus to reinforce his image as the protector of religion and as a supporter of Islam against the Communists.[26] Besides having been periodically revisited for political ends, the story of al-Andalus, as Menocal has demonstrated, is also emblematic of the many ways in which myths of origin and national mythologies, such as the story of the Cid and of the Battle of Poitiers with roots in the history of the medieval province under Muslim rule, have been manipulated politically to foster national unity and spread the belief that national histories and literatures are internally homogeneous and were born out of the clash with other civilizations.[27]

Ltaif's journey to the historical province of al-Andalus ends with the poem "San Sebastián." This time the speaker is traveling on a plane taking her from Spain back to North America. The speaker identifies herself with Saint Sebastian, a mythical figure and a Christian martyr, thus blurring the boundaries separating reality and myth, life and death, historical account and popular religious creed. The figure of San Sebastián in this poem mirrors the in-between condition of the speaker as being caught between two "worlds":

San Sebastián

Martyr
J'étais sur un cheval
Je combattais les Maures
Le cheval encore vivant
Moi le poitrail transpercé
d'une lance
Pégase m'emmène
dans l'au-delà
C'est un avion
qui me transporte
vers le Nouveau Monde.[28]

Saint Sebastian

Martyr
I was on a horse
I was fighting the Moors

The horse still alive
my chest pierced
by a lance
Pegasus leads me away
in the afterworld
It's a plane
carrying me
to the New World.

Ltaif intermixes here Greek mythology, Christian hagiography, historical reconstruction, and her own imagination, representing the speaker fighting against "the Moors" and being rescued by a Pegasus. Life and death, survival and annihilation, reality and myth blur in this poem thanks to the figures of Saint Sebastian—a protector against the plague, according to the popular creed, which had revived earlier Greek and Roman myths—and that of the Pegasus. The association of the New World with an otherworldly dimension further confounds clear-cut categories separating a plane trip from a spiritual journey, life from resurrection. It is precisely this constant blurring of sharp divisions that complicates Ltaif's writing and renders it unique. Her work is located at the crossroads of secular and religious dimensions, ancient and modern times, opposite cardinal points. This intricate tangle will become clearer in the following section, as we move further east, toward India.

At the Crossroads of Wonder and Dread: Journey to India

In the section "Elles devaient être neuf pour avoir la force de l'éléphant, Inde 16 janvier 2006" (They had to be nine to have the strength of the elephant, India January 16, 2006), Ltaif writes about her journey to India and addresses a set of gender concerns by engaging once again in historical excavation and subjective reconstruction.

The poem celebrates the stylistic openness of Islamic art and the capacity of Islamic rulers in India to reshape local cultural elements promiscuously. The speaker looks with wonder at some human-made 'ajā'ib, such as the Jami Masjid, the mosque in New Delhi that was built by the

Mughal emperor Shah Jahan (r. 1628–58) and became the largest mosque
in India at the time of its construction,[29] and the majestic palaces of Rajaput, in Northern India, an area from which some of the stories of *The
Thousand and One Nights* originated and then traveled to Europe via Persia, the Abbasid caliphate, and Egypt.[30] What stupefies the speaker is not
only the massive size of the building but the fusion of cultural elements
in their rich ornamentation. The speaker's appreciation of the aesthetic
beauty of the buildings, however, cannot be separated from an ethical
judgment. During the visit to one of the royal palaces, in particular, some
dreadful details begin to emerge. As she wanders through the rooms, the
speaker has the impression of being followed by a spectral body, whose
vision evokes many other female figures of the ancient times:

> At times voiceless at times
> the philosopher Sappho
> at times dancer of the Temple
> Ishtar the sacred prostitute
> or Greek cariatyde
> A comrade follows me
> I meet her in different places
> At times mother
> at times sister.[31]

The mysterious woman mentioned in these lines follows the speaker as
she advances physically in the palace and bounces back temporally. We
witness the convergence in this ghostly figure of other women, who have
been sexually exploited or oppressed.[32] From the sacred temple of Innana/
Ishtar in ancient Babylon, readers are catapulted into the palace of a Raj-
pute prince (Maharaja) in twelfth-century India. As the speaker drifts
through the rooms of this palace, where the women were kept imprisoned,
it is her own exile that resonates with theirs:

> Yamouna had no wish to be chosen
> by the Maharajah to join his harem
> She sticks to Radika and her other sisters

They are nine and they will have the strength of the elephant
to fight the injustice
. . .

In their golden cages
they live an exile.[33]

The speaker is shocked by the sudden realization that the palace she is
visiting is not simply a touristic attraction but was in fact a place of confinement and torment for the women held captive there. The ghastly sighs
she hears confirm her dreadful impression.

As she leaves the palace and wanders off into the streets of an unknown
Indian city, the speaker is hit by the view of yet another female figure, this
time a young, veiled bride who uncovers her face in front of her eyes. This
act of unveiling leaves the speaker deeply unsettled:

I am surprised
how to understand
this offering
this desire to unveil oneself
in front of us who come
from the West?[34]

This time, the speaker no longer identifies with the female figure that
stands in front of her but with a more general "nous," a collectivity that
is said to be coming from the West. The speaker's unraveling of what she
perceives to be yet another Indian "mystery" continues as follows:

Peut-être voulait-elle qu'on transporte son image avec nous
    en Occident
pour qu'elle exhale un parfum de liberté
Car elle sait qu'ailleurs
la liberté existe
pour elle aussi
Je tente encore
d'essayer de comprendre
mon malaise face

à ce don du visage
de la jeune mariée
toute orange
voilée.[35]

Perhaps she wanted us to carry her image over to the
        West
for it to exhale a fragrance of freedom
For she knows that elsewhere
freedom exists
even for her
I'm still trying
to understand
my unease vis-à-vis
the gift of her face
of this young bride
all orange
veiled

The unease expressed by the speaker in these lines derives from her interpretation of the woman's act of unveiling as an invocation for help. The
speaker perceives the woman's appeal and her own incapacity to intervene
and liberate her as troublesome.

Overall, in the collection, Ltaif situates gender issues in a global context and in a historical frame. Her reflection on gender oppression and
sexual exploitation stretches from ancient Mesopotamia to today's India.
Still, despite her sensitivity, when addressing gender oppression, the poet
appears to remain entrapped in the East/West divide. Her portrait of the
Indian maharani, for instance, is still soaked with the harem fantasy typical of nineteenth-century Orientalist writers, such as Gerard de Nerval
and Gustave Flaubert, who portrayed women as wrapped up in veils and
relegated to a secluded space.[36] As Marilyn Booth has convincingly shown,
the term "harem" has multiple meanings, and its understanding has
changed over time and across geographical locations.[37] While, in the previous poems, Ltaif represented the East and the West as intimately inter-
related although at times conflicting, when addressing gender concerns

the two appear to be at the antipodes. It follows that the speaker finds herself located in an uncomfortable position because caught between the two. Ltaif's representation of the Indian bride, who uncovers her face in a spectacular way, is particularly problematic, since it reproduces the colonial/imperial representation of veiling as the visible sign of the oppression of women and of unveiling as a precondition for their emancipation.[38] Despite these ambivalences, Ltaif's poems raise interesting points on the tense relationship between secularism and religion, gender oppression and women's self-determination, Islam and the so-called principle of laïcité, which has exacerbated the debate on the Muslim veil, particularly in France.[39] Eventually, Ltaif's poems appear to anticipate the travel of that heated controversy from France to Québec, where an anti-Muslim ban on face coverings was approved in 2017, six years after France became the first European country to impose a ban on full-face covering.

At the Crossroads of Memory and Guilt: Montreal and Beirut

In the section "Square Saint-Louis," Ltaif's attention switches back to Québec. In "Acrobate du matin," for instance, the speaker identifies herself with an acrobat, who struggles hard to find a precarious balance and to skillfully control her body, as she walks along a wire stretched above urban zones of exclusion and marginalization.[40] What puts her balance at risk in one single morning is the shocking view of a homeless person in the city's public park and the news of a man aged twenty-one, who committed suicide. As in the case of Rawi Hage's gloomy novel *Cockroach* (2008), Ltaif's poems are reminders that the immigrant contact zones of Montreal have not been always treated as pure conviviality and that the Canadian metropolis is no mythic al-Andalus.[41]

In "Fourmilière" (Anthill), in particular, the speaker observes passersby and compares them to industrious ants and mechanical automates, performing a series of repetitive operations while being afflicted by the weight of an unknown crime. The poem echoes Georges Abou-Hsab's "Rue St. Catherine. 20 September 1997; 18h38," in which Montreal is once again outlined as a "crepuscular city / crucified anonymous."[42] A similar sinister atmosphere can also be found in "Anthill":

Il y a le poids la lourdeur du crime
que nos enfants n'ont pas commis
que nous-même n'avons pas commis
un mal qui n'a pas connu sa rédemption
et qui pleure
de siècle en siècle
un pardon non exaucé
en cette ville du Yom kippour.

There is the weight the burden of the crime
that our children did not commit
that we ourselves did not commit
an evil that has not known its redemption
and that implores
century after century
a forgiveness unrealized
in this Yom Kippur city.

The most solemn religious fast of the Jewish year—Yom Kippur—transcends its strict sectarian boundaries in this poem, since the atonement and repentance invoked by the Jewish believers during this festivity spreads over to include all passersby, who need to be forgiven for the wrongs inherited by their ancestors.

Historical wrongs and the blame but also forgetfulness that follows them link the cities of Montreal and Beirut in unexpected ways. In the section " . . . Et autre voyages" (. . . And other journeys), the speaker abandons the Nordic city of Montreal and travels South to the Mediterranean, engaging in the impossible task of circumscribing Beirut in a few lines.[43] The poet outlines the city as gleaming in daylight and scintillating at night, while its religions cannibalize each other silently. A Phoenix that has arisen from its ashes many times, Beirut appears to be jeopardized by the treacherous residues of the civil war, the "muffled grudges" that, like a highly inflammable substance, can set the city on fire at any time.

A stroll across the downtown, in particular, prompts the speaker to excavate the traumatic history of the civil war and to capture in a snapshot the few tangible traces left by the war on the urban landscape:

Centre-ville

Je photographie seule, lors de ma déambulation brûlante sous le soleil.
Les vieilles maisons d'Achrafiyé. Et puis, deux immeubles encore
criblés de balles. Des passoires restées pour mémoire de l'horreur.
Enfin, Lui, le centre-ville, nouveau, astiqué. Je place dans mon cadre
une mosquée et une église.
J'essaie toujours de me placer sous cet angle. L'horloge de l'Etoile. Des
souks et Le Petit Café. Le soir: ce sera le narguilé qui fume de partout.

Difficile de faire le point dans tout ce méli-mélo historique.
Culturel. Multiconfessionnel. Pourtant je me sens appartenir encore
à toutes ces différences. C'est une chance de pouvoir revenir sur place
comme on retourne à son ancienne vie.[44]

Downtown

I take photos all by myself, during a stroll under the burning sun.
The old houses of Ashrafiyah. And then, two buildings still riddled
with bullets. Colanders standing to commemorate the horror. Finally,
Him, the downtown, in a new guise, glossy. I place in my frame a
mosque and a church.
I always try to put myself in this angle. The clock of Nadjma square.
Some souks and Le Petit Café. In the evening: it will be the narghile
that smokes everywhere.

How difficult it is to take stock of all this historical mishmash.
Cultural. Multifaith. Quite surprisingly, I feel to belong to all these
differences still. It's a real luck being able to come back here as one
returns to her early life.

By navigating Beirut's most contested urban space—the Burj or downtown
area—the speaker retrieves the city's precarious topography divided along
ethnic lines, which was razed first by bombardments and later by bulldoz-
ers.[45] The poet sketches here an intimate portrait of the city center, refusing to support either a nostalgic and idealized reconstruction of it as an
interethnic and interfaith utopia or a neglectful and profit-oriented devel-
opmental plan, as advertised by the private real estate company Solidère

with the slogan "Beirut—An Ancient City for the Future."[46] Indeed, as Adrienne Fricke notes, "by providing a sanitized and safe vision of a happy, prosperous past, the Solidère architects are producing a nostalgia whose commercial and tourist value is as significant as it is repressive of more personal, troubled memories."[47]

In "Downtown," Ltaif acknowledges and mourns the material and human losses caused by the war, thus competing with the state-sponsored amnesia and the narratives of progress and profit circulated by real estate agents and businesspeople. For Ltaif, the downtown is not "a cleared-out blankness" invoking with force a reconstruction plan,[48] but a wounded urban fabric haunted by painful memories, spectral buildings, and an incommensurable void.[49]

No other city exemplifies the paradoxical condition of lyrical beauty and brutal reality better than Tyre, a town south of Beirut that had been a major Phoenician port but also a city periodically under siege.[50] Ruled by the Assyrians and the Achaemenian kings of Persia, Tyre was conquered after a seven-month siege by Alexander the Great in 332, who completely destroyed the mainland portion of the town and massacred or sold into slavery its inhabitants. The town was later destroyed again by the Mamluks in 1291 and, more recently, bombarded several times during Israeli attacks in Southern Lebanon. One should note that this town, which few today would be able to locate on a map, became renowned during antiquity for the "highly desirable and expensive" purple dye that was extracted from a shellfish and exported by the Phoenicians first to Carthage and later to Rome, where it became a symbol of power, prestige, and wealth.[51] We need to excavate Tyre's rich and multilayered history to understand fully Ltaif's mournful representation of this postapocalyptic city and her firm stance on nonviolence, as epitomized by the following lines:

But suddenly Tyre calls me and obsesses me

It is empty
It is emptied of its inhabitants
It's a dead city
They have all fled the enemy bombs.[52]

The sudden memory of Tyre functions for the speaker as an epiphany, as she suddenly realizes that the city with its ghostly silence and empty streets is both a reminder of past sieges and an admonishment for the future. The sense of weariness expressed by the speaker is particularly evident in the following lines, where she laments having spent most of her life watching men fight against each other:

On passe des vies
à regarder se battre
les hommes.

Je ne suis pas là
alors que je prépare
un guacamole
Ma tête s'est envolée
elle se trouve au Liban
alors que les avions
survolent la région
et se préparent à lancer
des bombes.

Les faibles bruits de la rue Clark
sont amplifiés dans ma tête
et j'écoute les bombardements
de l'autre côté du monde.[53]

We spend our lives
watching men
fight against each other.

I am not t/here
as I prepare
a guacamole
My head has flown away
it is in Lebanon
as airplanes
fly over the region

and prepare to launch
their bombs.

The hushed noises of Clark Street
are amplified in my head
as I listen to the shelling
on the other side of the world.

Even if physically distant from the conflict, the speaker in this poem feels
emotionally involved and deeply affected by the news that report of bombardments in Southern Lebanon. And yet the hushed noises of the rue
Clark in Montréal are deafening only for the speaker, an indirect sign of
the general indifference to the plight of the people in Lebanon.

Reflecting on the relationship between crisis and memory in Lebanon,
Andreas Pflitsch and Angelika Neuwirth have noted the following: "One
may even state that virtually all the Lebanese literature written during and
after the civil war is a work of processing memory, predominantly with a
de-mythisizing, integrative objective."[54] I see Ltaif's poetry as contributing
to this type of project, one that uses memory to defy the brutality of violence
and the cruelty of oblivion.

The poet's emphasis on memory is not new in the literary panorama
of Lebanon, even less in that of France and Québec. Yet Ltaif's tireless
historical excavation and accurate reconstruction of historical facts and
places takes on an unexpected and original look in the Québécois context,
since it offers a precious counterpoint to the widespread and indistinct
Québécois statement "je me souviens." Indeed, as Dahab notes:

> the Québec motto, *je me souviens* (I remember), also used on Qué-
> bec issued license plates, a motto that pertains to the multiple heri-
> tage of Québec, has evolved, according to Québécois noted historian
> Yvan Lamonde, into an intransitive aphorism that has forgotten what it
> should be remembering in the first place, thus becoming strictly self-
> referential: reminding one to remember (that which one has forgotten).[55]

Ltaif's sharp use of memory is different from the self-referential and
vague Québécois motto mentioned by Dahab; her act of remembrance is

lucid, precise, and sympathetic. It further distances her from a French canonical figure like Marcel Proust, the pioneer of a rather self-absorbed and ephemeral type of memory. In his monumental novel *In Search of Lost Time*, the aristocratic narrator involuntarily recovers the forgotten memories of his childhood years, the moment he dips a small madeleine—a national symbol of France—in a cup of tea. By contrast, in Ltaif's case, the speaker's memory is not activated by a quintessentially French sponge cake but by some disturbing noises coming from afar, that the speaker hears as she is preparing a Mexican, transnational dip: a guacamole. More important, the memories she retrieves are not of family comfort and bedtime habits but of urban destructions and human devastations. The faint noises heard by the speaker in Montreal resonate with Tyre's bombardments that no one hears, bringing back to life a familiar childhood landscape: that of war-torn Beirut. This spontaneously resurgent memory with lasting effects echoes Andrée Chedid's personal account reported by Francine Bordelau, according to which, whenever she heard a horn, no matter what city she was in, the sound would immediately bring her back to the streets of Cairo during her childhood years. As she states: "It is also the landscape of my childhood, this landscape that impresses one to death. So when I hear a horn in any corner of the world, all the streets of Cairo suddenly come up again."[56]

Organized at the MAXXI Museum in Rome in 2018, the exposition *Home Beirut: Sounding the Neighbors* while celebrating the cultural effervescence and sonic vitality of Beirut also reminded visitors of the deafening sounds of its bombs. Most of the visual works displayed in the museum's rooms echoed the hushed voices and moral outcry that follow unacknowledged atrocities and the (loaded) silence that Ltaif's collection so aptly captures and reverberates.[57] The Rome exposition highlighted in particular Beirut's baffling condition as a producer of world-renowned poignant melodies as well as a reverberator of global detonations. In the curators' own words: "Beirut is a unique musical instrument that, oscillating between deafening explosions and romantic songs, constantly expresses the cacophony of the world. More precisely, it is a home resonating with the outcries of its neighbors, near and far."[58] Fouad Elkhoury's installation "Le plus beau jour" (The most beautiful day), in which gorgeous photographs are projected on two white bedsheets lightly moved by a cooling fan, epitomizes Beirut's pure splendor while also indirectly hinting at its bursting fury. Its fascinating soundtrack interrupted by the feverish lines of Etel Adnan's "To Be in a Time of War" captures at best the contradictions, tensions, and breaks that make up Beirut particularly, and the contemporary world more generally.[59]

The Funambulist's Ultimate Challenge:
The Surreptitious Ascent to the Canon

Ltaif's poetic imaginary is populated with a plurality of myths, ghostly figures, and themes that span from North America to the Middle East and further east. A swarming Canadian metropolis with its zones of exclusion functions as counterpoint to the spectral downtown of the Lebanese capital, marketed alternatively as touristic attraction, archeological site, ultramodern and economically exclusive hub.[60] Ltaif's poems not only address typical feminist topics from a subjective perspective but also reiterate traditional Québécois themes with a surprising twist. The North, for instance, which traditionally represents in Québécois writing the mythical frontier and the end of the world coincides in Ltaif's poetry with Lebanon's South, which is perceived as inaccessible and out of reach. The Mediterranean sea rather than the river St. Laurent is reconfigured in her collection as a mythical gateway to access the larger world and, in Karla Mallette's own words, as an incredible "engine of cultural transmission."[61]

Ltaif's poems chronicling her journeys eastward evoke the rich Arabic *rihla* (travelogue) tradition, which "involves travelers whose journeys are replete with references to lands, cities, and countryside."[62] Whereas Ibn Jubayr (d. 1217) and Ibn Battuta (d. 1368) took the pilgrimage to Mecca as the impetus for their travel narratives, Ltaif revisits the traditional Islamic pilgrimage, since in her poems the pilgrimage is not meant for worship but rather for an act of remembrance and mourning.[63] Moreover, in opposition to Anne Blunt's Orientalist travelogue A *Pilgrimage to Nejd*, which, as Ali Behdad has demonstrated, was heavily edited by her husband, Ltaif's poetic account of her travels is not interrupted by a masculine voice that gives discursive authority to her narrative.[64] The poet is nobody's "traveling appendage" and her position is not that of a "note taker or sketcher" but of an authoritative writer.[65] Nor does Ltaif follow what Behdad has called "the hedonistic tradition in Orientalism that viewed travelling in the Orient as a leisurely stepping out of the familiar reality of European home, a journey that would ease the cultural ennui associated with daily life."[66] In her case, traveling is not meant for sightseeing but for "making sense," and it is animated by a true desire to know, understand, bear witness to the injustice, and eventually forgive.

Ltaif's evocative and far-reaching poetics contests monolithic identities and a univocal sense of belonging. This is why her poetry can be included among the postwar Lebanese diasporic texts, which, as Syrine Hout notes, "inscrib[e] a homing desire while simultaneously critiquing discourses of fixed origins."[67] Hers, however, is not a poetics of the "non-lieu" nor a celebration of happy nomadism and hybridization. Her speaker, in other words, travels not lightly, to use Nadje Al-Ali's apt formulation.[68] She is neither a flaneuse—in the tradition of Charles Baudelaire's nineteenth-century literary rendition: a stroller who lazily criss-crosses the urban center—nor a disengaged idler or simple voyeur. On the contrary, she is a lucid and participative observer who is alert to history and attentive to the time and place she happens to occupy.

Ltaif's writing is never indifferent to local, national or transnational tragedies, no matter their scale. The poet participates to the private plights and sorrows of a young maharani imprisoned in a twelfth-century Rajaput palace as well as to the tragedy of the inhabitants of Tyre and Guernica forced to flee the bombardment of their city. Hers is a poetry in the tradition traced by Anne-Marie Alonzo, a poetry that is both "ici ou/et ailleurs" (here or/and elsewhere) and that takes on the duty to "tracer sans dire/ expliquer: ceci est sable ou neige" (tracing without saying/explaining: this is sand or white snow).[69] Finally, in line with the writing of Andrée Chedid, Ltaif's poetry performs a constant investigation of the human condition in the attempt to escape the risk of "*l'étroite peau*," of navel-gazing.[70]

Clearly, the poet is well aware and feels the weight of French as a language with a high status and a prestigious literary tradition, as was the case long time ago in the two colonial outposts of Québec and Lebanon. Her style is lucid, polished, and restrained, her aesthetics disciplined, formally rigorous, and harmonious. Ltaif's linguistic craftsmanship, which avoids experimentation and linguistic disruption, may seem incongruous with her poetics of ruins ("la poétique des ruines"), yet responds to her attempt to patiently piece together the fragments of her own identity and of the bombed-out cities she visits or evokes.[71] Her poetry takes the form of a solo recital, in which the speaker provides her listeners with a detailed account of things seen, heard, and experienced. Hers is a poetry that well fits Judith Butler's double formulation of poetry "as evidence and as appeal, in which each word is finally meant for another."[72]

The poet, in particular, breaks out of the traditional frame of war and counters its quotidian acceptance through an emphasis on vulnerability, grief, and loss. This is why she vehemently condemns the instrumental use of history and the biased or sanitized reconstruction of historical events that reinforce divisions, hatred, and sectarianism. It is precisely to counter institutional distortions and official silences together with the social forgetfulness engendered by political myopia that she engages in a complex literary project aimed to excavate memory, rescue it from oblivion, and employ it as a tool to redirect the future.[73] Instead of commodifying and marketing a glorious past, Ltaif invites readers to carefully cultivate and preserve the memory of historical atrocities so that future wrongs can be avoided. Since she tightly binds together past and present, Ltaif joins Nicole Brossard's idea that one should not cultivate memory out of a form of nostalgia but to stimulate an observation and critical questioning of the present. In Brossard's own words: "The photo album does not make me nostalgic, it stimulates me, encourages me to observe and to question the visible and the invisible of our presence in the world. We must maintain our memory as we maintain a garden, with its roots and its life cycle, because in it hides largely what constitutes our living identity."[74] The danger of a recrudescence of the specters of the past in the form of sectarian divisions, ethnic conflict, religious fanaticism, and political amnesia is indeed always lurking. Nor is non-violence an uncontested and untroubled position, as Butler reminds us in this passage: "Non-violence is precisely neither a virtue nor a position and certainly not a set of principles

that are to be applied universally. It denotes the mired and conflicted position of a subject who is injured, rageful, disposed to violent retribution and
nevertheless struggles against that action (often crafting the rage against
itself)."[75]

Ltaif's narrative, although bleak and painful, is not disheartening. In
"Voilà" (Look here), the poet invites readers to take notice of and be rein-
vigorated by the sight of a nature that cyclically revives after the long winter: "Look here everything is to start over again, restarting from scratch,
the lawn, the grass, the first shoots, the stems, the plants, and so on and
on."[76] These, I suggest, are Ltaif's "āyāt," the miraculous signs of survival
of which she is also a great celebrant.

As I see her, Ltaif's speaker positions herself in between conflicting
temporal plans and geographical dimensions. Hence, the speaker's private
drama of exilic death and diasporic rebirth comes to mirror the urban
drama of Beirut itself, whose iconic status has been compressed by Nadja
Tuéni in this laconic line: "Elle est mille fois morte, mille fois revécue"
(She is thousand times dead, thousand times reborn).[77] As in the theater
and fiction of her fellow compatriots Wajdi Mouawad and Abla Farhoud,
Ltaif uses a self-reflexive mode and a series of nonrealistic strategies—
ghostly apparitions, frightful sights, and reemerging visions of the past—to
revisit a traumatic history. The past in her poetry still haunts the present,
and the survivor feels the obligation to mourn, remember, and bear witness. Her poetic oeuvre, I claim, represents a memo—in Djelal Kadir's
poignant formulation, "a reminder of the past and . . . an advertence for a
time to come."[78]

All in all, Ltaif's poetry is a recital that takes the form of a lamentation
in the tradition of the Bible and of ancient tragedies. This is why her poetic
work is directed to a chorus of planetary size, whose role is to observe,
listen to, comment on, and make sense of the main recitation. Besides
being a living testament, the collection is also a written dedication. The
book is explicitly dedicated to Monique Bosco but also addressed to an
anonymous female figure who, as the title and the opening poem make
clear, will not be able to read the book, despite having been a source of
inspiration and motivation throughout. In the closing poem, the speaker
addresses this mysterious woman as follows:

Aujourd'hui chère madame
vous auriez fêté vos quatre-vingts ans
Il est 8h du matin
sur le toit un vent chaud
prépare une douce journée
on annonce 30 degrés
vous n'auriez pas aimé
cette journée

Ceci achève le livre de votre vie
votre corps a décidé de mettre fin
à sa vie matérielle
combien nous allons nous sentir seuls
dans notre quotidien
ce qui reste de vous
votre rire
votre présence
votre absence
et l'été sans vous
et l'automne sans vous
et l'hiver sans vous
le plus dur
sera le printemps
sans vous.[79]

Today dear lady
you would have turned 80
It is 8 a.m.
and on the roof a warm wind
prepares a sweet day
30 degrees are being announced
you would not have liked
a day like this

This one accomplishes the book of your life
your body decided to put an end
to its material life

how lonesome will we feel
in our daily life
what remains of you
your laugh
your presence
your absence
and summer without you
and autumn without you
and winter without you
the toughest
will be spring
without you.

As is typical of Ltaif's writing, the closing poem is not cleansed of but soaked with pain; the cultivation of the memory of the speaker's friend functions once again as a powerful tool to counter an otherwise unbearable loss.

A recognized and acclaimed poet with a thirty-year-long career, Ltaif today rejects the label "migrant writer," striving instead to be included in the literary canon of the country in which she has been residing for so many years and whose culture she—together with so many other writers, poets, and intellectuals of non-Canadian or mixed descent—has contributed to enrich, diversify, and revitalize. As she poignantly asserts: "There was a time when the label 'migrant writing' was needed. It gave us a voice. Yet this same label has ended to lock us in a box from where we find it difficult to get out today."[80]

A clear-sighted funambulist, Ltaif has managed to fearlessly cross the global landscape to bring together devastated lands and people. After this arduous tightrope walk, she is now ready to start a new challenge: the dazzling ascent to the canon.

PART 3

BREAKS

5

Breaking Love as an Ideal

Maram al-Massri's A Red Cherry on a White-Tiled Floor

Born in Latakia, Syria, Maram al-Massri moved to Paris in 1982 and currently resides there. Her first poems appeared in Arab magazines in the 1970s and have been translated into many languages. Today, she is considered one of the most fascinating female voices in contemporary Arab (diasporic) poetry. Her poems, as I will show, grapple with loss in myriad ways, thus amplifying the affective cost of her severed relationship with the Syrian community. As Adrienne Rich notes, "Whether her or his social identity, the writer is, by the nature of writing, someone who strives for communication and connection, someone who searches, through language, to keep alive the conversation with what Octavio Paz has called 'the lost community.'"[1] Al-Massri's poems, however, are not nostalgic and sorrowful compositions; rather, they are quotidian and deeply sensuous poems in Rich's sense of the term, "poems good enough to eat, to crunch between the teeth, to feel their juices bursting under the tongue, unmicrowable poems."[2]

Included in the 2004 bilingual collection *A Red Cherry on a White-Tiled Floor* translated by Khaled Mattawa, the poems discussed in this chapter are short and labeled with numbers from 1 to 100, which were composed, respectively, in 1996 and 2000. Al-Massri talks with frankness about physical love and female lust, represents the female lover in rather unconventional ways, and challenges romantic fantasies of wedded bliss. In particular, the poet spoils the performance of deference and loyalty expected not only from the faithful wife but also from the submissive

111

citizen, thus breaching the traditional separation between the private and the public domain. In line with other post-1967 Arab writers, al-Massri unrelentingly exposes the silent complicity between patriarchy and authoritarianism, while also showing how affects such as shame, blind loyalty, and fear perpetuate what Tuula Juvonen and Marjo Kolehmainen have termed "affective inequalities" in both the private and public domains.[3]

A defiant funambulist, al-Massri's female speaker audaciously walks on the tightrope of love, training hard to find a precarious balance between two opposite poles: the pursuit of her own sexual pleasure and the social constraints that limit her liberty. The tension between sensual passion and the rigidity of social norms is exemplified in the title through the image of the red cherry—a symbol for carnal love and sensuality—placed against the background of a white, aseptic tile. The reference to the sanitized, germ-free floor evokes what Judith Halberstam has defined, with reference to the cycle *Alguna Parte* by photographers Cabello/Carceller, as "the clean and hygienic spaces of hetero-normative domesticity."[4] Like Cabello/Carceller's photographs, showing the debris of human interaction in empty bars (e.g., the stickiness of the floor, the broken glass, the dirt), al-Massri's lyrics disturbingly lay bare the failure of love to last and, by extension, the failure of political hope. The collection reads like an archive of "broken intimacies," to borrow an expression from Heather Love, in which love is never romanticized or idealized but foregrounded in all its contradictions, disappointments, and failures.[5] The poet indeed represents a series of occasional encounters between two clandestine lovers, whose infatuation is ardent but most of the time short-lived.

Al-Massri's poems, as I will show, are poems in chiaroscuro: they describe relationships between light and dark, where shining moments of euphoria and optimism make darker affects such as loss and delusion really stand out. Her poetry, despite its intensity and beauty, frustrates fantasies of eternal love and makes palpable, in Halberstam's own words, "the failure of love to last, the mortality of all connection, the fleeting nature of desire."[6] In that sense, it contradicts the ideology of love in societies governed by religious norms, where (indissoluble) married life is seen as the only regulated and socially acceptable context for love and sexuality.[7] On the other hand, since it underlines loss and the suffering that comes with it, al-Massri's poetry further challenges the ideology of love in neoliberal societies governed by commodification, in which, as Alain Badiou notes, "relationships are made and remade in the name of a cosy, consumerist permissiveness."[8]

Al-Massri's poetry, I claim, is not only thematically but also stylistically innovative. Her straightforward, bare language, her emphasis on the quotidian, and her use of simple, unsophisticated metaphors set her at odds with the conventions of classical Arabic love poetry. The poet breaks with the stylistic artifices and formally stringent rhyme scheme of traditional poetic love forms, particularly the pre-Islamic *qaṣīda*, with its binding tripartite structure, and the *ghazal*, grounded on syntactically and grammatically complete couplets.[9] She further breaks free from the fixed gender roles that frequently characterize these two forms, with the male poet-speaker lamenting and articulating the severity of his love in clearly audible words, and the female beloved relegated to the role of an impossibly beautiful and habitually unattainable object of love. By contrast, al-Massri's female speaker has an active sexual role and is animated by physical desire, which has no cathartic or elevating power but rather functions as a shattering and destabilizing force. And yet, despite these formal breaks, al-Massri's lyrics keep the typical somber and emotionally intense mood of canonical love poetry in Arabic intact.

Few women poets before her had taken the courage to turn their back to the classical tradition. Among them, as Muhsin J. al-Musawi claims, Nazik al-Mala'ika (the female pioneer of the free verse) and Fadwa Tuqan, who had put herself in a direct line of descent with classical male poets yet had also expressed the urgent necessity for female poets to engage with more pressing, everyday concerns and to develop an honest style freed from the affectation of her male predecessors.[10] To quote Tuqan: "The pre-Islamic, the Umayyad and the Abbasid poets lived with me. They ate, drank, did household chores and bathed with me. They talked to me and I talked to them. . . . From that time, I turned my back on the Abbasid style, my main ambition being to write poetry deriving its beauty from simplicity, flexibility, truthfulness, and poetic expression free from affectation."[11]

Like Tuqan's poetry, al-Massri's writing is simple, unadorned, and crystal clear. This is why she has also been associated with the ancient Greek poet Sappho, particularly for her refined and essential language, her intense and candid imaginary, her spontaneous style, and her colloquial tone. Exiled to Sicily, Sappho's plainspoken verses had received incendiary attacks from Christian censors in Alexandria, Rome, and Constantinople.[12] Despite having been the target of vehement condemnations, Sappho's verse fragments outlived the cries of the censors and were unearthed by a group of archeologists in Egypt during their excavations in Oxyrhynchus (1898–1907).[13] Quite ironically, they were brought back to life, thanks to some ancient papier-mâché coffins that contained some of her verse fragments.[14] This was poetry that had been consigned to the grave and that had sprang up again against all expectations.

Opened on Valentine's Day in 2017 in the crypt at the St. Pancras Church in London, the art exhibition *Radical Love: Female Lust* presented the paintings of forty-eight contemporary female artists from around the world, whose works had been inspired by poems written by premodern Andalusian and Arab female poets who had unapologetically addressed the topic of female lust.[15] As in the case of Sappho's fragments resumed through excavations in an ancient burial spot, these long-forgotten poetic fragments were recovered and publicly displayed in a London crypt. The generative force of these poems functioned as a source of inspiration for new radical artworks created by contemporary visual artists. I suggest that a similarly underground and regenerative force can also be found in al-Massri's lyrics.

"Broken Intimacies": Female Lust and the Body

Female lust and the body play a key role in al-Massri's collection, where physical love is outlined as a *surprise*, in Laurent Berlant's sense of the term, "the encounter with what disrupts our expectations by breaking through the defensive barriers associated with routine."[16] Since it is a driving force that cracks open customary habits and traditional standards of morality, physical love is perceived by the speaker as silly and ill-advised. Poem 2, in particular, manifests love as hazard and folly.[17] The speaker's availability in this poem reveals a dangerous exposure, an imprudent openness; the internal dynamism, resulting from the swift actions performed by the speaker's heart, increases the liveliness and exuberance of the whole scene. In this strikingly succinct and terse poem, al-Massri outlines female lust as an experience that overwhelms the speaker; in Elizabeth Grosz and Elspeth Probyn's terms, hers is a sexuality that "spills the boundaries of its proper containment, the unease of bodies breaking and flowing over the limit."[18]

Al-Massri's female speaker does not only voluntarily open the doors of her heart to her occasional lovers but also deliberately ignites their passion. As in Sappho's fragment 105, where the red apple embodies sensual passion, in poem 64 al-Massri displays a consuming desire, epitomized by the red cherries, which the lover wears as an ornament to embellish herself and arise her lover's lust.[19] The poem is based on the tension between passion and short-lived satisfaction, hunger and voracious appetite, which highlights the ephemeral and deceptive nature of love. Poem 1, which opens the collection, exemplifies these tensions:

أنا سارقة السَّكَاكِرِ،
أمام دكانك
دَبَّقْتُ أصابعي،
ولم أنجح
بوضع واحدة في
فمي.

I am the thief
of sweetmeats
displayed in your shop.
My fingers became sticky
but I failed
to drop one
into my mouth.[20]

Through a figurative language that combines eroticism with stealing and associates the speaker with an inveterate shoplifter with sticky hands, al-Massri ambiguously describes the speaker's unrestrained sexual appetite. A "sticky" element, physical love remains visible and persists on the surface of her fingers through its gluey texture, thus activating contradictory affects such as attachment and disgust, which pertain both to the individual and collective spheres.[21] The skin, in particular, is reconfigured here as a border, a boundary that separates the subject from its object of desire but also from the rest of the community that shuns her, as the reference to the social affect of distaste indirectly indicates.

Trajectories of modernity and tradition intersect in this poem. Al-Massri clearly writes here against the traditional image of the male poet-speaker weeping at the memory of his virginal love as in the pre-Islamic *qaṣīda* but also against the construction of the female body as a "pure," almost angelic object of love, as in the troubadour lyrics of the Middle Ages and the romantic poems of, among others, Jibran Kahlil Jibran.[22] The female speaker in al-Massri's poem does not mourn the absence of her beloved, nor does she abandon herself to nostalgic remembering. Rather, she is an active agent who makes concrete, albeit unsuccessful, attempts to satisfy her sexual hunger. This is a radical performance even for modern times. Indeed, as Rosella Dorigo Ceccato notes with reference to the Arabic theatre of the twentieth century, "in a strongly male-oriented society such as the Arab one, the role of the lover had to be assigned basically to the man. The woman could appear either as a defenseless victim of male desire, or alternatively, she could be presented as the clever instigator of his desire, the astute dominator of his naïve mind, the enemy to be fought. She rarely appeared in an actively sexual function."[23] It is precisely against this tradition that al-Massri writes, by refusing to compose a poetry of platonic adoration and by preferring instead to celebrate female lust and the contradictory affects (i.e. euphoria and delusion, confidence and self-deception) that come with it.

Desire of the senses and the imperatives of the body are the fulcrum also of poem 3, where female lust emerges as an inflammable and devilish amalgam.[24] Originally created as an angel according to the Qur'an, the Devil later lost its privileged status due to its disobedience, becoming a jinn made of fire. The association of the Devil to fire is also present in "Stories of the Prophet," which narrate that the Devil was created from fire, and in the New Testament, where the devil is thrown in the fire as a punishment for its disobedience and misdeeds.[25] Al-Massri therefore mixes in poem 3 sacred and profane literary sources as well as tropes belonging to overlapping poetic traditions of premodern times. The representation of love as an inflammable substance that burns the heart is indeed a wide-spread religious image but also a trope in premodern (Arabic) love poetry, which traveled to al-Andalus, the Aquitanian courts, and the Kingdom of Sicily under Norman rule, as clearly documented in the verses of the Sicilian Romance poets Giacomo da Lentini and Guido delle Colonne.[26]

The combination of images belonging to both religious and secular sources is particularly evident in poem 52. Here, the poet uses typical rhetorical turns and a set of Qur'anic references—the holy spirit as a source of prophetic and divine revelation, the anonymous "he" blowing his holy spirit into a human body, thunder and lightning as signs of divine power that inspire reverence—combining them creatively with mundane acts and a lexicon related to the body.[27] In this poem, the figure of the speaker oscillates between innocence and guilt, shyness and immodesty, self-control and unrestraint. Initially represented as a cautious and diffident creature, the speaker metamorphoses toward the end of the poem into a fervent devotee and zealous believer.

One finds another direct reference to the Qur'an in poem 59, where the speaker admits having stumbled while advancing on a "straight" path:

كنت أسير على الصراط
المستقيم
عندما اعترضت طريقي
اختل توازني
إلا أنني
لم أقع.

I was on the straight
path
when you blocked my way.
I stumbled
but I did not
fall.[28]

The poet performs here formal and religious discontinuity, by separating with a line break the expression "straight path" (ṣirāṭ al-mustaqīm), a Qur'anic enunciation that is conventionally continuous. She further enacts a gender suspension. Indeed, the "you" mentioned in this poem by al-Massri, who chooses not to qualify its gender, is voluntarily left unmarked. The "you" blocking the speaker's advancement and forcing her to lose her balance cannot be unequivocally identified as either male or female; the gender of the "you" remains forever unknown.

The idea that female lust provokes moral downfall and sociopolitical havoc has a long tradition both in Islamic as well as in Jewish and Christian thought. Drawing on the works of Fatima Mernissi, Samira Aghacy clarifies this point, stating that "woman is a source of *fitna* possessing an active and insatiable sexuality that if unchecked would release chaos . . . not only in the domestic space but also in the public sphere, thus constituting a threat to the patriarchal social and political order that determines male/female behavior."[29] The conviction that eros represents a threat to the subject's personal equilibrium, particularly to her rectitude, is a widespread belief since antiquity. As Adriana Cavarero notes in her introduction to *Inclinations* (2016), "In the library of the West, whenever discussion turns to the dangers of inclinations, women are regularly in the mix."[30] Sexual and emotional inclination on the part of women, Cavarero observes, has historically stirred serious apprehension, particularly among philosophers, who have blamed female lust for being "a threat to the subject's equilibrium—a deep quiver, a slippery slope."[31]

Since it is most of the time performed outside the regulated channels of marriage and family life, physical love in al-Massri's poetry is seen as a threat not only to the speaker's own personal equilibrium but also to the stability of the patriarchal family and to that of the larger society. A ripe, mashed cherry on a white-tiled floor thus anticipates the loathsome destiny of the transgressor, the exemplary punishment for those who follow the imperatives of the body and their passions, as exemplified in poem 72.[32]

What happens—I ask in the next section—both on an individual and collective level, when the erotic as a vilified and repressed resource is finally released?

The Erotic as Rupture: Confronting Inequality in Intimate Lives

In *Love and Sexuality in the Arab World* (1995), Hilary Kilpatrick underlines the tight connection between intimacy and public life, sexual self-expression and the social order. As she claims: "The search for love is intimately connected with the individual's desire for freedom and fulfillment, while the frank affirmation of sexuality, of whatever kind, represents a challenge to a rigid and hypocritical social order."[33] Throughout the collection, al-Massri emphasizes the connection between physical love and personal freedom, addressing globally sensitive issues such as gender inequality and domestic violence with extreme frankness. Poem 14 is a clear case in point.[34] In it al-Massri breaches the usually impenetrable walls surrounding the domestic space, thus providing readers with a representation of marital life that challenges romantic fantasies of wedded bliss. The repetitive image of the silenced and repressed women in particular echoes Cavarero's idea that since antiquity for patriarchy "the perfect woman would be mute—not just a woman who abstains from speaking, but a woman who has no voice."[35] The poem reads like a choral denunciation, in which the speaker (and perhaps the reader, too) joins the rank of these abused and vilified women, who are just like her (al-nisā' mithly), thus offering to her audience a new vocabulary to talk about gender violence not as a private disgrace or shame but as a social and cultural malaise, the result of distorted because unbalanced intimate relations.

Poem 20, with its insistence on hallucination and a phantasmagorical reality, suggests that the possibility of pursuing personal and collective liberation can only happen in dreams.[36] The speaker in this poem avows having killed her father and buried him in a beautiful shell, as if he were an immaculate pearl or an aquatic sleeping beauty. What is initially represented as the innocent victim of a terrible parricide metamorphoses toward the end of the poem into a cruel and frightening ogre. The patriarch's true nature is revealed in bright daylight: he is no candid gem, but a scary even if ghostly Bluebeard. The story is set in a fairy-tale time, where the boundaries separating past and present, day and night, innocence and cruelty are blurred, and in a fantastic universe, where aquatic and terrestrial worlds intermingle. In contrast to Charles Perrault's canonical tale, however, this poem has no moral lesson to teach its supposedly naive female readers. Moreover, in opposition to Angela Carter's feminist rewriting of the famous fairy tale, there is no maternal figure who comes and rescues the heroine. Al-Massri's feminism indeed fails to save her speaker (let alone other women), and readers find her antiheroine trembling under her bed in total solitude.

A liminal figure, simultaneously fragile and cold-blooded, childish and mature, the female protagonist in this poem openly confronts a ghostly paternal figure that haunts and torments her. Her temporary escape from his grip offers moments of euphoria and liberation, which are, however, not destined to last.

In al-Massri's collection, insurgent acts can only happen at night and belong mainly to a nocturnal, underground world, in which the speaker spends her insomniac nights running on untamed horses in wild open spaces—for instance, in poem 24. As soon as dawn breaks, however, this utopic world ends, with the speaker inexorably going back to her customary rational and sober behavior.[37]

Since it is the undiscussed reign of the patriarch, the home in al-Massri's poetry offers no relief, let alone any space for personal freedom and fulfillment. This representation confirms Geraldine Pratt and Victoria Rosner's statement on the oppressive nature of many intimate relations: "Intimacy, after all, is equally caught up in relations of power, violence, and inequality and cannot stand as a fount of authenticity, caring, and egalitarianism."[38] In poem 91, the speaker bluntly reveals the affective imbalance that reigns in her relation and the macroscopic extent of her delusion:

مللت البقاء
على هامشك
في مسوداتك
على أدراجك
أمام أبوابك.
أين
فسيح جنانك؟!

I am bored with being
in your margins,
in your notebooks,
in your traces,
before your doors.

Where
are the wide spans of your heavens?[39]

Here, the speaker contrasts her marginal and dependent condition, under-
scored by the repetition of the possessive pronoun "your" with its persistent
Arabic rhyming sounds, to the immense breadth of her lover's false prom-
ises. The caesura, separating "your heavens" from the speaker's hellish
condition, makes the antithesis between the two lovers really stand out.
Everyday and spiritual dimensions, sacred and profane worlds, intermingle once again in this poem to emphasize the magnitude of the speaker's
frustration and the death not only of romance but also of an illusion.

By and large, al-Massri's poetry contradicts Abdelwahab Bouhdiba's
interpretation of sexuality in Islam as "a full positivity," showing instead
that the hierarchy of sexes and the inequalities produced by patriarchy
engender misrecognition, domination, and abusive behaviors, which
clearly falter that indisputable positivity.[40] In the attempt to alter these distorted because asymmetrical relations, al-Massri provides readers with an
unconventional representation of femininity, one that boldly defies the
social norms of docility, blind loyalty, and reverent fear, while also des-
tigmatizing adultery. Poem 48 is particularly telling in this sense, since it
represents the adulterous woman neither as a sinner nor as a miserable and
failed creature, as happened previously in iconic nineteenth-century novels such as *Effi Briest, Anna Karenina,* and *Madame Bovary.*[41] Al-Massri
indeed troubles the innocence vs. guilt binary, refusing to represent the
woman at the center of her poem either as an evildoer or as a "celestial
body," to borrow the term from the title of a recent Omani novel by Jokha
Alharthi, that is a woman who is sublime, self-contained, and forever grav-
itating around her male partner.[42] In poem 48, the female figure has no
beatific qualities and follows only her carnal desires without any hesitation
or second thought.[43] In doing so, the poet boldly removes associations of
sin and shame from the figure of the adulteress, talking frankly about a
kind of love that, as Cavarero rightly notes, since antiquity had been historically "forbidden to women and tolerated in men."[44]

The woman portrayed in poem 48 is neither a happy wife nor a good
mother, but just a woman following her own desires. The poet privileges

erotic adventure to the stability of domesticity and family life, deempha-
sizing the institution of marriage as a stronghold against social chaos.
Al-Massri further writes against traditional constructions of the female
body as inherently vulnerable and fragile, refusing, for instance, to represent femininity as in need of masculine protection and guardianship.
Accordingly, in poem 103, unloving men are equated to "grains of salt,"
shining yet also melting fast, while in poem 99 the speaker appears to
possess an autogenerative force, with her beauty incrementing steadily
after each loss.[45]

Far from being simply positive and generative, al-Massri outlines in
poem 8 femininity as a mercurial category—active, daring, and at times
even nasty, thus contributing to bend the classical representation of
women as being bred for silent endurance, self-denial, and mothering.[46]
Desire in this poem has no redemptive or generative function but, rather,
a disruptive force; in Halberstam's words, it "devours rather than gener-
ates, obliterates rather than enlightens."[47] In this sense, it contradicts the
religious imperative of creation and procreation, thereby situating female
sexuality outside this traditional paradigm.

I argue that al-Massri's poetry plainly expresses her social critique by
representing a queer femininity, one that deviates from the established
heteronormative and patriarchal order and shifts the ground upon which
binary constructions are based. Al-Massri's political radicalism, by contrast, is expressed in latent rather than straightforward ways: it is tightly
enmeshed with her complex poetics and mediated through intricate
poetic choices, as I show in the next section.

Breaking Romantic Phantasies of Wedded Bliss: Challenging
the Popular Image of the Happy Wife (and Happy Citizen)

In al-Massri's poetry, the domestic space is imbued with estrangement
and simulation; the home is reconfigured as an *unheimlich* place, where
the body feels at odds with itself and unappealing affects such as boredom and weariness circulate. Married life, in particular, emerges from
the collection as a still life. Like Giorgio Morandi's achromatic paintings,
which were completed under the shadow of Fascism, al-Massri's poems

are, emotionally speaking, arid and plain.⁴⁸ Poem 34, in particular, with its emphasis on moldiness and disaffection together with its oppressive repetitions, reveals the shortcomings and monotony of domestic life.⁴⁹ A pervasive sense of loss runs through the poem together with the idea that the relationship between the two partners has inexorably reached its end station.

Through monotonous repetitions and ghastly metaphors, al-Massri brings to light the speaker's emotionally sterile domestic life with its stagnant and musty atmosphere, thereby killing the very fantasy that happiness can be found in marriage and the family, while also adumbrating the iconic image of the happy wife. This is clearly a feminist act, since, as Sara Ahmed reminds us, "feminist genealogies can be described as genealogies of women who not only do not place their hopes for happiness in the right thing but who speak out about their unhappiness with the very obligation to be made happy by such things."⁵⁰

There is no space in al-Massri's poems for the feel-good qualities of successful resolution or absolute mediation, and little space even for dreams of reconciliation; hers is a poetry in Audre Lorde's terms, "as a revelatory distillation of experience."⁵¹ Feelings of disillusion and loss abound also in poem 87, where the speaker is confronted with the debris of love, when it turns into apathy, loneliness, and affective detachment between the two (ex-)lovers:

عندما تخرج
من حذائك
وتتركه
وحيداً
على عتبة الباب
أو تحت السرير
يحتله الضجر
وأقدام الانتظار الباردة.

When you take off
your shoes
and leave them
lonely

on the doorstep
or under the bed
they are filled by boredom
and the cold feet of waiting.[52]

The empty shoes left on the doorstep or under the (marital) bed become
the symbol of the gulf that separates the two lovers; they epitomize a
presence that has inexorably turned into an absence. I suggest that the
speaker and the reader share an affective disorientation, since they both
feel vaguely confused and unsettled by the lack of goals expressed by the
passive act of waiting, with which the poem ends. Indeed, the dominant
affects mobilized here do not express vehement passions, as one would
expect from a love poem, but a lack of intentionality that leaves the reader
disoriented. Drawing from Sianne Ngai, I suggest that "the unsuitability
of these weakly intentional feelings for forceful or unambiguous action is
precisely what amplifies their power to diagnose situations, and situations
marked by blocked or thwarted action in particular."[53] There is nothing
sublime or heroic in the two poems; what we witness here is a lack of intent
and a feeling of suspension and hopelessness, which reveal the home—
and, by extension, the nation—to be loveless and unlivable. The poet's
insinuation that happiness cannot be found in the domestic space combined with a hinted desire for liberation breaks the image of the happy wife
and, by extension, of the happy citizen as joyous and fulfilled. This rather
hidden act of denunciation, as I will argue in the conclusion, irrevocably
breaks the public façade of harmony and unity, exposing the illegitimate
(and detestable) character of both intimate and social relations based on
subordination, as bonds backed up by a general consensus that may seem
granitic but is in fact volatile. Indeed, as James C. Scott notes with reference to the subtle ways, both covert and bursting, in which subordinate
individuals and groups express their discontent with the state of things:

the initial act that publicly breaks the surface of consent owes a part of
its dramatic force to the fact that it is usually an irrevocable step. . . . If
it is not beaten back, it will fundamentally alter those relations. Even if
it is beaten back and driven underground, something irrevocable has

nonetheless occurred. It is now public knowledge that relations of subordination, however immovable in practice, are not entirely legitimate.
In a curious way something that everyone knows at some level has only
a shadowy existence until that moment when it steps boldly on stage.[54]

A Daredevil Act: Clandestine Walks to Inspire
Individual and Collective Liberation

All in all, al-Massri addresses in her collection controversial topics, such
as female lust, adultery, physical love, thus awakening women—as Nizar
Qabbani did back in the 1970s—"to a new awareness of their bodies and
their sexuality, wrenching them away from the taboos of society, and making them aware of its discriminatory treatment of the sexes, of its inherent
cruelty."[55]

Al-Massri writes about these issues in Arabic, using a vocabulary, style,
and imaginary deeply rooted in the tradition of Arabic classical love poetry
but also breaking free from its most binding conventions, particularly
those concerning stylistic artifices and stereotypical representations of
gender norms and roles. In doing so, she joins a long line of literary predecessors thereby confirming Fadwa Malti-Douglas's conviction that "consciousness of gender and arguments about the roles of men and women
were not brought to the Arab world by Western feminists, like serpents in
the Garden of Eden. These issues have always been major and fully conscious preoccupations of Arab writers who have filled their literature with
chapters and books on women, their roles, their problems, and the like."[56]

What is new in al-Massri's treatment of femininity, I argue, is her
skepticism about the old feminist credo that sees feminist agency as
fully progressive, empowering, and, in the end, triumphant. She indeed
shows readers that agency can sometimes take, as Kathleen Stewart notes,
"unpredictable and counterintuitive forms," and that, most importantly,
"it's lived through a series of dilemmas."[57] Liberation, for instance, can be
followed by moments of regression, and even revolutionaries must expect
potential pitfalls, as Love shows in *Feeling Backward*.

Far from being a clear "call to arms" to end women's subjugation
under patriarchy, al-Massri's minimal poems have no glorious mission to

accomplish or (moral) lesson to teach. Al-Massri is indeed not interested in investigating the psychological, moral, or religious aspects of love in order to educate her readers about its virtues and complex codes, as was the case with the exemplary medieval treaty *The Neck-Ring of the Dove* (1022) by the Andalusian poet Ibn Hazm.[58] Her delicate and withdrawn lyrics further diverge from more contemporary and daring literary experimentations, such as Joumana Haddad's explicit and blunt equation of writing about love as "an orgasmic act of ejaculation."[59] Finally, since al-Massri's poems play heavily with obscurity, allusion, and ambiguity, they deviate from the recent trend in Saudi novels to display female sexuality in a rather blank, straightforward, and uncomplicated way, thus providing readers with the perhaps pleasurable yet ultimately barren position of the voyeur.[60]

In Al-Massri's poetry, on the contrary, the erotic is performed as a powerful affective tool to concretely alter unbalanced power relations both in the intimate and public spheres. In this sense, her writing is closer to the short stories of Yusuf Idris and Layla al-Uthman and to Ghada Samman's poems and novels, which employ surrealistic tones to express a corrosive yet latent social critique involving, among others, the institution of marriage, the idyll of the couple, and the supposed happiness of the nation.[61]

Since Al-Massri is a poet-funambulist who holds herself stoically on a rope stretched taut above the globe, her poems further include debates and preoccupations about love and the nature of relationships that are relevant not only in the here but also in the elsewhere. Consequently, by representing love both as surprise and risk, al-Massri simultaneously rejects more traditional conceptualizations of love as an arranged matter and an imposed duty, while also joining Badiou's critique of a neoliberal, consumerist form of love, where partners are meticulously selected online and love is "comprehensively insured against all risks."[62] Badiou's interpretation of love as a quotidian reinvention, a commitment to a construction that is creative, effervescent, and potentially breakable yet that ultimately defies separation, echoes al-Massri's mercurial representation of love as a never-accomplished act, as a process always in the making, and as an intense engagement with what is different, perhaps refractory, and in the end unwilling to lose itself within a symbiotic union. Her representation further resonates with the Surrealists' celebration of love as "a magnificent poem of the encounter," and as a "potential support for a revolution in existence."[63]

Negativity in al-Massri's poetry is indeed not the opposite of a radical politics, but a practice of detection and contestation to challenge social norms and values that perpetuate structures of inequality both in the intimate and public spheres. Since it relies on a conceptualization of love as a recalcitrant and insubordinate substance, her poetry inspires and supports acts of rebellion at the private level and perhaps at the public level as well. Al-Massri, I claim, lays bare the risks and perils of a love that has been conceived in unequal terms as submission, domestication, and reverent fear, on the one hand, and as domination, control, and violence, on the other.

As Wilhelm Reich (1933) notes with reference to the Fascist regime, sexual repression went hand in hand with authoritarianism: the patriarchal family mirrored the power relations between the authoritarian leader and its people.[64] To quote Reich: "The authoritarian state has a representative in every family, the father; in this way he becomes the state's most valuable tool, since he in turns reproduces submissiveness to authority."[65]

Shifting her attention from Fascism to authoritarian regimes in the Arab world, Samira Aghacy argues in her latest book that in contemporary Arabic fiction since 1967 "there is a clear correlation between authoritarianism, censorship, repression and patriarchal sexuality."[66] Shifting her attention from masculinity to femininity, al-Massri performs in her work a shrinking politics, one that reveals the frustrations, misery, and submissiveness of women in the private domain, while also hinting at the oppression of citizens at the political level. The moldiness of the speaker's home and her lover's abandoned shoes, for instance, evoke the immobility and sense of impotence of the citizens under authoritarian rule, as expressed, among others, by the protagonist of Hanna Mina's *Journey at Dusk* (*Al-rahīl 'inda al-ghurūb*, 1992): "We do nothing, because we don't have the courage to do anything. They have domesticated us."[67]

Al-Massri's intimate poems offer a privileged though furtive and oblique peek into the political, enabling readers to observe how distorted social relations based on domination and violence transform the home, and even the nation, into a real inferno. Her audacious poems contribute to make audible "what has historically had to be whispered, controlled, chocked back, stifled, and suppressed" in the domestic space.[68] By disturbing the very fantasy that happiness can be found in marriage and family life, whenever they are conceived in unequal terms, the poet shows readers how much there is to be unhappy about the patriarchal family and, by extension, the "neopatriarchal state"[69]; both are indeed "the product of arbitrary power, violence, control, surveillance, and physical confinement."[70]

Neither the domestic space nor the existing political can be experienced in al-Massri's poetry as a site of comfort, where mutual recognition and personal fulfillment can take place; they are both intolerable, hostile environments, the personal fiefdom of a terrible (hereditary) marquis. I see al-Massri's poetry as opposing this feudal interpretation of love as blind attachment and fidelity at all costs, which are extorted through control, coercion, minimal concessions, and the fantasy of protection. Her poetry, I suggest, contributes to the realization of what Nadine Naber (2012) has called a project aimed at "ending injustice and oppression" and at forming "new definitions of family and kinship, new ideas of affiliation and belonging, new grounds for the fostering of community."[71] These alternative forms of affiliations, I wish to add, should be based on the understanding of trust as in Annette Baier's apt formulation: a "vulnerable good, easily wounded and not at all easily healed."[72]

As we have seen, al-Massri's female speaker is neither a model wife nor an exemplary citizen: she is no obedient pawn and refuses to participate in the cult of the patriarch or the national leader. Despite her indisputable active role, al-Massri's speaker is not a model activist, either: she expresses her opposition to the status quo latently rather than overtly, not in the chaos of the street but on the whiteness of a blank page.

Like the queer fairy-tale heroine of poem 20, Al-Massri forgets family and biological ties but also national, sectarian, and class connections in the attempt to forge alternative forms of affiliation that are less violent and potentially more liberating for all.[73] Her female speaker, like the protagonist of Sylvia Townsend Warner's novel *Summer Will Show* (1936), as Heather Love describes her in *Feeling Backward* (2007), "waits for the revolution as one waits for the beloved: with hope and with despair, but without certainty."[74] This is why, in the end, al-Massri clings on to the poetic word to (re-)create that vital, perhaps tumultuous, and always inse-cure hope:

حيث الأحصنه
لا تستطيع الركض.
حيث لا يوجد
ثغرة
تسمح
لشعاع من الضوء أن يدخل.
حيث لا عشب
ينبتُ؛
أتشبث
بأقدام الكلمة

Where horses
cannot gallop,
where there is no
crack
to allow
a beam of light to pass,
where no grass
grows,
I cling
to the feet of the word.[75]

6

Afro-Arab Beats

Suheir Hammad's breaking poems

Born in a refugee camp in Amman (Jordan) in 1973 to Palestinian refugees, Hammad grew up in Beirut and, later, in Brooklyn, a tense interracial and intercultural milieu, as she evokes in her memoir, *Drops of This Story* (1996).[1] Influenced by the Black artistic tradition of spoken-word-based performance but also metaphorically moving toward her (original) home in search of inspiration, Hammad adapts the Arab classical practice of publicly reciting incandescent verses to the needs of the present time, binding this specific Arab tradition with African American and African Caribbean spoken word/dub poetry.[2] Michelle Hartman has been among the first to have extensively explored the "political and poetic solidarity . . . within the worlds of Arabs and Black Americans."[3] As she explains: "Being marked as different, alien, and generally understood as non-white or outside mainstream in the United States has prompted many Arab Americans to seek out and build links to other groups of color, including African Americans."[4] While it is important to acknowledge the creative influences and political alliances between these two ethnic groups, readers should also not forget that this history of mutual recognition, exchange, and solidarity has additionally been characterized, as Therí A. Pickens notes, by a "growing set of tensions between the two communities, particularly in areas where they were in close contact."[5]

This double dialectic of relation and rupture marks not only the circulation of cultural influences and political alliances between Blacks and Arabs in the United States and abroad—as described, for instance, by Alex Lubin in *Geographies of Liberation* (2014)—but also Hammad's poetry itself, particularly her latest collection, *breaking poems* (2008). Hammad, I claim, situates herself within the tradition of spoken word/ dub poetry, a rhythmic and politicized genre originating in Black and particularly West Indian culture.[6] Following the example of Audre Lorde and June Jordan, Hammad uses the creative force of spoken word poetry to confront the injustices of racism, (neo)imperialism, gender oppression, and militarism, thus employing, in Nadine Naber's own words, "performance art [as] a viable medium for expressing multiple oppressions simultaneously."[7] Hammad's double emphasis on brokenness and relation, rupture and continuity produces a tangible effect on traditional conceptualizations of history as a progressive march toward amelioration and emancipation, as well as on fanatic constructions of religion as a pure, sealed-off, and homogeneous whole. A resolute funambulist, Hammad takes intrepid steps on the tightrope of global violence, offering readers the possibility not only to see its destructive force but also to imagine new forms of kinship outside the usual patterns.

Breaking Global Violence in the Name of Kinship: "break" and "break (bas)"

The term "break," which gives the name to the collection and recurs in the title of each single poem taking on new forms and meanings, is clearly a keyword for Hammad; it represents the germinal element of her compositions. A recurring built-in rhythmic pattern but also a thematically laden term, the word "break" conveys an idea of damage, injury, separation while also communicating change and new beginning, as in the poem "break (rebirth)."[8] It further suggests an act of disobedience and transgression, as in the expressions "to break the law" or "to break a silence"—or, alternately, the intention of ending a process, stopping an action, resting and taking a pause after a long period of resistance.

In Hammad's collection, the break not only functions rhythmically and thematically, but also syntactically and linguistically. As Barbara Jane Reyes rightly notes, Hammad's "syntax is broken, her lines are clipped, and her poems are bombardments of images and words, demonstrations of brokenness and piecing together of selves, of languages, histories, and geographies."[9] Powerful incursions of Arabic terms, such as *diwan, baalbek, bas, habibi, khalas, yamma,* and *al bab* (to name just a few), blast English as the dominant language with the double aim of destabilizing its structure and defamiliarizing its readers, while contributing to opening up a space of visibility and audibility for the Arabic language and self.

The tension between rupture and relation is particularly evident in "break," the poem that opens the collection. Here, the poet draws a horizontal cartography, linking together distant geographical locations that seem to have little in common: New York City, Bombay, New Orleans, Gaza, Tel Aviv, Baghdad, Houston, and the Palestinian refugee camps of Deheisha (West Bank) and Khan Younis (Gaza Strip). As the poem opens, the speaker is wandering slowly and in total solitude in New York City in search for human connections:

(nyc)

humidity condenses breath

bodies stick and stones gather in a lower back

gray thick moving slow and alone[10]

Right from the outset, Hammad's speaker appears to be a profoundly broken yet also a deeply relational being. She is indeed "looking for [her] body / for [her] form in the foreign / in translation."[11] Writing, in particular, represents for her the only available resource to overcome her traumatic past and patch up the broken pieces that compose her life:

what had happened was
i wrote myself out of damage

this is the body of words and spaces
i have found to re-construct[12]

Mirroring the inner fragmentation but also the relational, hybrid nature of the self, the places that Hammad mentions in her poem are torn apart by violent destructions and natural calamities. They call to mind Mona Hatoum's installation 3D *Cities*, in which the maps of Beirut, Kabul, and Baghdad show paper depressions, evoking the detonations, economic recession, and moral degradation that those cities witnessed during the war. Beirut, in particular, is outlined in Hammad's poem as a city maddened "by all male religion," a place where violence reigns undisturbed and creepily makes its way across "olive oil sweat camps resorts."[13] A sensitive "contact zone" traversed by creative cultural frictions as well as a hot spot of sectarian conflict and political unrest, Beirut emerges as a simmering and potentially blustering place. As the writer recalls: "we lived there once my parents sisters and me / i left my skin there still boiling."[14]

Far from considering her family history unique, Hammad connects her personal story of dispossession, uprooting, dispersal and relocation to other tragic histories of material destruction and human devastation on a global level. Accordingly, the distress of a Palestinian woman deploring the slaughter of her family in Gaza—as expressed in the lines "a woman's hand cups bloodied sand bits scalp ooze / to the camera and says this is my family"[15]—resonates with the fear experienced by people living in Bombay under permanent threat, as suggested by the sound explosions "bomb bay bomb bay bomb bay bomb bay," and with the sense of abandonment that overpowered the Katrina refugees (in large part Blacks) in the aftermath of the 2005 hurricane that hit New Orleans, anticipating the 2010 oil spill in the Gulf of Mexico.[16] Their hopeless condition, as expressed in the lines "there is no wading in this water / a body can be polluted inside and out,"[17] echoes the distress of Palestinians in the Khan Younis camp crying "yamaaaaaaaaa / yamaaaaa,"[18] as well as the sense of abandonment of Iraqi children in Baghdad "fall[ing] in love with the soldiers killing them / . . . / wish[ing] for something to follow / a star an idea called hope sick as it sounds."[19]

The brusque juxtaposition of a scene set in Houston, portraying a self-absorbed family, whose members are concerned uniquely with their physical appearance and the price of gas, breaks the previous web of relations, raising uncomfortable questions regarding vanity, privilege, and blindness to the suffering of others:

(houston)

a family says this is the summer of sacrifice
no vacation no new car no addition to the study
but pedicures and hair relaxing and shape-ups and gyms
mandatory a body must keep up must be presentable

a husband says i wake up and sleep and wake up
and all i think about is gas prices[20]

Hammad's smoothly flowing lines seem to reproduce also visually the safe bubble in which the family lives; all its members appear to be totally unaware of and disconnected from the atrocities happening around them. No wonder that also the section stands happily on its own, showing no connection whatsoever with the previous part.

In his provocative article "What Does the Comparative Do for Literary History?," Djelal Kadir warns us against the danger of a self-centered approach and highlights the power of "contrastive correlation and comparative differentiation" to pursue mutual recognition.[21] "Absent the comparative," Kadir writes, "all recognition, then, devolves into self-recognition in the purified rhetoric of the tribe and in the pellucid mirror of the self, in which the tribal acquires universality."[22] By abruptly juxtaposing a deadly scene set in Baghdad with a privileged bubble set in Houston, Hammad underlines the contrast between the two situations, thus countering insularity and self-sufficiency while stimulating awareness, recognition, and solidarity.

The poem closes with the speaker waiting for a "storm," a clear metaphor for destruction contrasted with the promising image of a newborn baby girl. Through the delicate image of her niece sleeping in her mother's arms and being nursed by her, Hammad contributes to reconstructing an atmosphere of regained harmony, human connection, and nourishing care:

(exactly brooklyn)

my niece sleeps light
my sister feeds her her body
my clan holds one breath[23]

Through the image of her baby niece sleeping peacefully in her mother's arms, Hammad mobilizes feelings such as mutual trust, affection, and hope, where there previously were desolation and despair. The term "clan," normally a synonym standing for violent faction or tribe, is poetically reimagined by Hammad to indicate a group of women held together not by blood ties but by reciprocal care and by a shared understanding of human life as "one breath."

Hammad's horizontal geography purposefully breaks up the undiscussed centrality of New York City, a metropolis that is aligned in this poem to Beirut, Baghdad, and even to the refugee camps of Deheisha and Khan Younis. This alternative geography based on disjunctive alignments destabilizes the traditional binaries (North vs. South, West vs. East, center vs. periphery, metropolis vs. refugee camp, occupier vs. occupied) and the hierarchical orders attached to them, allowing these places to become-in Barbara Johnson's own words—"readable in new ways."[24] Since they stress interconnection and interdependence rather than separation and self-sufficiency, Hammad's disjunctive alignments further expose the asymmetries, divisions, and privileges that produce tensions and breaks in those relations, opening the way to violence.

This is particularly evident in "break (bas)," a poem in which the speaker rages against the pervasiveness and omnipresence of human violence, demanding with force that the deaths and destructions that storm the planet immediately stop:

bas
bastana
ana bastana
bas

daily papers photo babies
charred bread no life

venus chaired motionless shaking
bleed currents

astonished stars cry

bas[25]

Through a strong self-affirmative voice and specific linguistic and rhetorical strategies, such as the reiteration of the beating sounds "b," "t,"
and "p," Hammad turns the reader's attention to the turbulent reality of
global violence, performing a kind of brief percussion solo to awaken a
collective consciousness in danger of atrophy. The poem reveals a clear
tension between individual poetic voice and collective demands, Arabic
vernacular and English written language, orality and writing. The opening lines in crescendo ("bas / bastana / ana bastana") produce a mounting
effect and express the speaker's increasing anger and indignation in front
of the terrible escalation of violence; by creatively stretching on the page
the word "bas," Hammad increases the intensity of her appeal, while the
absence of punctuation signals urge, rage, and unrest.

Hammad carefully selects her words according to their distinctive
beat and their capacity to affect her audience. In so doing, she follows
the steps of her predecessor, the singing Diva Umm Kulthum, who
enchanted her audience with the virtuosic prolongation of few syllables,
the hypnotic repetition of short passages, and the introduction of minimal changes.[26] The legacy of *tarab*, or the affective component of Arab
music exemplified by Umm Kulthum's solo performances, which enrap-
tured the ecstatic audience, is not the only influence visible in these
lines.[27] Hammad's incendiary lyrics also resonate with the sounds and
rhythms of prominent figures belonging to the Black Arts movement,
such as Amiri Baraka and Sonia Sanchez, that in turn followed the Harlem Renaissance poets and were later retrieved by the Black Mountain
poets and the (mostly white) Beats, who wanted to bring poetry "back to

the streets" and wrote free, unstructured verses that followed the rhythm
of speech to convey the immediacy of their experience and express powerful emotions in a spontaneous and straightforward manner.[28] Clearly
situating herself in this double line of descent, Hammad interrupts her
writing with cadenced breaks, spinning words, and sonic attacks; she further writes down or leaves out words to produce a very specific effect of
(dis)continuity and (en)rupture.

Writing on African Caribbean dub poetry, Christian Habekost underlines the effects produced by minimal expression and a rhythmic language, arguing that "minimal expression and the short line, in this case,
combined with repetition and multiple rhyming, not only emphasize the
riddim (in performance) and visualize it (in print); they are themselves a
thematic reflection. Minimal expression is the best way to channel rage
into a poetry structure."[29]

The world Hammad outlines in this poem is indeed a cruelly simpli-
fied and chaotic universe on the brink of disaster where even the ancient
Greek goddess Venus has lost the enchanting qualities of her personifica-
tion of beauty and love, to be frozen by horror and immobilized by fear. In
a world where even mythological gods have lost their supernatural powers
and violence is equated to an unstoppable force, Hammad still clings on
to poetry as a useful means to document and denounce the spreading violence and promote a radical change in the ways we react to, acknowledge,
and mourn the loss of distant others:

gather armless
gather heart broke
gather just broke
gather harvest
gather blood
gather thirst[30]

Through the repetition of the verb "gather," Hammad hastens readers to
collect proofs to document and preserve the memory of those who were
killed or whose life broke under the pressure of violence; she further
invites them to gather courage, strength, and come together as a group

to contrast the scattering force of violence. And yet the speaker's persistent demand to "gather armless / gather heart break / gather just broke" is somewhat problematic, since it calls to mind a compulsive act of hoarding, thus raising uncomfortable questions regarding the real possibility of making sense of loss and publicly mourning those deaths. I argue that by effect of this unusual call to gather proofs and implicitly congregate, the poem becomes an instrument of intervention and participation in history rather than being merely an aesthetic object untouched by historical occurrences. Hammad's poetry, in other words, contributes to unearth the "unhappy archives" that make up history conceived in its standardized version as a regular and onward march toward progress, amelioration, and emancipation. Her poems raise awareness, promote an ethical rebellion, and stimulate the desire for immediate change.

Since they dissolve clear temporal distinctions and precise geographical locations, both "break" and "break (bas)" help to deconstruct the stereotype of the postcolony as "a place of danger and deficit" standing opposite to a secure and nonviolent colonial center.[31] In contrast to these simplifications, Hammad rewrites violence as a continuum, a reiterated historical event afflicting different areas and people on earth in very distinctive ways.

By and large, violence is represented in her poetry in a rather impressionistic way through the use of nonlinear, disjointed, and conflicting bombardments of images and sounds that reproduce both visually and sonically its damage to the individual, the collectivity, and the urban space. In line with the poetics of improvisation performed by her predecessors, Hammad embraces a poetry of spontaneity that resists formal polish and closure. It is precisely in this task of decrying social and political injustice through the mobilization of beating sounds, explosive words, powerful affects that Hammad's poetry aligns itself in ultimate analysis with Arab hip-hop particularly and global rap music more generally.[32] All of these musical forms, in which words are not sung but spoken in a rapid, rhythmic way, have proved to be a first-rate receptacle of the frustration, anger, and indignation of a whole group of disenfranchised people and a catalyst for change. Indeed, as Alex Lubin notes: "In hip hop the local is always already formed by transnational sonic migrations, and because of this, hip hop is uniquely capable of articulating solidarities and extranational belongings, while also being grounded in specific localities."[33] To the articulation in words and the practical implementation of this perhaps still utopic, yet highly needed future we will now turn.

Breaking News and the Living Room as Obligation: "break (still)"

In "break (still)," Hammad's indebtedness to Jordan is not only hinted at but directly expressed, as the reference to Jordan's poem "Moving towards Home" (1985) clearly suggests. Written in the form of a litany, the poem traces an unprecedented link between the Atlanta child murders (1979–81) and the mass killing of civilians that took place in the Sabra and Shatila Palestinian refugee camp in Beirut in 1982. In a very original way, the poem juxtaposes and contrapuntally reads together two very distinctive massacres taking place in two different geographical locations that have in common the involvement of innocent people.

Jordan's poem opens with the speaker refusing to lend her voice to the criminal acts that were committed while others looked away. By openly refusing to directly talk about violence, Jordan disempowers it; she further blocks the consumption of violence as a spectacle, favoring instead a completely different approach based on proximity and connection:

> I do not wish to speak about the bulldozer and the
> red dirt
> not quite covering all of the arms and legs
> Nor do I wish to speak about the nightlong screams
> that reached
> the observation posts where soldiers lounged about
> Nor do I wish to speak about the woman who shoved
> her baby
> into the stranger's hands before she was led away
> Nor do I wish to speak about the father whose sons
> were shot
> through the head while they slit his own throat before
> the eyes
> of his wife[34]

By naming one by one the shocking atrocities that were committed while the soldiers (and the international public) "lounged about," Jordan refuses to let the violence go unnoticed. Her poem counters the invisibility of war and the acceptance of violence as inevitable, bringing readers in close proximity to those tragic events. And yet her poetry does not provide catharsis; in fact, it refuses to offer a purifying release. By effect of her direct and straightforward words, readers become directly involved in the massacre and feel as if they were physically present and personally witnessing the bloodshed that took place that silent night. Readers sharply see, for instance, "the / red dirt / not quite covering all of the arms and legs"; they also unequivocally hear "the nightlong screams" breaking the silence with a terrible howl. By effect of Jordan's colloquial tone and precise words, readers cannot look away and are forced to take notice of that distant drama now incredibly proximate. I suggest that the immediacy through which Jordan communicates these killings together with the absence of univocal temporal and geographical references stir in the reader the memory of other carnages, that took place at other latitudes and in other historical periods yet involved, as in this particular case, the deliberate murder of an entire community. I am thinking, among others, of the Cilicia massacres of Armenians in 1909, of the roundup of Jewish people in the Roman ghetto in 1943, of the inferno of Amazigna Washa in Ethiopia in 1939, of the 1995 Srebrenica massacre in the former Yugoslavia. And the list could sadly continue.

Quite surprisingly, however, Jordan's attention is not fixed in this poem on violence itself but is directed instead toward desire. In the following stanza, the speaker expresses what at first glance may appear as a rather whimsical need in the face of such mass murder. She expresses the desire and invokes the need for a living room, which becomes the real fulcrum around which the entire poem gravitates and a flickering light among the darkness cast by those tragic events:

> I need to speak about living room
> where the land is not bullied and beaten into
> a tombstone

I need to speak about living room
where the talk will take place in my language
I need to speak about living room
where my children will grow without horror
I need to speak about living room where the men
of my family between the ages of six and sixty-five
are not
marched into a roundup that leads to the grave[35]

In this poem, the intimate space of the living room, the familiar room where people across all cultures welcome and honor their guests, gather, and spend time together, becomes through Jordan's poetic reconfiguration a utopic site of familiarity, peace, and comfort that extends from the private home to include the entire planet. In Jordan's creative re-vision, the living room takes a planetary size and is outlined as a collective zone where people regardless of their different origins, cultures, and faiths come together to comfortably talk to each other in their native tongues. It is a protective and intimate space, where horror and violence are kept at bay, and life continues naturally, generation after generation, without the fear that an entire community may be wiped out of history. Jordan's metaphor of the living room, I suggest, gives a concrete, almost architectural shape to what would otherwise remain a rather evanescent longing for global peace and nonviolence; it expresses an urgency and, in ultimate analysis, an obligation that the survivors have toward those who were killed.

Both inheriting and departing from Jordan's legacy, in "break (still)," Hammad poetically denounces the fact that Jordan's desire for a planetary living room has remained unfulfilled, that the promise she asked us to keep alive in order to honor those deaths is constantly being broken:

and always happening
in june's living room

    the children who can't run are the charred dead
    privilege will not save it is the noose
    people get off on this shit they must

> beirut is still sexier than gaza
> gaza is still closer than sudan
> sudan still iraq still
> you your own civil war still[36]

As Hammad underlines here, "june's living room" is still a bullied land cramped with broken, massacred bodies. Her poem thus functions as a powerful j'accuse; her words are bleak and prophetic, reminding readers that violence is a "noose" that entraps anyone, and that no one can be happy with things as they are.

In *Politics of Happiness* (2006), Sara Ahmed draws a tight connection between consciousness of the world and feelings of unhappiness. As she writes: "Opening up the world, or expanding one's horizons, can thus mean becoming more conscious of just how much there is to be unhappy about."[37] By indicating the persistence of violence in various areas of the planet, Hammad stubbornly declares her unhappiness with this persistence. She further offers readers a different angle from which to observe the world, by estranging them from the happiness of the familiar. In "break (still)," Hammad attacks the widespread tendency to aestheticize the violence taking place elsewhere, in those "other places" so far from the here, and the voyeuristic attitude that considers "beirut still sexier than gaza," as if the cities were involved in a macabre beauty contest.

Since the poet-speaker seems to weep alone in front of a devastated "camp," Hammad appears to retrieve in this poem the classical Arab poetic topos of "standing by the ruins" (*al-wuqūf ʻalā al-aṭlāl*), bending it however to the needs of the present time.[38] The poet-speaker is indeed not lamenting the destruction of the encampment of her own tribe but rather offering desolate visions of devastated cities and inevitable human loss. Far from weakening her demand for justice, her incongruous juxtapositions and disjunctive correlations ("beirut—gaza—sudan—iraq—your own civil war") make her claims more powerful, since they point to a disaster of global proportions. Moreover, by unearthing a forgotten archive of unhappy stories that keep repeating themselves all over again, Hammad carefully recreates the ground on which those massacres were committed and wars broke out, so that readers can reencounter what happened and prevent it from happening again. As Ahmed writes: "To learn about possibility is to do genealogy, to wonder about the present by wondering about how of its arrival."[39] In the next section I will show how this hard labor of genealogy, analysis, and re-vision breaks not only triumphalist representations of history as a forward march but also fanatic conceptualizations of religion as an unmixed, entrenched, and unchanging system.

Breaking Religion in the Name of Interfaith: "break (rebirth)" and "break (cross)"

Hammad's attempt to break religion to counter its extremist interpretations is particularly evident in "break (rebirth)" and "break (cross)." In both cases, the poet gathers her poetic raw materials from a variety of sources belonging to different faiths (Jewish, Christian, Muslim) and even to other more controversial beliefs (astrology, Greek mythology, magic). I suggest that these heterogeneous elements coexist—albeit in tension—on the written page, giving cultural depth and richness to Hammad's poetic work; they all conduce to the rupture of religion as an exclusivist, pure, and unitary construction, by revealing instead its "outright contradiction" and its mixed interfaith substratum.[40] The opening lines of "break (rebirth)" are particularly telling in this sense:

> jesus left at thirty three
>
> full saturn revolution returning messiah
>
> math a myth wa language a lie
>
> scorpio sun wa libra amar[41]

In these condensed lines, the departure of the lover at thirty-three evokes in the speaker the death of Jesus; his loss is compared to a cataclysm and a full revolution of planets and constellations. Hammad performs here a rather ingenious trespassing from the holy figure of Jesus to that of the returning messiah and, ultimately, to the beloved. This desacralizing poetic gesture is even more evident in the following couplet, where the speaker ties the resurrection of Jesus—a crucial Jewish figure in the Christian tradition that Islam recognizes as a prophet—with the boiling of morning coffee:

> ana sawah wa thousand wa one nights wa ahwak
> morning ahwa boiling resurrection no sugar no touch[42]

Religious and profane dimensions intermix in these lines, where the boiling of morning coffee is associated with the "resurrection" of the messiah, while the wandering and ascending Jesus refracts the speaker's self-representation as a traveler ("ana sawah"). Sacred texts, such as the Qur'an and the Bible, are intricately woven together with the lovelorn lyrics of the song "Sawāh" by 'Abd al-Halim Hafiz and the popular stories of *The Thousand and One Nights*, where daybreak signals the victory of life over death, thus evoking a symbolic resurrection. Furthermore, the religious act of waiting for the missing messiah (a figure that distinguishes the Shi'ite current within Islam, but also Judaism) overlaps with the speaker's profane waiting for her beloved, this latter association being in line with a certain Muslim mystical tradition, where the boundaries separating divine from profane love overlap.[43] This syncretism is reinforced in the closing lines, where the speaker laments the absence of her "habibi," her "missing messiah":

> habibi writ his name in water
> rhymed sixteen bars wa sang mawal blue heavy brass hair
> wool wa ana still waiting missing messiah zei self missing my
>
> habibi don't see me
> he gaze stars of different flame[44]

What we witness here, I claim, is the breaking down of religion as an impermeable and homogeneous system. Hammad, as a skillful funambulist, performs a smooth slide from the Christian and Islamic Sunni faiths to Shi'ism to the absolutely profane belief of the lover who faithfully awaits the return of her beloved. We find a similar glissade also in "break (cross)," a poem in which Hammad recovers perhaps the most important Christian icon—the Cross—and performs this time another skillful glide. She indeed attributes the cross not to Christ but to Mary—rather, to a plurality of "maries," each one representing vertiginous variations of a female archetype that is, alternatively, a mother, a weeping woman, a single woman who sleeps alone, a woman who sleeps in more than one bed, and even a woman who does not sleep and wants a child:

> marie mary mariam
> our golden ladies
>
> maria weeping
>
> women in hats   women in veils   women in crowns
> beheaded women   braided women   dyed women
>
> miriam sleeps alone   aches for touch   kisses lipstick
> marie sleeps around   longs for bond   mirrored face
> mary does not sleep   wants child   bears herself
> maria weeping[45]

Hammad clearly writes here against standard male representations of the Virgin Mary as a symbol for maternal love and devotion in a way reminiscent of Jean "Binta" Breeze's poem "The Wife of Bath Speaks in Brixton Market," which powerfully revises Geoffrey Chaucer's negative portrait of a medieval woman.[46] Mary is a figure that is recognized by Islam and to which the Qur'an devotes an entire surah (the nineteenth) and other fragments in surah 3. Hammad thus recovers this central figure represented widely by traditional Christian iconography as a model woman, who is venerated around the globe for her modesty, chastity, and submission to God's will. The poet, however, breaks up this female icon to a certain extent, responding in her own specific way to classical male iconography. Her "maries" are indeed not all chaste and not all mothers; most importantly, they agree on the necessity to form an integrated coalition against the often violent will of their men rather than submitting voluntarily to such will:

yamma we in need of fellowship
our hearts do not trust
men yamma our hearts
do not trust themselves yamma.[47]

Women's solidarity is outlined in this poem in a transnational way as an antidote to various forms of gender based violence perpetrated by the single male individual, by the authoritarian state, and by religion as an oppressive system based on and reproducing patriarchal norms.

Clearly, then, Hammad intervenes here poetically to reflect on the female condition both at the local and global level; she grounds her representation in a precise historical moment and in a specific geopolitical location, by recovering the figure of the Holy Mary and the religious symbol of the Cross, which are at the same time local and global icons. In particular, the figure of the "mary weeping" calls to mind multiple variations of the same archetype. Among others, it stirs up the memory of the Mothers of Plaça de Mayo, whose children officially "disappeared" during the military dictatorship (1976–93) in Argentina, and who gathered for years defiantly a few steps away from the center of power—the Casa Rosada of the president—wearing white scarves and demanding justice for themselves and their offspring. I am reminded of them today, as I see the mural of al-Nā'iḥāt (The Mourning Women), drawn by Alaa Awad on the walls of the Mohammed Mahmoud Street in Cairo. All of these weeping women, real or mythical, despite their indignation and anger, have voluntarily chosen to counter violence through nonviolence. Adriana Cavarero's emphasis on Mary's altruism in Leonardo's painting, as "a type of altruism that is not abnegation and martyrdom, suffering, and renunciation and does not require a privileged connection with the horizon of death (as Lévinas, like so many others, would prefer)," aptly describes these mourning women who demand justice and whose actions are directed by a sure, spontaneous, carnal love and by an altruistic desire, rather than by doomed affects such as violent revenge and despair.[48]

In "break (cross)" then, Hammad clearly transgresses national, religious, and cultural confines as well as the so-called ḥudūd that Fatima Mernissi mentions in Dreams of Trespass.[49] They represent, as her female narrator explains, those sacred yet invisible confines that establish and differentiate what is admissible (*ḥalāl*) from what is inadmissible (*ḥarām*); her female protagonists perform a set of creative acts to trespass such borders, in a place that is per se a threshold, the terrace of the narrator's home situated between the sky and the earth. I cannot read Hammad without mentioning Mernissi, a crucial figure of Islamic feminism, who has provided us with new readings of the sacred texts of Islam and emphasized the leading political role of women within Islam. As Miriam Cooke writes in *Women Claim Islam*, several Muslim feminists around the globe have attempted to extend the right to reread sacred sources from a female perspective, if not by going directly to the sources, at least by calling into question certain interpretations of the sacred texts that they consider misogynistic and tendentious and by multiplying the tools used for their rereadings.[50] Hammad's original re-vision of traditional religious figures and symbols calls to mind, in addition to Mernissi's feminist rereadings of female leaders within Islam, Assia Djebar's experimental work. As Cooke explains in *Far from Medina*, Djebar proposes a re-vision of the seventh century *umma* by tracking down the different trajectories and destinies of an utterly diverse group of women after the Prophet's death (Bedouin queens; anonymous, wandering women; military leaders; female prophets; migrants; and historical figures recognized by Islam, such as Fatima and Aisha).[51] Djebar's methodology is both imaginative and mixed; it includes orality and is by necessity polyphonic. In Cooke's own words: "Djebar interweaves the classical chronicles of men like Tabari, Ibn Hisham, and Ibn Saad with imagined verbatim accounts of three women transmitters, or rawiyat."[52] To Mernissi and Djebar's chorus of female voices of imperfect consonance, constantly hovering between the sacred and the profane, the past and the present, what is admissible and what is not, I wish to add the numerous "maries" that Hammad outlines in this poem.

Before concluding, however, I would like to perform my own trespassing, by reading a poem that is not included in the collection discussed so far but in Hammad's previous collection, *ZaatarDiva* (2005). In "talisman," Hammad blurs the boundary that safely separates religion from superstition, holy objects from talismans, prayer from poetry, writing from orality, underlining the holiness of writing and the sacredness of words:

it is written
the act of writing
is holy words are
sacred and your breath
brings out the
god in them

i write these words
quickly repeat them
softly to myself
this talisman for you
. . .
may these words always
remind you your breath
is sacred words
bring out
the god in you[53]

Simultaneously a prayer and a talisman, a religious invocation and a material object filled with magical powers capable of protecting the person
for whom it was written, this poem defies rigid definitions of poetry and
narrow interpretations of religion and the religious, as it confounds the
confines separating profane writing from sacred invocation. Exploring the
function of talismans, in *Stranger Magic*, Marina Warner notes that in
classical Arabic literature and in the Islamic world more generally, talismans had the function of securing those wearing them the alliance of the
natural forces. They were "charmed things," bringing good luck and protection to the people wearing them.[54] Since it is in particular the inscription that gives to the talisman its supernatural power, it is not surprising to
find the words themselves becoming magic and giving blessings in Hammad's poetry. Indeed, as Warner writes with reference to the words on
the talisman: "The writings which charm it are magical, holy, and often
hermetic and they frequently depend on underlying enigmatic systems,
signs as casting horoscopes and geomancy."[55]

Artifacts issued from a prestigious literate culture that placed great
value on the written word, as well as on the human being for which the

talisman had been created, talismans were very popular in ancient times before the consolidation of Christianity and Islam; they were also present in Hellenic and Judaic culture and were never really uprooted in later times. As Eugenio Trías notes with reference to early Christianity, *superstitio* represented before the supremacy of Rome a kind of fossil, a hardened residue belonging to an ancestral world, that *religio* with its detailed and scrupulous rituals came to supplant in the late empire.[56] Religious orthodoxy, either Islamic, Christian, or Jewish, later banished these objects that were suspected of black magic, although it never managed to root them out completely. This poem, in which the voice of the speaker counterpoints the chorus of the censors, undeniably proves their survival and together with it the belief that words themselves can become magic, offer consolation, and bring blessing.

Poetic Funambulism: An Art That Clarifies Vision

Hammad's poems are simultaneously linking and breaking, linear and syncopated compositions, which illuminate silenced histories and religious syncretism, thus shaking the grounds on which history as a teleological and theological narrative and religion as a unitary and intrinsically wholesome construction rest. Faith itself is multiplied almost ad infinitum: it is faith in the written word and therefore also in literature; faith in the act of coming together, preserving the memory of, and mourning the dead; faith in the communal; faith in the sacredness of the human; and faith in the breaking as well as in the relational force of the arts, particularly of poetry and music.

Originally monophonic, Greek Orthodox Byzantine music became polyphonic once it started to travel abroad, particularly to Georgia. Hammad's poetry, I claim, follows a similar trajectory. As soon as it starts to travel outside the strict contours of the United States, it begins to include a variety of sources, figures, voices, thus necessarily losing its monadic character. The ensuing polyphony breaks with its amazing richness, intrinsic heterogeneity, and unusual beauty the monotonous *cantus datum* of religious fundamentalists.

I recognize Hammad's solo voice as part of the great tradition of the Arab singing divas Umm Kulthum and Fairuz, who managed to win over even their detractors with their incredible vocal impact, musical talent, and strong personalities. In a similar way, Hammad's voice also clearly stands out because, to quote Adrienne Rich, "it reminds us of the beauty, precisely there where it seems impossible, remind[s] us of kinship where all is represented as separation."[57] Hammad's distinctly fierce and amazingly intense chant breaks, interrupts, suspends the dogma of religious doctrines, and reveals the partisanship inherent in the history of the winners, inviting readers to bend themselves over to capture the whispers, cries, and outrage of those who perished or were wronged by history.

Hammad not only replaces devastated lands with the image of a planetary "living room" but also breaks religion by unearthing a rich intercultural and interfaith common ground. Islam together with Christianity and the Jewish faith appear in her poems to be historically intertwined as well as broken today by unhealable rifts. The traditional unity of "the people of the book" (ahl al-kitāb, in its Islamic formulation) is implicitly reappropriated, critically interrogated, and problematized to reveal a set of inner tensions that do not mine, however, the common substratum that these faiths in fact share. This is the difficult glissade and "contortion" that the funambulist Hammad invites us to perform.

I would not argue together with Pickens that Hammad's poetry "privileges sight over sound," since the poet shows readers broken places and revises traditional religious icons while also making very audible claims and interrupting the musicality of her verses with potent sounds, incursions, and breaks.[58] Poetry in her hands becomes a slippery object, a genre with porous borders that the poet uses not just to comment on the present but to make both audible and visible interventions in history, religion, and the political, inviting readers to take notice and put an end to religious extremism and global warfare. In doing so, Hammad responds to Marc Augé's recent call for a new type of art that is simultaneously expressive as well as reflexive. To quote Augé: "Art must express society (which today means the whole world), but it must do so purposely. It cannot be simply a passive expression, a mere aspect of the situation. It has to be expressive and reflexive to show us anything beyond what we see every day in the supermarket or on TV."[59]

It is precisely in her indefatigable attempts to bind together distant geographical places, forgotten histories, and supposedly antagonistic faiths that Hammad proves to be a true funambulist. From her bird's-eye view readers get to see the world at large with its injustices as well as its transnational coalitions, its "weeping maries" along with the healing force of the poetic word. Hammad has the rare talent to be visionary, without letting the ravishment provoked by her funambolic art compromise the clarity of her own and her readers' vision. On the contrary, poetry in her hands functions as a workshop where readers encounter conflicting alterities that nonetheless precariously coexist on the written page despite the tensions and potential breaking points. Most important, it is a powerful instrument to counter comfort, self-absorption, and oblivion, one that offers the unique opportunity to prepare the ground for political change, by instilling the desire for things to be different. As in the case of Lorde, poetry for Hammad is certainly not a luxury, but rather a vital and creative tool aimed at stimulating concrete action directed to produce change in the present and to build more solid and nonviolent futures. In Lorde's simultaneously very concrete yet also highly imaginative words:

> For women, then, poetry is not a luxury. It is a vital necessity of our existence. It forms the quality of the light within which we predicate our hopes and dreams toward survival and change, first made into language, then into idea, then into more tangible action. Poetry is the way we help give name to the nameless so it can be thought. The farthest horizons of our hopes and fears are cobbled by our poems, carved from the rock experience of our daily lives.[60]

I see Hammad's funambolic art, performed high above the heads of violent perpetrators and religious fanatics, as participating in Lorde's poetic project of inspiring tangible actions to pave the way toward survival and change.

Conclusion

The Stunning Vistas of Funambolic Art

The poets at the center of this study write from multiple geographical locations, perform provocative changes in perspective, and reconfigure conventions of scale, shifting the reader's attention from spectacular events and major global actors to everyday occurrences and minor agents. These poets juxtapose, bind together, and contrapuntally read divergent histories without ever falling victim to generalizations or to the danger of erasing crucial differences. As Susan Stanford Friedman writes with reference to the nature and methods of a comparative approach based on juxtaposition: "Juxtaposition can potentially avoid the categorical violence of comparison within the framework of dominance. The distinctiveness of each is maintained, while the dialogue of voices that ensues brings commonalities into focus."[1]

The everyday as a heterogeneous common ground emerges as versatile and enchanting in the case of Nye; it is, however, also stale and monotonous in the poetry of Mersal and al-Massri. Disturbing repetitions, cold observations, and compressed sentences with no punctuation, together with the evocation of enclosed spaces and spectral objects, are the aesthetic strategies through which these two poets convey the atmosphere of apprehension, tedium, and weariness that pervades a socially and politically oppressive milieu. I claim that such an aesthetics of defamiliarization, which reveals the familiar either as uncanny or, alternatively, as enchanting, provokes a revision of habitual looks and attitudes and propels a desire for political change. Nye's poetry, for instance, which pays attention to the marginal and the overlooked and celebrates queer assemblages that defy rigid compartmentalizations and bring the "odd one out" in again, offers readers the opportunity to see neglected things as relevant and to reencounter Others as significant and charming again. Nadine Ltaif, on the other hand, crosses temporal and geographical boundaries and combines objective and phantasmagorical reconstruction to unearth a traumatic history marked by religious strive, gender oppression, and collective amnesia, so that the resurgent specters of the past do not find us unprepared.

The poets included in this book liberate poetry from traditional aesthetic constraints, such as rigid rules of versification, fixed thematic motifs, predetermined structures, as well as from the impressive yet often vain linguistic virtuosism of their classical and neoclassical male predecessors. All of them unanimously refuse to "go . . . back to an old, venerable model, and to relive the glorious experience of ancient poets," preferring instead to adopt free verse (shi'r hurr) as their means of poetic expression.[2] Unlike their Modernist predecessors, however, they do not use "referents and shared codes [that] target the more educated public" and succeed in reaching a wider, more popular audience.[3] Nye, for instance, employs a spontaneous tone and a language that is fresh and easily understandable. Al-Massri's style too is crystalline and unaffected; her tone is frank and straightforward, while the images she selects are easily recognizable. By embracing a conversational format and colloquial tone, moreover, Nye structures her poems on a form that is clearly antihierarchical and bears the influence of Mahmoud Darwish's cadenced and dialogical compositions. Hammad's choice to abolish capital letters is equally guided by democratic principles and calls to mind the radical linguistic experimentations of an antiwar poet like e. e. cummings, bell hooks's attempts to deemphasize the self as well as the experience of the bauhaus at the end of 1925, whose founder Walter Gropius wanted to remake the world from the bottom up, saw no essential difference between a prototype for industrial production and a unique artisanal piece, and practiced a teaching that was not modeled on predetermined results.[4]

Multiple artistic traditions and literary sources play off one another within each single collection. In Nye's case, the US tradition of travel writing is interwoven with the typical anecdotes and framed tales of popular Arabic literature and folklore. The influence of surrealism, as a local as well as a regional and global avant-garde movement that rejected art for art's sake and used surprise and shock to upset and reverse old habits and preconceived ideas, is evident both in Nye and Mersal.

Regional literary motifs, such as the Maghrebi trope of *al-ghurba*, are engraved in Mina Boulhanna's poems, while ancient Greek and Roman myths and symbols mark Ltaif's poetic oeuvre together with typical, though twisted, Québécois themes. Classical Arabic tropes and genres, such as the "standing at the ruin" trope (or *aṭlāl* motif), the great *ghazal* (love poetry) tradition, and the elegiac genre (*marthiya*), which have been part of the Arabic literary tradition since the pre-Islamic era, are reworked and updated to the needs of the present time. Even sacred texts, such as the Qur'an and the Bible, and ancient tragedies and epics, such as Medea and the Odyssey, are a source of inspiration for the poets included in this book. Al-Massri employs images, rhetorical turns, and lexical terms drawn from the Qur'an to challenge traditional gender roles and conservative views of love in society, while Mersal plays around with Pharaonic vestiges and purposefully blocks the sentimentality mobilized by Egyptian melodramas, refusing to cultivate heated patriots and overemotional women. The Arab singing diva Umm Kulthum is a clear source of inspiration for Hammad; her poetry further bears the influence of the astonishing wordplay and syncopated rhythms of Audre Lorde, June Jordan, and Jean "Binta" Breeze's spoken word poetry.

All the funambulists considered here execute their remarkable leaps with extreme precision and rare agility. They have indeed learnt to accord their steps to the vibration and mood of the distinctive wires on which they walk. Ltaif, for instance, treads on a rope vibrating with grief and loss, while Mersal's cable oscillates with nervousness and impatience. Affects are therefore ubiquitous yet distinctive. Hammad, for instance, uses minimal expression and the short line to communicate urgency, rage, and indignation, while al-Massri mobilizes tedium, unease, and fatigue to pinpoint, amplify, and possibly alter (affective) inequalities in the private as well as in the public domain. Patriarchs and political leaders may indeed change over time, with one bloody ruler being followed by a more "enlightened" one. What does not change, however, are the affects of deferent fear, blind attachment, and extorted loyalty that these male guardians and national guides command.

Still, the funambulists discussed in this book walk high above the heads of frightening patriarchs and tyrannical religious and political authorities, performing stunning acrobatic moves—jumps, glissades, and balancing acts—that leave the viewers spellbound. Their art is radically imaginative but also deeply grounded, and meant for an alert, reclined, and responsive viewer—one whose gaze is not fixed on the ground but whose eyes look up towards the sky.

Recurrent literary motifs such as the home, and, by extension, the nation, are rewritten in unexpected ways. In al-Massri's poetry, for instance, the home metamorphoses into a nightmarish site: it is burdensome, dull, and flavorless. The intimate is indeed hooked into the national and the global dimensions, which exert an inescapable pressure on it. Mobility, another recurrent theme, is invoked when it is a free choice; when it is the only available option to find relief from an oppressive political that blocks one's self-realization, it is cursed. Immobility, on the other hand, is presented only in dark light, as the product of despotic obstruction or neoliberal securitization, which increasingly cast the public space as dangerous and insecure and gradually encroach on basic civic liberties such as walking, traversing, and occupying public space.[5]

Overall, the poets considered in this book sabotage a unified narrative of fixed identities, mythic origins, and a univocal sense of belonging by showing instead that life trajectories are, as Ella Shoat argues, always "situated and conjunctural, shifting and transmuting across histories and geographies."[6] Since they all have good reasons to distrust filial forms of kinship, such as blood and sectarian ties, affiliation is what these poets emphasize throughout. Hammad, for instance, reinforces Afro-Arab cultural ties and political alliances and digs up the intercultural substratum from which monotheistic faiths originate, while Ltaif sympathizes with a remote and secluded group of twelfth-century maharanis as a symbolic act of sisterhood. The one performed by these funambulists is a form of "minority cosmopolitanism," to borrow a term coined by Susan Koshy. Theirs is a cosmopolitanism that rests on "translocal affiliations that are grounded in the experience of minority subjects and are marked by a critical awareness of the constraints of primary attachments such as family,

religion, race, and nation and by an ethical or imaginative receptivity, orientation, or aspiration to an interconnected or shared world."[7] I see Nye's
careful observation of the everyday, which captures unforeseen affinities
between apparently distant things, as a clear participation in this project
and a stimulus to seek forms of kinship outside the biological or sectarian
framework.

Language, too, emerges from their collections as heterogeneous and
mixed. Hammad, for instance, subjects English to incursions of Arabic
words, while the Arabic in Mersal is interspersed with untranslated or
transliterated English words to express typical North American experiences, such as buying organic food or using the remote control to open
and close an automatic gate. This linguistic mix contributes to inflect
what Werner Sollors has called with reference to the United States the
"monolingual ideal" on which the nation-state is based.[8] Still, the rather
timid openings performed by Hammad and Mersal toward bilingualism
do not lead to the radical and at times barely intelligible transformation
of the dominant language that one finds, for instance, in the vernacular
literatures of Zora Neale Hurston or M. NourbeSe Philip, as documented
by Ahmad Dohra in *Rotten English.* Nor is their linguistic manipulation
comparable to the weirding of English performed by bicultural writers
such as Maxine Hong Kingston and Junot Díaz in prose, as shown by
Evelyn Nien-Ming Ch'ien in *Weird English.*

And yet, as historian María Rosa Menocal and literary critic Karla
Mallette have shown, multilingual writing is not a new phenomenon; in
al-Andalus and the Kingdom of Sicily under Norman rule, to name just
two examples discussed in this book, Arabic coexisted with Latin, Greek,
Hebrew, and the local vernaculars.[9] Rather, what has changed through
time are the reasons that have pushed writers to borrow from and adopt
other languages. As Khaled Mattawa has shown, in the first half of the
twentieth century, poets T. S. Eliot and Ezra Pound borrowed Greek and
Latin words to situate themselves in a direct line of descent with canonical
figures and great literary geniuses such as Homer and Dante.[10] By contrast, the linguistic experimentations carried out by poets in the United
States since the 1960s and 1970s were meant, in Mattawa's own words, "to

express the poet's identity and perhaps aid the poet's struggling subculture from being subsumed."[11] A similar intent, I suggest, animates also the writing of the poets considered here.

As funambulists who try the impossible, the poets discussed in this volume write against normative masculinities and femininities, emphasizing desire, self-determination, and personal fulfillment. By representing their female speakers as traveling alone, having an authoritative voice, and openly confronting tyrannical patriarchs, these poets write against the appropriation of the female body and the cooptation of feminist claims by ruling men and the political ideologies they support (nationalism, Marxism, neoliberalism, and Islamism).[12] They further expose the silent connivance between authoritarianism, religious conservatism, and patriarchy, thereby confirming poetically what sociologist Nadje al-Ali has called "the centrality of woman and gender when it comes to constructing but also controlling an entire community."[13]

What type of feminism, then, do the poets discussed in this book embrace? I think we should not speak of one unitary or overarching feminism, but of a plurality of feminisms. Mersal, for instance, is suspicious of the state as champion and supporter of gender equality, while Ltaif is still imbricated in the old diatribe dividing first world and third world feminism. All of them, however, seem to agree with al-Ali's claim that "sisterhood is not global," and that women must actively come together, gather forces, and build local, regional, and global alliances to combat gender oppression and violence worldwide.[14] Together with Lila Abu-Lughod, the poets considered here are indeed skeptical about a single formula or solution that works for all women across the planet.[15] They are convinced that the hardships that women face, both in the here and in the elsewhere, are disparate and discrete. Al-Massri's feminism, among others, refuses to rescue women; hers is a feminism that, by blurring the figure of the patriarch with that of the authoritarian leader, inspires a desire for liberation capable of overcoming dichotomous and hierarchical gender divisions.

Since human bodies are at the center of the political order, the poets addressed include questions of embodiment into their analysis of politics. The body emerges from their collections as the site on which patriarchs, authoritarian leaders, and religious extremists extend their grip. It is, however, also one of the few available tools that individuals have at hand to express their discontent and rebel against a hegemonic power meant to crush them. The image of Mersal's speaker biting her nails, while observing a disgusting army and a grotesque head (of state) is a good case in point. Her bodily affliction immediately communicates her refusal to let the importunate political figure go without saying.

Since high-wire walking is not only about clandestine acts but also about movements in space, the funambulists included in this study break the myth of universal mobility and of the arrival of the migrant in the new country as essentially good and thriving. They further oppose an almost purely academic version of nomadism, which refuses to see the innumerable barriers, obstructions, and blockades that many people in the real world encounter, as soon as they decide to leave their home. Since they promote both a radical re-vision and a political change, these poets-funambulists develop a new aesthetics aimed at changing standardized views and global imaginaries. From the heights of their wire, the Mediterranean Sea is not the sun-drenched and clear blue water advertised in touristic depliants but the burning front line of an undeclared global war, while Europe's southern border has stretched into the Sahara, a desert that has been forcefully pushed into the line of fire. Not only the Mediterranean basin but also the planet at large look from the standpoint of these funambulists unfamiliar and bizarre: Egypt and Alberta have become adjacent lands, while "Europe's veritable centre," to borrow Menocal's expression, has shifted from Mittleuropa to the peripheral province of al-Andalus and even to that burdening South so often blamed by Europe's northern countries.[16] From Hammad's wire, in particular, America comes into view as an annex of the West Bank, while the Gaza Strip with the refugee camp of Khan Younis rubs shoulders with the similarly populous yet otherwise largely opulent cities of New York and Houston. If Mersal bemoans Europe's recent metamorphosis into an entrenched citadel, she simultaneously bows her head to, salutes, and rejoices at the survival of a tiny village that has the size of a dot.

In *Globalectics*, Ngũgĩ wa Thiong'o underlines the crucial role played by orality in anticolonial struggle, explaining the following: "In the anti-colonial resistance, song and dance played a pivotal role in recruiting, rallying, and cooling the social vision. The colonial authorities feared orature more than they did literature."[17] By being receptive to and giving prominence to the oral tales that a bunch of foreigners tell each other in a tiny map store in the heart of Manhattan, Mersal joins their struggle for recognition, self-determination, and liberation, implicating readers in her own anticolonial and decolonial practice.

In opposition to the exclusionary policies and violent acts carried out by neocolonial and neoliberal powers, who have erected walls, set up detention camps, and adopted deportation policies aimed at keeping out "undesirables," these funambulists take illegal walks and voluntarily depart from the familiar to reach its far end. With their trespassing, they circulate and endorse a vision of the world based on love for (absolute) alterity, thereby performing a public, nonviolent breach of the law that prescribes separation, confinement, and isolation.

One finds a harsh critique of the proliferation of walled states and of surveillance measures in Mersal. Her poetry exposes international airports as high-security incarceration systems, while also turning the "official" spying of dictators on its head. After all, as Nanni Moretti's documentary on General Pinochet's coup d'état *Santiago, Italia* (2018) clearly shows, whenever a civil right is violated and a wall is erected, there will always be people ready to fight against those violations and to jump over those walls, trying the impossible. This is also what Emanuele Gerosa corroborates in *One More Jump*, a documentary on the Gaza Parkour Team founded in 2005 by Abdallah Inshasi and Mohammed Aljakhbir.

Far from feeding fantasies of self-sufficiency, complacency, and insularity, the poets discussed in this book emphasize human precariousness and interdependence, advocate shared actions in the name of individual and collective well-being, demand accountability for the material destructions, human rights violations, and horrible atrocities carried out by political authorities who most of the time reject responsibility. They also illuminate the privileges of the few and the frustrations of the many, warning readers against the violent reactions of those who feel dispossessed.

Through their unlicensed art, the poets-funambulists included in this book develop a harsh critique of apparatuses of the state, particularly of ruling elites, armed forces, and authoritarian leaders. They further invoke a renewal of existing democracies, showing, for instance, that neoliberal democracies have failed to live up to the expectations of the people they rule, since the lures of finance capitalism and the erosion of public goods, spaces, and services together with the encroachment of fundamental democratic principles such as equality, solidarity, nondiscrimination, and justice have almost neutralized not only the state's commitment to the people's welfare but also the citizens' belief that politics serves precisely to improve individual and collective lives.

These funambulists do not simply hold up the mirror to reflect a political in crisis but poetically imagine an alternative political, inclusive, just, and participatory, in order for readers not to lose sight of the possibilities that are at hand. Theirs is a political that passionately engages in a set of considerate actions inspired by the principles of equality, justice, and sustainability; a political that does not monopolize the scene and darken the street, but patiently prepares the ground so that citizens can trustfully walk towards personal fulfillment and collective amelioration. The one imagined by these poets-funambulists is a "democracy to come," in Derrida's famous formulation—one that takes on responsibility for the actions it adopts and is not immune from prosecution; a political that foresees, anticipates, and cleverly governs the negative consequences of neoliberalism, globalization, climate change, global pandemics and wars, not one that is taken by surprise, held hostage, and runs at its best after them. Ltaif, among others, invokes a political that, instead of commodifying and marketing a people's historical and cultural heritage, cares for and safeguards it, considering it a fundamental brick to build a constructive sense of "we." The one imagined by Ltaif is, moreover, a political that engages in urban planning choices that do not exacerbate preexisting divisions increasing social tensions, but one that collaborates with the civil society to realize more sustainable and livable urban environments. Overall, the political imagined by the selected poets envisages future scenarios and, quoting Mahmoud Darwish's famous lines, "invent[s] a hope, invent[s] a direction, a mirage to extend hope."[18]

Since they have witnessed a series of historical and political failures that have frustrated their belief and trust in salvific figures, the poets addressed in these pages do not fuel the romantic phantasy of the intellectual as prophet, so in vogue in the *nahḍa* period. As Rasheed El-Enany under-lines: "From the very beginning of the *nahda*, the Arab intellectual has borne the burden of the educator, the moderniser, the connector between East and West, the importer and adaptor of foreign thought and values, the very prophet of a brave new world."[19]

Voluntarily breaking the relation between intellectual work and proph-ecy, the poets included in this book engage wholeheartedly in historical excavation and genealogy to understand the root causes behind apparently obscure events. The insights they gain are worth considering. First, colo-nization for these poets is not a thing of the "past," and anticolonial and decolonial work is more necessary today than ever before. This implies not only decentering Europe and criticizing a knowledge and an education still permeated by a colonial outlook, but generating countermaps and counterhistories that offer, in Claire Gallien's words, "alternative ways to conceptualize and experience the world."[20] This is work that one does not find in textbooks or anthologies and that remains to be done. Engaging in decolonial work also implies listening to and learning from "homegrown," autochthonous, and therefore potentially different and disorienting views; it means being prepared to accept that antitheses, contradictions, and paradoxes are natural and productive and may not be easily diluted into a synthetizing whole. In Franco Cassano's own words: "Every tradition remains and cannot but remain itself, but if it is pushed into a journey, it can come home having learned much and thus re-read its own history in a new way, valorizing something that it once knew but has since forgotten. Differences remain but can now host other points of view and all have taken a step not toward a unilateral universalism but rather a complex one traversed by a multiplicity of paths."[21]

Even though "scholars of the new generation," as Edward Said notes in his 2001 article "Globalizing Literary Studies," "are much more attuned to the non-European, genderdized, decolonized, and decentered energies and currents of our time," the structures in which these scholars operate—syllaba, curricula, canons, department organizations—are rather impermeable to change.[22] According to Said: "Two aspects seem more in need of revision than others—first, the idea that literature exists within a national framework, and, second, the assumption that a literary object exists in some sort of stable or at least consistently identifiable form."[23]

Let me take up Said's challenge and provocatively ask: How does the study of literature and the evolution of literary genres and forms change in an increasingly globalized and interconnected world marked by international migration, global economic crises, environmental risks, and pandemic diseases? Are national curricula and syllaba offering the necessary tools to our students and to ourselves to understand the huge transformations we are currently witnessing? In Donatella Izzo's compelling words, how can we "redeem . . . the humanities—and in particular literary studies—from charges of irrelevance?"[24]

In this book, I have favored a wide-ranging yet also close reading of literary texts to highlight their permeability and instability. Whereas Nye and Mersal experiment with the "slippery" genre of prose poetry, which, as Peter Johnson explains, "plants one foot in prose, the other in poetry, both heels resting precariously on banana peels," Hammad's poetic performances blur the boundaries separating performance art, music, and poetry, while also disrupting the traditional antagonism between literature and orature.[25] Indeed, as Ngũgĩ wa Thiong'o writes with reference to the hierarchical order in which writing and orality are normally placed: "The problem has not been the fact of the oral or the written, but their placement in a hierarchy. Network, not hierarchy, will free the richness of the aesthetic, oral or literary."[26] For her part, Al-Massri adopts and deviates from classical love tropes that abound in both secular and religious writings, while the epic genre is disliked by all the poets because burdened by a nationalistic mythology that rests on the us vs. them binarism. Finally, Mersal's black humor confounds the fine line separating tragedy from comedy, showing that even humor, when it travels to new locations, takes an unexpected guise.

The controversial rubric of world literature, as a field that either pretends to study the literatures of the world by reading a strict selection of masterworks in translation or engages in distant reading practices that privilege "the system in its entirety" and accepts losing the text with its singularity, is put in question in this study.[27] How can *Weltliteratur* in

Johann Wolfgang von Goethe's eighteenth-century Mittleuropean formulation be revised so that our students today may find it still interesting and helpful rather than obsolete and elitarian? To what extent would the practice of looking at literary texts as unruly and animated entities, which refuse to stand still, be generative and valuable? I agree with Ngũgĩ wa Thiong'o when he notes:

> Works of imagination refuse to be bound within national geographies; they leap out of nationalist prisons and find welcoming fans outside the geographic walls. But they can also encounter others who want to put them back within the walls, as if they were criminals on the loose.
>
> Equally important, if not more so, are approaches to the text, how we read it. Do we want to welcome it or do we want to put it back into prison—or even a new prison? One can read a literary text with a narrow, short, or wide angle of view. It makes a difference whether one's view is through a concave or convex lens.[28]

In my reading of these poetry collections I have attempted to adopt a "convex lens." In order to do so, I have followed Erich Auerbach's methodological approach as theorized in "Philology and *Weltliteratur*," particularly his invitation to locate a circumscribed "point of departure (*Ansatzpunkt*)," from where it is possible to radiate outward.[29] I see the poetry collections discussed in each chapter of this book as representing a good *Ansatzpunkt*, a concrete and precise point of departure with a "potential for centrifugal radiation."[30]

I hope my still limited study of these texts will work as a stimulus for further developments and be taken on, deepened, and refined by colleagues working in the neighboring disciplines of gender studies, Arabic language and literature, Islamic and Middle Eastern studies, postcolonial and decolonial studies, philosophy, and Romance languages and literatures, as well as in the more distant fields of sociology, urban studies, political theory, history, geography, and religious studies. In a time marked by lockdowns, restricted mobility, social distancing and polarization, the need for proximity, connection, and trustful overtures is particularly pressing. This is why I have taken the liberty and also the risk to connect distant fields of knowledge and wander off in territories that exceed my immediate disciplinary expertise. I agree with James T. Monroe when he writes that professional insularity and specialism in a particular subject can sometimes work against ourselves, as in the case of the study of the tangled *muwashshah*, a circled and strophic poetic form, whose origin dates back to the eleventh- and twelfth-century al-Andalus. This is Monroe's valuable reflection, which we find in Mallette's *European Modernity and the Arab World*:

> There is no room in this difficult field for simplistic or one-sided solutions, nor for narrow appeals to professional insularity. Little can be gained from putting Arabists against Romanists. A serious study of muwashshah poetry requires that one be an Arabist, a Hebraist, a Romanist, and much else beside (musical expertise and literary competence are essentials), yet since it would be unrealistic to expect all of these areas of knowledge from a single individual, modesty and a spirit of collaboration are the least that may be expected.[31]

This reflection can also be ascribed to the literary works analyzed in these pages. In line with the poets-funambulists celebrated in this book, I am deeply suspicious of categories and organizing principles based on practices of demarcation, partition, and separation. These divisions have historically circulated the myth of homogeneous and impermeable identities, literary cultures, and nations. I see the authors included in this book as sabotaging with their intrinsically mixed and far-flung poetic projects these narrow and exclusionary narratives. Hammad, for instance, connects the Arab icon Umm Kulthum, who trained in religious singing and captivated her public with her vocal virtuousism, with radical Black spoken word poets and political activists Audre Lorde and June Jordan, a poetic move that complicates national, linguistic, cultural, and racial divisions together with the religious and secular divide.

The funambulists considered here have indeed situated their high wire far above the national, reattuning their walks to the vibrations and telluric undercurrents currently shaking the global world. As they get hold of these shocks, they urge us to change not only our societies but also our personal and collective libraries.

Comparing the occupation movement at Gezi Park in Istanbul, Zuccotti Park in Manhattan, and Syntagma Square in Athens, and the assembling in those squares of an alternative "people's library," Aamir R. Mufti notes: "The people's library embodies the desire not just for different books—than those enshrined in national curricula or literary cultures or in globalized commercial publishing, for instance—but for different ways of reading, circulating, valuing and evaluating them."[32] I believe that this is also the demand that the poets included in this book make: to diversify canons, include new voices, circulate less-known books, especially those that are receptive to local tensions, regional changes, and global shocks as well as to minorities, noncanonical literary figures, and forms of expression belonging to popular traditions.

I see in the vision endorsed by Rabih Alameddine in *An Unnecessary Woman* (2013) of world literature as an intimate and yet cosmopolitan reading practice that contests colonial hierarchies, historical periodizations, and the logic of national and linguistic purity a valid antidote to abstract conceptualizations of world literature, which, as Rajagopalan Radhakrishnan claims, is primarily "a metropolitan and academic" preoccupation.[33] I share Jane Hiddleston's conviction that the grounded Saidian definition "worldly literature" is far more apt than the standard terms of *Weltliteratur* or "world literature" to keep critics, readers, and students down-to-earth, since it "suggests a way of thinking, an alertness to different cultures but also a worldly wisdom about the text's limits that attenuates the utopianism of some theories of world literature."[34]

The poets included in this book write "worldly texts"—that is, literary works that respond to concrete, mundane happenings, are created at a particular temporal juncture and in a specific geographical location, yet are deeply entangled in the world's global net. These works, I claim, are inclined toward, listen to, speak together with, and respond to a variety of audiences, simultaneously local, regional, and global. Since they write in Arabic, al-Massri and Mersal's primary interlocutor is clearly an Arabophone reader, yet one that lives either in an Arab country or in the Arab diaspora. These texts, which were originally conceived with an Arabophone reader in mind, become global, once they start to travel abroad and are translated into foreign languages and especially into English as the global language par excellence. While al-Massri and Mersal's Arabophone readers may be more able to see through the density of their writing and manage to catch the nuances, double entendre, and innuendos enmeshed in their complex poetic creations, global readers may not always be able to find their way through that thickness and crowdedness, ending up feeling frustrated and disoriented. These poets-funambulists, however, are not interested in easing our way through the process of reading; on the contrary, they require serious engagement on the part of their readers as well as a willingness to leave the familiar and experience some level of estrangement. In Vilashini Cooppan's words: "This is an ethics of reading whose goal cannot be conversion of otherness to sameness, an ethics of reading that must instead choose to stay blocked from the final assimilative moment, at home in the very moment of nonrecognition."[35]

As Brian T. Edwards has shown regarding the strange ways in which US culture travels today to the Middle East-North African region collecting new and unexpected meanings, the cultural production of contemporary artists from the Arab region (and, I would add, also from artists living in the Arab diaspora) follow strange routes and get enriched with original imports. As Edwards has shown, these worldly wise cultural producers willfully refuse to adhere and respond to the expectations of what they perceive as distant and often unresponsive global readerships and at times even "jump publics," refusing to take those publics seriously into consideration.[36] It is precisely in their capacity to be so self-reliant and fierce and to dodge a global audience pretentiously convinced that it can do without them, that their irreverence and independence becomes more manifest.

Despite their initial intractability though, all the poets-funambulists included in this book offer stunningly broad vistas to those willing to follow them, which are worth the journey and the effort. Places as peripheral as the Texan countryside, the green fields of Oklahoma, the empty streets of Tyre or of an anonymous provincial town in Italy are reconfigured here as nodal points—sometimes even as "end points," as Edwards would have it—in which the tensions and moods of the contemporary age are felt most powerfully.[37] I claim that only by paying attention and listening to the marvelous views and frightful cries but also to the imperceptible shivers and intimate desires captured and put down in words by these poets-funambulists will we be able to forge a more accurate, nuanced, and perhaps also less catastrophic vision of our time. These funambulists have indeed learnt at their expenses how to move upwind, to conquer their fears, and to cultivate the patience of those who have fallen once. As we move forward and follow their steps to achieve a much needed balance and a long-expected opening of horizons, Darwish's hopeful words may encourage us one final time:

> Let us go,
> Let us go into tomorrow trusting
> the candor of the imagination and the miracle of the grass/[38]

Notes

Bibliography

Index

Notes

Introduction

1. Mersal, "Writing on the Threshold."

2. For an overview of recent debates about world literature, see Damrosch, *What Is World Literature?*; Casanova, *World Republic of Letters*; and Moretti, "Conjectures on World Literature."

3. Gunn, "Introduction," 19.

4. For a broad overview of cultural and political issues involving the Arab diaspora and its relation with the so-called West, see Salhi and Netton, *Arab Diaspora*.

5. For a historical and critical discussion of Arab Anglophone literature produced worldwide, see Al Maleh, *Arab Voices in Diaspora*. On the development of the Arab novel in English from its early stages to its most recent examples, see Gana, *Edinburgh Companion to the Arab Novel*. For an examination of the post–civil war Anglophone Lebanese novel, see Hout, *Post-War Anglophone Lebanese Fiction*.

6. The only exception is Nadine Ltaif's collection *Ce que vous ne lirez pas*. A selection of poems has been translated into English by Christine Tipper in the collection *Journeys*. However, the book was published in the spring of 2020 when the chapter on Ltaif had already been completed.

7. On Said's notion of the contrapuntual, see *Culture and Imperialism*, 51. For an in-depth and fascinating illustration of Said's practice of contrapuntual criticism, see Radhakrishnan, *Said Dictionary*.

8. Ramazani, *Transnational Poetics*, x.

9. Ramazani, xiii.

10. On the theorization of diaspora from a feminist and poststructuralist perspective, see Brah, *Cartographies of Diaspora*. On recent developments in diasporic literature and theory, see Shackleton, *Diasporic Literature and Theory*. For an analysis of diaspora in connection to identity, locality, and religion, see Alfonso, Kokot, and Tölölyan, *Diaspora, Identity, and Religion*. In *Global Diasporas*, Cohen has examined the changes the term diaspora has undergone on a global scale. On the theoretical and methodological debates relating to diaspora and transnationalism, see Bauböck and Faist, *Diaspora and Transnationalism*.

11. On the potential of poetry and the imagination for changing traditional visions of geography, see Dematteis, *La geografia come immaginazione*.

12. Holzhey, *Tension/Spannung*, 7.

13. Kuhn, *Essential Tension*, 227.

14. Lee, "Foreword," x.

15. Arkoun, *Essais sur la pensée islamique*, 10, emphasis in the original.

16. My translation from the original French, which reads: "La société musulmane contemporaine est en pleine effervescence révolutionnaire. Pour la comprendre et s'addresser à elle, il importe de s'installer dans sa proper perspective qui est socio-dynamique et dialectique," 291.

17. Caputo, *Deconstruction in a Nutshell*, 70.

18. Said, *Reflections on Exile*, 145.

19. On the underreppresentation of women as agents in migration and diaspora studies, see Andrijasevich, *Migration, Agency and Citizenship*. See also Boyd, "Immigrant Women in Canada" and "Family and Personal Networks." On the increasing vulnerability of migrant women to structural inequality, see Boyd and Pikkov, "Gender Migration, Livelihood, and Entitlements." On the contribution of feminist theory to migration studies, see, among others, Nawyn, "Gender and Migration." Among critical works countering the invisibility of women migrants in the arts, see Willis, Toscano, and Nelson, *Women and Migration*. Ruba Salih has explored the challenging experience of Moroccan women living in-between Morocco and Italy in *Gender in Transnationalism*.

20. Arendt, *Men in Dark Times*, ix.

21. Arendt, ix.

22. Arendt, ix.

23. Cooke, *Women Write War*.

24. Cooke, *War's Other Voices*, 27.

25. Ngai, *Ugly Affects*, 1.

26. Rancière, *Disagreement*, 99.

27. Hirsch, "What We Need Right Now," 1779.

28. On the ways in which ordinary people in the Arab region contribute to introduce political change through everyday actions, see Bayat's *Life as Politics*.

29. Among the first anthologies that have contributed to map the field of Arab-American literature, see Orfalea and Elmusa, *Grape Leaves*; Mattawa and Kaldas, *Dinazard's Children*; Mattawa and Akash, *Post Gibran*; and Charara, *Inclined to Speak*. For an anthology of writings by Arab-American and Arab-Canadian feminists, see Kadi, *Food for Our Grandmothers*.

30. For a literary and social analysis of modern Arab American fiction, see Salaita, *Arab American Literary Fictions* and *Modern Arab American Fiction*. For a far-reaching exploration of the vast literature produced by Arab émigrés writing in English, see Hassan, *Immigrant Narratives*. On present-day articulations of US citizenship by Arab American

writers and their lasting connections to the land of their ancestors, see Fadda-Conrey's *Contemporary Arab-American Literature*. The political engagement of contemporary Arab-American poets and their literary acts of resistance have been explored by Sirène Harb in *Articulations of Resistance*. For a broad overview of Arab-American aesthetics across different media, see Pickens, *Arab American Aesthetics*.

31. Romeo, "Racial Evaporations," 231.

32. Dimock, Wai Chee, "Literature for the Planet," 174.

1. The Everyday as Protean and Enchanting: Naomi Shihab Nye's *Tender Spot*

1. For more information on Nye's biography see the Poetry Foundation's website, https://www.poetryfoundation.org/poets/naomi-shihab-nye (accessed March 12, 2022).

2. Felski, "Introduction," 609.

3. For a thorough exploration and critical evaluation of modern and contemporary Palestinian art, see Boullata, *Palestinian Art*; and Ankory, *Palestinian Art*. On the poetry of Mahmoud Darwish and his relationship to the Palestinian cause, see Mattawa, *Mahmoud Darwish*. On the living legacy of Mahmoud Darwish's experimental aesthetics and its impact on the practice of contemporary Palestinian artists, see Rahman, *In the Wake of the Poetic*. Fadwa Tuqan's autobiography *A Mountainous Journey* published in 1990 offers useful insights into her lived experience, poetic work, and political stance.

4. Felski, "Introduction," 608.

5. Nye, *Tender Spot*, 60.

6. Nye, 60, emphasis in the original.

7. See Said, *Orientalism*; and *Covering Islam*.

8. Hornung and Kohl, *Arab American Literature and Culture*, 1.

9. De Certeau, *Practice of Everyday Life*, 612.

10. Nye, *Tender Spot*, 60.

11. Nye, 31.

12. Nye, 31.

13. Nye, 31.

14. Kaplan and Ross, "Introduction to Everyday Life," 3.

15. Nye, *Tender Spot*, 55.

16. Ahmed, *Queer Phenomenology*, 27.

17. Diprose, *Corporeal Generosity*, 151, 102.

18. Nye, *Tender Spot*, 55.

19. Derrida, among others, has raised questions regarding the media construction of certain incidents as "major events." See on this, Derrida's dialogue with Habermas in *Philosophy in a Time of Terror*.

20. Bonazzi, "Touching Tender Spots," 17.

21. Ahmed, *Queer Phenomenology*, 164.

22. Nye, *Tender Spot*, 41.

23. Nye, 41.

24. Najmi, "Naomi Shihab Nye's Aesthetic," 168.

25. Nye, *Tender Spot*, 41.

26. See Halberstam, *Queer Art of Failure*, particularly chapter 1.

27. Nye, *Tender Spot*, 41.

28. Bennett, "Force of Things," 353–54, emphasis in the original.

29. Nye, *Tender Spot*, 41.

30. Nye, 42.

31. On this ambiguity, see Marchi "Engaging with Otherness."

32. See Harb, *Arabic Poetics*, 202.

33. Gardiner, *Critiques of Everyday Life*, 35.

34. Gardiner, 208.

35. On magic states and animated objects in the *Arabian Nights*, see Warner, *Stranger Magic*.

36. Warner, 5.

37. Nye, *Tender Spot*, 98–99.

38. As a surname, Flinn is an anglicized version of an Old Gaelic form meaning "son of a red(dish) person." See the Surname DB, https://www.surnamedb.com/Surname /Flinn (accessed March 12, 2022).

39. Derrida, *Shibboleth*, 36

40. Derrida, "Passages," 377.

41. Derrida, 378.

42. On the Oklahoma City car bomb attack, see Johnston, "At Least 31 Are Dead."

43. Nye, *Words Under the Words*, 99.

44. Derrida, *Spectres of Marx*, 18, emphasis in the original.

45. Nye, *Words Under the Words*, 112–13.

46. Nye, 112.

47. Mercer and Strom, "Counter Narratives," 37.

48. Nye, *Tender Spot*, 112.

49. Mercer and Strom, "Counter Narratives," 37.

50. See Hass, "How Israel Prevents Palestinian Farmers." On problems and prospects involving the Palestinian Agricultural Sector, see UNACTAD, *Besieged Palestinian Sector*.

51. Kurson, "Poet Naomi Shihab Nye."

52. Nye, *Words under the Words*, 28.

53. Nye, 28.

54. Nye, 28.

55. Darwish, "Edward Said," 181–82.

56. Butler, "What Shall We Do," 48–49.

57. Kerouac, *On the Road*.

58. For a nuanced and intimate literary biography of Jack Kerouac as a writer struggling to come to terms with his mixed ethnic identity, see Johnson, *Voice Is All*.

59. Cavarero, *Inclinations*, 40, 43.

60. Aart, Molini, and Nye, "Poet's Humble Answers."

2. The Everyday as Claustrophobic and Stale:
Iman Mersal's *These Are Not Oranges, My Love*

1. For more information on the avant-gardism of the Daughter of the Earth Group, see Hammad, "Other Extremists." As Hammad explains, the members of the group managed to negotiate their own space of action in opposition to three major forces: the authoritarian state, the Islamists, and Western-funded activism. For a compelling investigation of feminism in Egypt and the broader Muslim world, see, among others, Badran, *Feminism in Islam*; and Sorbera, "An Invisible and Enduring Presence."

2. See Mersal's biography on Arab World Books, https://www.arabworldbooks.com /en/authors/iman-mersal (accessed March 17th, 2022).

3. For an analysis of the poets of the seventies in Egypt, who prepared the ground for the rebellion of the subsequent generation, see Mehrez, "Experimentation and the Institution."

4. See Fakhreddine, "Prose Poem," 243–45. As Mersal explains on her blog, her own poetry is more influenced by the Iraqi prose poets of the 1990s, such as Sargon Boulos and Salah Faiq. They had revitalized this poetic form, which had been first inaugurated by Nazik al-Mala'ika together with Mahmoud Matloub, Badr Shakir al-Sayyab and Ali Ahmad Bakatheer in the first half of the twentieth century. For a discussion of Mersal's own poetic choices, see Mersal, "S. J. Fowler interviews Iman Mersal." For a review of al-Mala'ika's pioneering role in the free verse movement, see Stevens, "Iraqi Woman's Journey."

5. Creswell, *City of Beginnings*, 19.

6. Mattawa, "Introduction," in *These Are Not Oranges*, vii.

7. On the turbulent and rough poetry developed in Cairo in the 1990s by the so-called Locusts, see Metwalli, *Angry Voices*.

8. For a discussion of Edwar El-Kharrat's experimental work, particularly its rich intertextuality, which deeply influenced the members of the 1990s generation, see Deheuvels et al., *Intertextuality in Modern Arabic Literature*, particularly 133–48 and 149–60. On El-Kharrat's modernist revolution and his role as mentor and supporter for a whole generation of young novelists and poets, see Amireh, "Edwar al-Kharrat and the Modernist Revolution."

9. Warner, "At the Tate Liverpool."

10. For an in-depth study of the Art and Liberty Group, see Bardouil, *Surrealism in Egypt*. For an overview of the recent exposition on this transnational artistic group organized at the Tate Museum, see Warner, "At Tate Liverpool," 28–29.

11. See Gioni et al., *Here and Elsewhere*.

12. Stanley Moss, back cover of Mersal, *These Are Not Oranges*.

13. Abu-Lughod, "Egyptian Melodrama," 116.

14. Mattawa, "Introduction," ix.

15. Mersal, *Mamarr muʿtim yaṣluh litaʿllum al-raqs*, 53.

16. Mersal, *These Are Not Oranges*, 20.

17. On the traditional Egyptian shadow theatre, see Amin, "Shadow Theatre."

18. Mersal, *These Are Not Oranges*, 14.

19. Mersal, *Mamarr muʿtim yaṣluh litaʿllum al-raqs*, 46.

20. Mersal, *These Are Not Oranges*, 14.

21. Bayat, *Life as Politics*, 142.

22. Mersal, *Mamarr muʿtim yaṣluh litaʿllum al-raqs*, 51.

23. Mersal, *These Are Not Oranges*, 19.

24. Mersal, 71. This is the original Arabic version of the poem from the collection *Jughrāfiyā badīla*, 63:

رأسٌ واحدةٌ ترسل إشارات آمرةً إلى كل هده القلوبِ والأطرافِ والأعضاءِ التناسلية

25. Mersal, 71. This is the original Arabic version:

جيلٌ لا يحتاجه أحدٌ

26. Mersal, 72. This is the original Arabic version of the poem from the collection *Jughrāfiyā badīla*, 53:

أما عنّي،
فأنا أقفُ على أطرافِ أصابعي منذ سنواتٍ، خلفَ شُبّاكه، أتلصّصُ عليه، لكنّي لا أستطيع متابعةَ الشاشِ
التي يتسمّرُ أمامها

27. Mersal, 72. This is the original Arabic version from *Jughrāfiyā badīla*, 54:

حيث أنه لم يغادر الكنبة منذ سنين

28. For a selection of works that have drawn attention to the creative spirit and explosion of cultural forms of expression witnessed during and after the 2011 Egyptian revolution, see Mersal "Revolutionary Humor"; Gröndahl, *Tahrir Square*; Mehrez, *Translating Egypt's Revolution*; and Mehrez and Abaza, *Arts and the Uprising*.

29. Mersal, *These Are Not Oranges*, 72.

This is the original Arabic version from *Jughrāfiyā badīla*, 54:

ولا أتصوّر أن اللّه يرسلُ له الفرينش فرايز هنا كمتعبدٍ تطعمُهُ الدنيا طعاماً ليس هناك ما هو أشهى
منه ولا أزكى.

30. See Ahmed, *Politics of Happiness*.

31. See Rakha, "This Is Not Literature."

32. Mersal, *These Are Not Oranges*, 59.

This is the original Arabic version from *Jughrāfiyā badīla*, 9:

لماذا جاءت إلى البلاد الجديدة؟ هذه المومياء؛ موضوع الفُرجة
ترقد بزينتها في كتّانٍ رماديّ: حياةٌ متخيلةٌ في فترينة متحف.

33. On the ways in which Egypt's ancient pharaonic cultural heritage has been historically perceived, appropriated, and contested both by European colonial and imperial forces and by the nascent Egyptian nation, see Reid, *Whose Pharaohs?* On the pharaonist movement of the 1920s and the post-1967 rise of pharaonist discourse, see Selim, "New Pharaonism." On the recent use of the Pharaonic tradition by Coptic social movements in their protests, see El Gendi, "Coptic Commemorative Protests."

34. Mersal, *These Are Not Oranges*, 59.

35. Mersal, *Jughrāfiyā badīla*, 10.

36. Mersal, *These Are Not Oranges*, 59.

37. Mersal, 59.

38. Ahmed, *Politics of Happiness*, 152.

39. Mersal, *Jughrāfiyā badīla*, 12.

40. Mersal, *These Are Not Oranges*, 60.

41. Mersal, 61.

The is the original Arabic version from *Jughrāfiyā badīla*, 14:

ما تعلّمتَهُ هنا لا يختلف عمّا تعلّمتَهُ هناك:
القراءةَ كتذكرةِ مرورٍ إلى تغييبِ الواقع.

42. Mersal, 62.

This is the original Arabic version from *Jughrāfiyā badīla*, 17:

لا شيء جدير بأن تتمرد عليه.
أنت مرْضيٌّ وميتٌ.
والحياةُ من حولكَ تبدو مثل يدٍ رحيمةٍ
أضاءت الغرفةَ لعجوزٍ أعمى
ليتمكّن من قراءة الماضي.

43. Love, *Feeling Backward*, 147, and Mersal, "Eliminating Diasporic Identities" 1583.

44. Ahmed, 157.

45. Brown, *Walled States*, 7.

46. Mersal, *Jughrāfiyā badīla*, 77.

47. Mersal, *These Are Not Oranges*, 83.

48. Brown, *Walled States*, 33.

49. Gordon, *Naked Airport*, 13.

50. Gordon, 238.

51. The *Ventotene Manifesto*, whose full title is *For a Free and United Europe: A Draft Manifesto*, was completed by Altiero Spinelli and Ernesto Rossi in 1941 when they were both confined on the island of Ventotene. Its first, clandestine edition was released

in 1944 and established "the equal rights of all nations to organize themselves into in-dependent States" as well as the "equal rights of all citizens to participate in the State" and "the value of the spirit of criticism against authoritarian dogmatism." It further pro-moted an extensive social, political, and economic reform. See Spinelli and Rossi, *Per un'Europa libera e unita. Il manifesto di Ventotene*. On the ways in which politicians in Europe have helped promote fear of migrants and a hostile social and political environ-ment, see Malik, "How We All Colluded"; and Trilling, "Irrational Fear of Migrants."

52. Brown, *Walled States*, 25.

53. Brown, 42.

54. Mersal, *Jughrāfiyā badīla*, 47.

55. Mersal, *These Are Not Oranges*, 69.

56. Mersal, *Jughrāfiyā badīla*, 47.

57. Mersal, *These Are Not Oranges*, 69.

58. Atkinson, "Constructing Italian Africa," 19.

59. De Certeau, *Practice of Everyday Life*, 121.

60. Mersal, *Jughrāfiyā badīla*, 48.

61. Mersal, *These Are Not Oranges*, 69.

62. De Certeau, *Practice of Everyday Life*, 123, emphasis in the original.

63. Mersal, *Jughrāfiyā badīla*, 49–50.

64. Mersal, *These Are Not Oranges*, 69–70.

65. On the pioneering experience of the Mahjar Group, see Majaj, "Arab-American Literature." For an interesting discussion of how writers of the mahjar group both partici-pated in and resisted Orientalism, see Hassan, *Immigrant Narratives*, especially chapter 2. For a social and historical study of emigration, gender, and the middle class in Lebanon (1890–1920), see Khater, *Inventing Home*. Elizabeth Claire Saylor and Marjorie Stevens have compiled a story map of the involvement of women writers in the Mahjar Group; see "Mapping Women Writers."

66. See Mersal, "Eliminating Diasporic Identities," 1584.

67. Mersal, 1583.

68. Ngai, *Ugly Feelings*, 1.

69. Mersal, "S. J. Fowler Interviews Iman Mersal."

70. Halberstam, *Queer Art of Failure*, 124.

71. Mersal, "Eliminating Diasporic Identities," 1583. For an anthology collecting both classics and less-known texts produced during the *nahḍa* in the nineteenth and early twentieth century, see El-Ariss's bilingual anthology, *Arab Renaissance*. See also El-Ariss, *Trials of Arab Modernity*. For a critique of the typical binaries (East/West, modernity/tradition) commonly used to discuss the *nahḍa*, see Halabi, *Unmaking of the Arab Intel-lectual*, particularly chapter 1.

72. Mersal, "S. J. Fowlers Interviews Iman Mersal."

73. Said, *Culture and Imperialism*, 6.

74. Said, 6.

75. Lamm, "Seeing Feminism in Exile."

3. Maritime Crossings: Mina Boulhanna's "Immigrata" and "Africa"

1. See Gnisci, *Nuovo Planetario Italiano*, 178–79.

2. Kosic and Triandafyllidou, "Italy," 185.

3. Kosic and Triandafyllidou, 194.

4. Ceola, *Migrazioni narranti*, chapter 7, note 165.

5. Boulhanna, "Immigrata," 178. This and the following translations from Italian to English are mine. This is the original version: "Nebbia, questa mia / È casuale, il mio cammino Eppure sono molto attenta."

6. Hajdari, *Ombra di cane / Hije qeni*, 50.

7. Mersal, *These Are Not Oranges*, 59.

8. Romeo, "Racial Evaporations," 231.

9. Lakhous, "Maghreb," 155–87, particularly 157.

10. Sayad, "El-Ghorba," 166–67.

11. Sayad, 166–67.

12. Boulhanna, "Immigrata," 178. This is the original version: "Il mio cielo è grigio Alberi e rami spogli Aria gelida, umida."

13. See Eliot, "Waste Land."

14. For an introduction of Rosi Braidotti's nomadic theory, see Braidotti, *Nomadic Theory*; on the relation between individual and global nomadism, see D'Andrea, "Neo-Nomadism."

15. Boulhanna, "Immigrata," 179. This is the original version: "Triste questa mia vita / Il mio destino che me l'ha scelta."

16. Eliot, "Waste Land."

17. Lombardi-Diop, "Postracial/Postcolonial Italy," 175.

18. Boulhanna, "Africa," 179. This is the original version: "Grappolo d'uva nera Dolce, calda e vera."

19. hooks, "Eating the Other," 380.

20. Boulhanna, 179. This is the original version: "Africa, semplice e sincera Selvaggia, spontanea Vittima della malvagità / Del tormento e della natura."

21. Boulhanna, 179. The original version is: "E chi ti capisce? / Sei nera e brutta / Sei povera maledetta / Sei l'Africa da rimanere in Africa."

22. Morrison, Playing in the Dark, x.

23. On the paradoxes, coverups, and hypocrisies of cultural expeditions sponsored by colonial France in the African continent, see Leiris, *Phantom Africa*.

24. On the persistence of negative representations of Africa in Western media, see Poncian, "Persistence of Western Negative Perceptions"; and Tsikata, "Historical and

Contemporary Representation of Africa." For an examination of the international media coverage of sub-Saharan Africa, see Bunce, Franks, and Paterson, *Africa's Media Image*.

25. Morrison, *Playing in the Dark*, xi.

26. On the representation of tropes of vision, visibility and vocality in postcolonial literature and film, see Moore, *Arab, Muslim, Woman*. For an analysis of imperial and postcolonial iconographies of Africa, see Landau and Kaspin, *Images and Empires*.

27. On the visual and material representation of gender, sexuality, and race by colonial powers, see Blanchard, Bancel, Boëtsch, Thomas, Taraud, *Sexe, race et colonies*. The book has sparked controversy, particularly regarding its unproblematic and morbid reproduction of erotic images of colonial bodies with little or no contextualization and its accumulation of degrading images and reactivation of violence on colonial bodies. On these two critiques, see Schneidermann's "Un beau livre des viols coloniaux"; and the indignation expressed by le Collectif Cases Rebelles.

28. For a contrapuntal reading of the Black Atlantic with today's Mediterranean, see Covi and Marchi, "Sweetly Dancing."

29. Ben-Ghiat and Fuller, *Italian Colonialism*, 3, emphasis in the original.

30. For a history of Italian colonialism in Africa, see Labanca, *Oltremare*; see also Labanca, *La guerra italiana per la Libia* and *La guerra d'Etiopia*. For a gender-based approach on Italian colonialism, see Stefani, *Colonia per maschi*. For a critique of the myth of "the good Italian," see Del Boca, *Italiani, brava gente?* On the topic of racism in contemporary Italy, see Lombardi-Diop and Giuliani, *Bianco e nero*; and Lombardi-Diop and Romeo, *Postcolonial Italy*. For an overview of everyday embarassing gaffes and "minor" misunderstandings as well as of episodes of violent racism in present-day Italy, see the creative works of Komla-Ebri *Imbarazzismi* and *Nuovi Imbarazzismi*; Aden, *Fra-intendimenti*; and Yimer, *Va' Pensiero*.

31. See Aden, *Fra-intendimenti*; Farah, *Piccola madre*; Ghermandi, *Regina di fiori e di perle*; Scego, *La mia casa è dove sono*, *Adua*, and *La linea del colore*; and Brioni's documentary *Aulò*. For a creative unearthing and remapping of Rome's denied colonial traces, see Scego and Bianchi, *Roma negata*. See also the interactive map "Roma imperiale" on "Postcolonial Italy," https://postcoloniality.com/roma-imperiale (accessed March 19, 2022). For a theoretical engagement with the durable impact of colonial histories on the present, see Stoler, *Duress*.

32. Cooke, Göknar, and Parker, *Mediterranean Passages*, xiii.

33. See Contreras, "Lybia."

34. Bensaad, "Mediterranean Divide," 56.

35. Bensaad, 52.

36. Adouani, *Ṣaḥrā'u al-baḥri/Meerwüste*.

37. Bensaad, "Mediterranean Divide," 59.

38. Generale, "When Migrants Do Not Arrive."

39. Dal Lago, *Non-persone*.

40. Butler, *Precarious Life*, xii–iii.
41. Malette, *Kingdom of Sicily*, 6.
42. Malette, *European Modernity*, 92.
43. Malette, 92.
44. Malette, *Kingdom of Sicily*, 30.
45. See Devet, van Belleghem, and Herrera Tobón, *Subjective Atlases*.
46. For a biography of Ibn Rushd/Averroes and a reflection on its legacy, see Sonneborn, *Averroes*; and Campanini, *Averroè*.
47. Maraini, *Ballando con Averroè*, 36.
48. Maraini, 36.
49. Maraini, 36.
50. Maraini, 38.
51. Maraini, 37. For a historical reconstruction of the dialectical relationship between Islamic scientific thought and the scientific discoveries in Europe during the Renaissance, see Saliba's *Islamic Science*. On the essential contribution of Arab astronomers to the field of astronomy and its influence on Copernicus, see Saliba's *History of Arabic Astronomy*.
52. Maraini, *Ballando con Averroè*, 38.
53. Maraini, 40.
54. See Campanini, *Averroè*, 113.
55. See Menocal, *Ornament of the World*, 201.
56. Maraini, *Ballando con Averroè*, 42.
57. Romeo, "Racial Evaporations," 231.
58. Merolla and Ponzanesi, *Migrant Cartographies*.
59. Said, *Beginnings*.
60. Morrison, *Playing in the Dark*, ix.
61. Said, *Beginnings*, 34.
62. Woolf, *Room of One's Own*.

4. Oceanic Crossings: Nadine Ltaif's *Ce que vous ne lirez pas*

1. This and the following translations from French into English are mine.
2. Gauvin, "Introduction," 10, emphasis in the original.
3. Ltaif, "Écrire pour vivre l'échange," 82. The original version sounds: "L'arabe reste l'inconscient de mon texte: le rythme qui scande la phrase, la composition musicale du poème. C'est comme chanter en français une langue arabe."
4. Dupré, "Women's Writing in Quebec," 21.
5. See Lalonde, "Speak White"; and Vallières, *Nègres blancs d'Amérique*. Lalonde's poem has inspired later revendications. In 1989, Marco Micone wrote a direct response to that poem and published it as "Speak What." This time, Micone complained about

the social and cultural marginalization that writers belonging to the non-Francophone minority were experiencing at the end of the 1980s. During the student contestations of 2012 following the 2008 global economic crisis, the poem underwent another metamorphosis, this time at the hands of Marie-Christine Lemieux-Couture, who wrote "Speak Rich en Tabarnaque." The poem attacked multinationals, wild capitalism, xenophobia, and political maneuvers aimed at shaping docile and disciplined citizens through terror.

6. For an extensive survey of the literature produced by Native and ethnic authors in Canada, see Kamboureli, *Making a Difference*.

7. Ireland and Proulx, *Textualizing the Immigrant Experience*, 2.

8. Some selected poems included in this collection have been recently translated into English by Christine Tipper in the volume *Journeys*.

9. Mailhot and Nepveu, *La poésie québécoise*, 10–11.

10. Verduyn, "Perspectives critiques," 84–85.

11. Carrière, "Des méprises identitaires," 67.

12. Carrière, 67.

13. Dahab, *Voices of Exile*, 4.

14. For a fascinating reflection on the possibilities offered by a "history without documents" to historians and artists, see El Shakry, "History without Documents."

15. Ltaif is not the only artist engaged in creative processes precariously positioned between historical and fictional narration aimed at recreating a missing historical archive or one that has been intentionally destroyed. See, among others, the artistic project *The Atlas Group* created by Walid Raad to fabricate an alternative, unofficial, and bottom-up archive of the Lebanese Civil War. For critical work that discusses this project, see Nakas, Schmitz, and Raad, *Atlas Group*. On the use of the imagination to fill-in historical gaps and absences, see Bowen, "This Bridge Called Imagination." On the presence of contradictions and anxieties, hidden and contested meanings in colonial archives, see Stoler, *Along the Archival Grain*.

16. The entire section "Exil Andalou, Espagne Novembre 2006" has been translated in English by Christine Tipper in *Journeys*, 13–27.

17. Ltaif, *Ce que vous ne lirez pas*, 19.

18. Faradj, "'Guernica' Connection."

19. Ltaif, *Ce que vous ne lirez pas*, 100.

20. For more information about Sevilla and the history of its cathedral, see Encyclopaedia Britannica, "Sevilla," https://www.britannica.com/place/Sevilla-Spain (accessed March 20, 2022). On the expulsion of Spanish Jews in 1492 and of the Moriscos in 1609, see Kamen, "Mediterranean and the Expulsion of Spanish Jews"; Jónsson, "Expulsion of the Moriscos"; and García-Arenal Rodriguez and Wiegers, *Expulsion of the Moriscos*.

21. Menocal, *Ornament of the World*, 271.

22. Menocal, 11. For works that critically analyze the conflicting reconstructions and interpretations of al-Andalus and its myths from a historical perspective, see Akasoy,

"Convivencia and Its Discontents"; Fanjul, *Al-Andalus*; Rubiera and De Epalza, "Al-Andalus"; Calderwood, "Invention of al-Andalus"; and Sardar and Tassin-Kassab, "Reclaiming al-Andalus."

23. Ltaif, *Ce que vous ne lirez pas*, 21. This is the original French version: "Une tour / et des murs / qui séparent les cultures / entre la cathédrale / somptueuse / tellement écrasante / de catholicité / et la tour arabe / à l'écriture épurée dans le Vieux Séville / dans le Veracruz—certains crimes / pouvaient rester / impunis."

24. On the ways in which religious ideas produced difference-making in the form of "race," see Heng, *Invention of Race*. For an unusually broad study of questions of gender, ethnicity, and religious identity in al-Andalus, see Coope, *Most Noble of People*. On the complexities of intimate interfaith relations in al-Andalus, see Barton, *Conquerors, Brides, and Concubines*.

25. See Irving, *Tales of the Alhambra*; and Calderwood, "Invention of al-Andalus."

26. Calderwood, "Franco's Hajj," 1102.

27. For an analysis of how the two historical events were later manipulated and became the basis for the creation of canonical Spanish and French medieval epics staging a Christian vs. Muslim holy war, see Menocal, *Ornament of the World*, particularly 58 and 71.

28. Ltaif, *Ce que vous ne lirez pas*, 29.

29. See Lewis, "Jami Masjid of Delhi."

30. Warner, *Stranger Magic*.

31. Ltaif, *Ce que vous ne lirez pas*, 67. This the original French version: "Tantôt sans voix tantôt / philosophe Sapho / tantôt danseuse du Temple / Ishtar la prostituée sacrée / ou cariatides grecques / Une compagne me suit / Je fais sa rencontre dans divers lieux / Tantôt mère / tantôt soeur."

32. For an overview of the diatribe concerning temple prostitution in ancient times, see Boudin, *Myth of Sacred Prostitution*; and Faraone and McClure, *Prostitutes and Courtesans*.

33. Ltaif, *Ce que vous ne lirez pas*, 69. This is the original French version: "Yamouna n'a pas voulu être choisie / par le Maharajah pour faire partie de son harem / Elle reste collée à Radika et ses autres soeurs / À neuf elles auront la force de l'éléphant / pour combattre l'injustice . . . Dans leur cages dorées / elles vivent un exil."

34. Ltaif, 73. This is the original French version: "Je suis surprise / comment comprendre / cette offrande / ce désir de se dévoiler / à nous qui venons / d'Occident?"

35. Ltaif, 75.

36. For an in-depth analysis of the belated encounter between nineteenth-century French and British writers and the Orient, see Behdad, *Belated Travelers*. The lives of the Maharanis in India have been the object of movies and memoirs, which have attempted to reconstruct from an insider's perspective their experiences of oppression and rebellion. See Devi, *Princess Remembers*; and Herpreet Kaur, "Rebel Queen."

37. See Booth, *Harem Histories*.

38. On this topic, see Elsadda, *Gender, Nation, and the Arabic Novel*.

39. On this debate, see Vince, "France, Islam and laïcité."

40. Ltaif, *Ce que vous ne lirez pas*, 36.

41. Simon, *Cities in Translation*, 147.

42. Abou-Hsab, *Le fleuve*, 37, my translation.

43. Ltaif, *Ce que vous ne lirez pas*, 79.

44. Ltaif, 82.

45. On the fraught relationship between state-sponsored amnesia and personal commemoration in Lebanon, see Sawalha, *Reconstructing Beirut*; and Hanssen and Genberg, "Beirut in Memoriam." On the reconstruction carried out by Solidère's developers and the popular contestations it provoked, see Makdisi, "Laying Claim to Beirut"; Fricke, "Forever Nearing the Finish Line"; and Larkin, "Reconstructing and Deconstructing Beirut."

46. Makdisi, 662.

47. Fricke, 171.

48. Makdisi, "Laying Claim to Beirut," 664.

49. On the recreation of an alternative, unofficial, and bottom-up archive of the civil war, see Raad, *Atlas Group*.

50. Encyclopaedia Britannica, "Tyre."

51. See Cartwright, "Tyrian Purple." For a comprehensive history of how the trade of textiles impacted far-flung locations stretching from the Mediterranean basin to the Indian subcontinent, see Phillips, *Sea Change*.

52. Ltaif, *Ce que vous ne lirez pas*, 91. This is the original French version: "Mais soudain Tyr m'appelle et m'obsède / Elle est vide / Elle est vidée de ses habitants / C'est une ville morte / Ils ont tous fui les bombes ennemies."

53. Ltaif, 91.

54. Pflitsch and Neuwirth, "Crisis and Memory," 15.

55. Dahab, "Introduction," 5, emphasis in the original.

56. Bordeleau, "Andrée Chédid," 58. This is the original French version: "C'est aussi le paysage de l'enfance, ce paysage qui nous impressionne jusqu'à la mort. Ainsi, quand j'entends un klaxon dans n'importe quel coin du monde, ce sont toutes les rues du Caire qui ressurgissent tout d'un coup."

57. On the ways in which a buried past of mass murder and violence breeds resentment, promotes impunity, and may open the way to new injustices, see Adam, *Hushed Voices*.

58. See Hanru and Ferracci, *Home Beirut*.

59. See Elkhoury, "Le plus beau jour."

60. For a historical study of the Bourj and its controversial reconstruction project, see Khalaf, *Heart of Beirut*.

61. Mallette, *European Modernity and the Arab Mediterranean*, 39.

62. Hassan, *Oxford Handbook of Arab Novelistic Traditions*, 79.

63. For an overview of the ways in which Muslim and Western travelers moved mutually across lands and cultures for worship or for thirst of knowledge, see Euben, *Journeys to the Other Shore*.

64. For an overview on the gender politics at play in colonial ethnography, see Behdad, *Belated Travelers*.

65. Behdad, 95, 98.

66. Behdad, 24.

67. Hout, "Last Migration," 144–45.

68. Al-Ali, "On Not Travelling Lightly."

69. Bordeleau, "Andrée Chédid," 56.

70. Bordeleau, 58, emphasis in the original.

71. Ltaif, *Élégies du Levant*, 27.

72. Butler, *Frames of War*, 59.

73. On the contemporary revival of the "standing by the ruins" trope in postwar Lebanon, see Seigneurie, *Standing by the Ruins*. On the tensions between memory and forgetfulness in postwar Lebanon, see Haugbolle, *War and Memory in Lebanon*; and Westmoreland, "Catastrophic Subjectivity."

74. Brossard, "Au fil de la narration," 7–8. This is the original French version: "L'album de photos ne me rend pas nostalgique il me stimule, m'incite à observer et à questionner le visible et l'invisible de notre présence au monde. Il faut entretenir notre mémoire comme on entretient un jardin, avec ses racines et son cycle de vie, car en elle se cache en grande partie ce qui constitue notre identité vivante."

75. Butler, *Frames of War*, 171.

76. Ltaif, *Ce que vous ne lirez pas*, 92. This is the original French version: "Voilà que tout est à recommencer, reprendre de zéro, la pelouse, l'herbe, les premières pousses, les tiges, les plantes, et ainsi de suite."

77. Tuéni, "Beyrouth."

78. Kadir, *Memos for the Besieged City*, 94.

79. Ltaif, *Ce que vou ne lirez pas*, 100–101.

80. Ltaif, "Écrire pour vivre l'échange," 82. This is the original French version: "Il a été un temps où la désignation 'écriture migrante' était nécessaire. Elle nous donnait une voix. Mais cette même désignation a fini par nous enfermer dans une boîte d'où nous trouvons difficile de sortir aujourd'hui."

5. Breaking Love as an Ideal: Maram al-Massri's
A Red Cherry on a White-Tiled Floor

1. Rich, *Arts of the Possible*, 159.

2. Rich, 109.

3. Juvonen and Kolehmainen, *Affective Inequalities in Intimate Relationships*.

4. Halberstam, *Queer Art of Failure*, 113.

5. Love, *Feeling Backward*, 24.

6. Halberstam, *Queer Art of Failure*, 105.

7. For an in-depth analysis of the (changing) institution of marriage and married life in the Arab world, with a specific focus on Egypt, see El Feki, *Sex and the Citadel*, particularly chapter 2.

8. Badiou, *In Praise of Love*, 7.

9. On the tripartite structure of the qaṣīda, see Al-Musawi, *Arabic Poetry*, 238. For a general discussion of the themes and variations in Umayyad ghazal poetry, see Jacobi, "Theme and Variations." For modern and contemporary English rewritings of the ghazal form, see Ali, *Ravishing Dis-Unities*.

10. Al-Musawi, *Arabic Poetry*, 2–23.

11. Al-Musawi, 18–19.

12. See Poetry Foundation, "Sappho."

13. Obbink, "Chapter 2."

14. See Poochigian, "Note on the Text."

15. For an overview of the London-based exposition, see the Crypt Gallery website, cryptgallery.org/event/radical-love-female-lust/ (accessed March 21, 2022) and Pollman's review "Lust for Life" in the *Art Radar Journal*. The classical Arabic poems that inspired the artists can be found in Al-Udhari's bilingual anthology *Classical Poems by Arab Women*.

16. Berlant and Edelman, *Sex, or the Unbearable*, 120.

17. Al-Massri, *Red Cherry*, 11.

18. See Grosz and Probyn, *Sexy Bodies*, xi.

19. Al-Massri, *Red Cherry*, 40.

20. Al-Massri, 11.

21. On the stickiness produced by certain affects, see Ahmed, "Affective Economies."

22. Ostle, "Romantic Imagination and the Female Ideal."

23. Dorigo Ceccato, "Figure of the Lover," 28.

24. Al-Massri, *Red Cherry*, 11.

25. See Kaltner and Mirza, *Bible and the Qur'an*, 63.

26. See Corrao, *Poeti arabi di Sicilia*.

27. Al-Massri, *Red Cherry*, 37.

28. Al-Massri, 39.

29. Aghacy, *Masculine Identity*, 7, emphasis in the original.

30. Cavarero, *Inclinations*, 4.

31. Cavarero, 3.

32. Al-Massri, *Red Cherry*, 45.

33. Kilpatrick, "Introduction," 15.

34. Al-Massri, *Red Cherry*, 17.

35. Cavarero, *For More than One Voice*, 117.

36. Al-Massri, *Red Cherry*, 19.

37. Al-Massri, 21.

38. Pratt and Rosner, *Global and the Intimate*, 3.

39. Al-Massri, *Red Cherry*, 50.

40. Bouhdiba, *Sexuality in Islam*, viii.

41. See Overton, *Novel of Female Adultery*.

42. Alharthi, *Celestial Bodies*.

43. Al-Massri, *Red Cherry*, 35.

44. Cavarero, *Inclinations*, 8.

45. Al-Massri, *Red Cherry*, 95.

46. Al-Massri, 62.

47. Halberstam, *Queer Art of Failure*, 105.

48. Smith, "Giorgio Morandi Creates a Universe."

49. Al-Massri, 27.

50. Ahmed, *Politics of Happiness*, 59–60.

51. Lorde, *Sister Outsider*, 87.

52. Al-Massri, *Red Cherry*, 49.

53. Ngai, *Ugly Feelings*, 27.

54. Scott, *Domination and the Arts of Resistance*, 215–16.

55. See Jayyusi, quoted in al-Musawi, *Arabic Poetry*, 98.

56. Malti-Douglas, *Woman's Body, Woman's Word*, 6.

57. Stewart, *Ordinary Affects*, 86.

58. Hazm, *Ring of the Dove*. The treatise illustrates love's principles, misfortunes, and accidents together with its vileness and virtues. Ibn Hazm's work has been read as an important Islamic source of courtly love, which had a prolonged and significant impact. In more recent times, the treatise has been accused of racism and misogyny. See Hickman, "Ibn Hazm"; and Fox Jr., "Ring of the Dove."

59. El Feki, *Sex and the Citadel*, 55.

60. For critical debates on these novels, see Al-Rasheed, "Economies of Desire"; Qualey, "Layla al-Othman"; and Laachir, "Saudi Women Novelists."

61. On Yusuf Idris's short stories, see Allen, *Critical Perspectives on Yusuf Idris*, particularly Cobham's "Sex and Society in Yusuf Idris"; and Malti-Douglas's "Blindness and Sexuality," respectively 77–84 and 89–96. On Layla al-Uthman's short stories, see Adang, Ansari, and Fierro, *Accusations of Unbelief in Islam*, particularly 360–62. See also Hassan, *Oxford Handbook of Arab Novelistic Traditions*, 386; and Tijani, *Male Dmination, Female Revolt*. On Ghada Samman's poetry, see Homsi Vinson, "Ghada Samman."

62. Badiou, *In Praise of Love*, 6.

63. Badiou, 79.

64. Reich, *Mass Psychology of Fascism.*

65. Reich, 44.

66. Aghacy, *Masculine Identity,* 9.

67. Mina qtd. in Aghacy, 61.

68. Scott, *Domination and the Arts of Resistance,* 227.

69. Sharabi, *Neopatriarchy,* 7.

70. Aghacy, *Masculine Identity,* 94.

71. Naber, *Arab America,* 9.

72. Baier, *Moral Prejudices,* 130.

73. On an alternative conceptualization of cultures and forms of kinship as creolized rather than pure, see Covi, "Creolizing Cultures and Kinship."

74. Love, *Feeling Backward,* 145.

75. Al-Massri, *Red Cherry,* 18.

6. Afro-Arab Beats: Suheir Hammad's *breaking poems*

1. See Hammad, *Drops of This Story.* See also Nathalie Handal's interview, "Drops of Suheir Hammad."

2. Allen, *Introduction to Arabic Literature.*

3. Hartman, "Dreams Deferred," 64.

4. Hartman, "This Sweet / Sweet Music," 146. On the cultural influences and political solidarities between African Americans and Arab Americans, see Hartman, *Breaking Broken English.*

5. Pickens, *New Body Politics,* 6.

6. On spoken word poetry, see Eleveld, *Spoken Word Revolution*; Smith and Kraynak, *Take the Mic*; and Olson, *Word Warriors.* On dub poetry, see Habekost, *Verbal Riddim*; and *Routledge Companion to Anglophone Caribbean Literature,* particularly Bucknor's "Dub Poetry."

7. Naber, *Arab America,* 241.

8. Hammad, *breaking poems,* 35.

9. Reyes, "Suheir Hammad."

10. Hammad, *breaking poems,* 11.

11. Hammad, 11.

12. Hammad, 11.

13. Hammad, 13.

14. Hammad, 13.

15. Hammad, 13.

16. Hammad, 14.

17. Hammad, 14.

18. Hammad, 13.

19. Hammad, 15.

20. Hammad, 14.

21. Kadir, "What Does the Comparative Do for Literary History?," 648.

22. Kadir, 650.

23. Hammad, *breaking poems*, 14.

24. Johnson, *Feminist Difference*, 13.

25. Hammad, *breaking poems*, 20.

26. For a in-depth analysis of Hammad's indebtedness to Arab popular music icons, see Marchi, *In filigrana*, particularly the analysis of Hammad's poem dedicated to the singing Diva Umm Kulthum "bint el-nil" included in the second chapter "Saldature afro-arabe."

27. See Frishkopf, *Music and Media in the Arab World*; and Frishkopf, "Tarab in the Mystic Sufi Chant." For an extensive study of tarab, see Racy, *Making Music in the Arab World*.

28. For a comprehensive analysis of the formation of the Black Arts Movement of the 1960s and 1970s and its deep influence on the production and reception of literature and art in the United States, see Smethurst, *black art movement*; and Bracey, Sanchez, and Smethurst, *SOS*. For an overview of the vitality and the generative force of the Harlem Renaissance, see Huggins, *Voices from the Harlem Renaissance*. On the experimental poetry of the Black Mountain poets in the 1940s and 1950s and their strong connections with the Beats, see Dewey, *Beyond Maximus*; and Olson's manifesto "Projective Verse," in which he theorized an improvisational, poem-form approach to poetic composition driven by breath and utterance. On the aesthetics of spontaneity and immediacy of the Beats, see Elkholy, *Philosophy of the Beats*, particularly chapter 3. For an introduction to the lives and works of the representatives of the Beat Generation as well as for an exploration of its long-overlooked female members, see Tytell, *Naked Angels*; and Knight, *Women of the Beat Generation*.

29. Habekost, *Verbal Riddim*, 96.

30. Hammad, *breaking poems*, 20.

31. Chakravorty, "Dead That Haunt *Anil's Ghost*," 555.

32. For a more conflicting view on hip-hop and rap music, see Hurt's documentary film *Hip-Hop*.

33. Lubin, *Geographies of Liberation*, 163.

34. Jordan, "Moving towards Home," 91.

35. Jordan, 92–93.

36. Hammad, *breaking poems*, 18.

37. Ahmed, *Politics of Happiness*, 70.

38. For an analysis of the contemporary reappropriation of the "standing by the ruins" topos, particularly in the Lebanese context, see Seigneurie, *Standing in the Ruins*.

39. Ahmed, *Politics of Happiness*, 218.

40. Ahmed, *What Is Islam?*, 72.

41. Hammad, *breaking poems*, 35.

42. Hammad, 35.

43. See Hoffman-Ladd, "Mysticism and Sexuality."

44. Hammad, *breaking poems*, 35.

45. Hammad, 27.

46. See Breeze, "Wife of Bath Speaks."

47. Hammad, *breaking poems*, 27.

48. Cavarero, *Inclinations*, 174.

49. Mernissi, *Dreams of Trespass*.

50. For an overview of Islamic feminism, see Cooke, *Women Claim Islam*; and Badran, *Feminism in Islam*. For specific examples of Islamic feminists' theorizations and practices, see Mernissi, *Islam and Democracy*; Wadud, *Inside the Gender Jihad*; and Khorasani, *Iranian Women's One Million Signatures*. See also Lamrabet's recent works *Women in the Qur'an* and *Femmes et hommes dans les Coran*.

51. Djebar, *Far from Medina*. Anjuli I. Gunaratne and Jill M. Jarvis have curated a fascinating collection of essays on Assia Djebar, which appeared in the journal *PMLA* in January 2016. See Gunaratne and Jarvis, "Introduction."

52. Cooke, *Women Claim Islam*, 65–66.

53. Hammad, *ZaatarDiva*, 59.

54. Warner, *Stranger Magic*, 216.

55. Warner, 220.

56. Trías, "Thinking Religion."

57. Rich, *Arts of the Possible*, 111.

58. Pickens, *New Body Politics*, 26.

59. Augé, *Future*, 56.

60. Lorde, *Sister Outsider*, 37.

Conclusion

1. See Friedman, "Why Not Compare?," 758.

2. Samekh, "Neo-Classical Arabic Poets," 36.

3. Al-Musawi, *Islam on the Street*, 211.

4. On the experience of the Bauhaus (1919–1933), see Magdalena Droste, *bauhaus, 1919–1933*; and the bauhaus-archiv, www.bauhaus.de (accessed March 21, 2022).

5. For a critique of conceptualizations of the public space as an ensemble of docile and monitored subjects, see Marchi, "Alchemy of Rawi Hage's Fiction."

6. Shohat, *Talking Visions*, 8.

7. See Koshy, "Minority Cosmopolitanism," 594.

8. See Sollors, *Multilingual America*, 2.

9. See Menocal, *Ornament of the World*, particularly 47 and 78; and Mallette, *European Modernity*, particularly 170.

10. Mattawa, "Resisting the Lapse into Monologue," 61.

11. Mattawa, 62.

12. Feminist scholars have written extensively on this complex issue from multiple perspectives. See, among others, Pepicelli, "Rethinking Gender in Arab Nationalism"; Weber, "Between Nationalism and Feminism"; and Hammad, "Other Extremists," as well as Mojab and Zia, "Race, Class, and Agency"; Newman, "Spaces of Power"; Rottenberg, *Rise of Neoliberal Feminism*; Badran, "Understanding Islam, Islamism, and Islamic Feminism"; and Jad, "Islamist Women of Hamas."

13. See Al-Ali, "On Not Traveling Lightly."

14. Al-Ali.

15. Abu-Lughod, *Do Muslim Women Need Saving?*

16. Menocal, *Ornament of the World*, 24.

17. Ngũgĩ wa Thiong'o, *Globalectics*, 81.

18. Darwish, "Tibaq/Antithesis."

19. El-Enany, "Preface," viii.

20. Gallien, "Decolonial Turn in the Humanities," 28.

21. Cassano, *Southern Thought*, lii.

22. Said, "Globalizing Literary Studies," 65.

23. Said, 64.

24. Izzo, "American Studies in Europe," 187.

25. Johnson, "About This Journal."

26. Ngũgĩ wa Thiong'o, *Globalectics*, 85.

27. Moretti, "Conjectures on World Literature." For recent theorizations of world literature, see Damrosch, *What Is World Literaure?*; Casanova, *World Republic of Letters*; and Moretti, *Distant Reading*. For a reflection on the challenges of teaching world literature, see Damrosch, *Teaching World Literature*.

28. Ngũgĩ wa Thiong'o, *Globalectics*, 58.

29. Auerbach, "Philology and *Weltliteratur*," 13–14.

30. Auerbach, 15.

31. Monroe qtd. in Mallette, *European Modernity and the Arab Mediterranean*, 174.

32. Mufti, *Forget English!*, 7.

33. Radhakrishnan, "World Literature, by Any Other Name?," 1398. For other critical views on world literature, see Cooppan, "Ethics of World Literature"; Apter, "Untranslatability and the Geopolitics of Reading"; Burns, *Postcolonialism after World Literature*; Bhattacharya, *Postcolonial Writing*; and Cheah, *What Is a World?*.

34. Hiddleston, "Writing World Literature," 1388.

35. Cooppan, "Ethics of World Literature," 38.

36. See Edwards, *After the American Century*, xv.

37. Edwards, xv.

38. Darwish "Edward Said." This the original Arabic version:

لنذهبْ،

لنذهبْ إلى غدنا واثقين،

بصدْق الخيال، ومُعْجزةِ العُشْبِ/

Bibliography

Aart, Greta, Sally Molini, and Naomi Shihab Nye. "A Poet's Humble Answers: Naomi Shihab Nye." *Cerise Press: A Journal of Literature, Arts, and Culture* 1, no. 3 (Spring 2010). http://www.cerisepress.com/01/03a-poets-humble -answers-naomi-shihab-nye (accessed August 29, 2015).

Abou-Hsab, Georges. *Le fleuve: poèmes.* Montreal: Lanctôt Editeur, 2006.

Abu-Lughod, Lila. "Egyptian Melodrama—Technology of the Modern Subject?" In *Media Worlds: Anthropology on New Terrain,* edited by Faye Ginsburg, Lila Abu-Lughod, and Brian Larkin, 115–33. Berkeley: Univ. of California Press, 2002.

———. *Do Muslim Women Need Saving?* Cambridge, MA: Harvard Univ. Press, 2013.

Adam, Heribert. *Hushed Voices: Unacknowledged Atrocities of the Twentieth Century.* Luton: Berkshire Academic Press, 2010.

Adang, Camilla, Hassan Ansari, Maribel Fierro, and Sabine Schmidtke. *Accusations of Unbelief in Islam.* Leiden: Brill, 2016.

Aden, Kaha Mohamed. *Fra-intendimenti.* Roma: Nottetempo, 2010.

Adouani, Najet. *Meerwüste / Ṣaḥrā'a al-baḥr.* Translated by Leila Chammaa. Berlin: Lotos Werkstatt, 2015.

Aghacy, Samira. *Masculine Identity in the Fiction of the Arab East since 1967.* Syracuse, NY: Syracuse Univ. Press, 2009.

Ahmed, Sara. "Affective Economies." *Social Text* 79, no. 22 (Summer 2004): 117–39.

———. *The Politics of Happiness.* Durham, NC: Duke Univ. Press, 2010.

———. *Queer Phenomenology: Orientation, Objects, Others.* Durham, NC: Duke Univ. Press, 2006.

Ahmed, Sara, Claudia Castada, Anne-Marie Fortier, and Mimi Sheller, eds. *Uprootings/Regroundings: Questions of Home and Migration.* Oxford: Berg, 2003.

Ahmed, Shahab. *What Is Islam? The Importance of Being Islamic*. Princeton, NJ: Princeton Univ. Press, 2015.

Akasoy, Anna. "Convivencia and Its Discontents: Interfaith Life in Al-Andalus." *International Journal of Middle East Studies* 42, no. 3 (2010): 489–99.

Al-Ali, Nadje. "On Not Travelling Lightly: Transnational Feminist Journeys to and from the Middle East." Accessed January 7, 2019. https://www.soas.ac .uk/staff/staff37137.php.

Alameddine, Rabih. *An Unnecessary Woman*. New York: Grove, 2013.

Alfonso, Carolin, Waltraud Kokot, and Khachig Tölölyan, eds. *Diaspora, Identity, and Religion: New Directions in Theory and Research*. London: Routledge, 2016.

Alharthi, Jokha. *Celestial Bodies*. Translated by Marilyn Booth. New York: Catapult, 2019.

Ali, Agha Shahid. *Ravishing DisUnities: Real Ghazals in English*. Middletown, CT: Wesleyan Univ. Press, 2000.

Ali Farah, Cristina. *Madre picoola*. Milano: Sperling & Knupfer, 2007.

Allen, Roger. "The Arabic Short Story and the Status of Women." In *Love and Sexuality in Modern Arabic Literature*, edited by Roger Allen, Hilary Kilpatrick, and Ed de Moor, 77–90. London: Saqi, 1995.

———. *Introduction to Arabic Literature*. Cambridge: Cambridge Univ. Press, 2001.

Allen, Roger, ed. *Critical Perspectives on Yusuf Idris*. Colorado Springs: Three Continents, 1994.

Allen, Roger, Hilary Kilpatrick, and Ed de Moor, eds. *Love and Sexuality in Modern Arabic Literature*. London: Saqi, 1995.

Al-Hirz, *The Others*. New York: Seven Stories, 2009.

Al Maleh, Laila, ed. *Arab Voices in Diaspora: Critical Perspectives on Anglophone Arab Literature*. Amsterdam: Rodopi, 2009.

Al-Massri, Maram. *A Red Cherry on a White-Tiled Floor*. Translated by Khaled Mattawa. Northumberland: Bloodaxe, 2004.

Al-Musawi, Muhsin J. *Arabic Poetry: Trajectories of Modernity and Tradition*. London: Routledge, 2006.

———. *Islam in the Street: Religion in Modern Arabic Literature*. Lanham, MD: Rowman & Littlefield, 2009.

Al-Rasheed, Madawi. "Economies of Desire, Fictive Sexual Uprisings. Saudi Chick Literature: The Girls Are Doing it." *Le Monde Diplomatique*, May 5, 2011. http://mondediplo.com/2011/05/05saudisexnovels.

Al-Sani, Raja. *Girls of Riyadh*. London: Penguin, 2007.

Al-Udhari, Abdullah. *Classical Poems by Arab Women: A Bilingual Anthology*. London: Saqi, 1999.

Amin, Nora. "Shadow Theatre: Performance and the Imaginary in Contemporary Egypt." *Theatre Times*, November 7, 2019. https://thetheatretimes.com/shadow-theatre-performance-and-the-imaginary-in-contemporary-egypt/.

Amireh, Amal. "Edwar al-Kharrat and the Modernist Revolution in the Egyptian Novel." *Al-Jadid* 2, no. 9 (July 1996). https://www.aljadid.com/content/edwar-al-kharrat-and-modernist-revolution-egyptian-novel (accessed November 7, 2020).

Anceschi, Luca, Gennaro Gervasio, and Andrea Teti, eds. *Informal Power in the Greater Middle East: Hidden Geographies*. London: Routledge, 2014.

Andrijasevich, Rutvica. *Migration, Agency, and Citizenship in Sex Trafficking*. London: Palgrave Macmillan, 2010.

———. "The Difference Borders Make: (Il)legality, Migration and Trafficking in Italy among Eastern European Women in Prostitution." In *Uprootings/Regroundings: Questions of Home and Migration*, edited by Sara Ahmed, Claudia Castaneda, Anne-Marie Fortier, and Mimi Sheller, 251–71. Oxford: Berg, 2003.

Ankori, Gannit. *Palestinian Art*. London: Reaktion, 2006.

Apter, Emily. "Untranslatability and the Geopolitics of Reading." *PMLA* 134, no. 1 (January 2019): 194-200.

Arendt, Hannah. *Men in Dark Times*. New York: Harcourt Brace Jovanovich, 1968.

Arkoun, Mohammed. *Essais sur la pensée islamique*. Paris: Éditions Maisonneuve et Larose, 1973.

———. *Rethinking Islam: Common Questions, Uncommon Answers*. Edited and translated by Robert D. Lee. Boulder, CO: Westview, 1994.

Atkinson, David. "Constructing Italian Africa: Geography and Geopolitics." In *Italian Colonialism*, edited by Ruth Ben-Ghiat and Mia Fuller, 15–26. New York: Palgrave Macmillan, 2005.

Auerbach, Erich. "Philology and *Weltliteratur*." *Centennial Review* 13, no. 1 (1969): 1–17.

Augé, Marc. *The Future*. Translated by John Howe. London: Verso, 2015.

Badawi, M. M., ed. *Modern Arabic Literature*. Cambridge: Cambridge Univ. Press, 1993.

Badiou, Alain. *In Praise of Love*. Translated by Peter Bush. Paris: Flammarion, 2009.

Badran, Margot. *Feminism in Islam: Secular and Religious Convergences.* Oxford: Oneworld, 2009.

———. "Understanding Islam, Islamism, and Islamic Feminism." *Journal of Women's History* 13, no. 1 (Spring 2001): 47–52.

Baier, Annette C. *Moral Prejudices: Essays on Ethics.* Cambridge, MA: Harvard Univ. Press, 1995.

Bardouil, Sam. *Surrealism in Egypt: Modernism and the Art and Liberty Group.* London: Tauris, 2016.

Barton, Simon. *Conquerors, Brides, and Concubines: Interfaith Relations and Social Power in Medieval Iberia.* Philadelphia: Univ. of Pennsylvania Press, 2015.

Bauböck, Rainer, and Thomas Faist, eds. *Diaspora and Transnationalism: Concepts, Theories, and Methods.* Amsterdam: Amsterdam Univ. Press, 2010.

bauhaus-archiv. www.bauhaus.de. Accessed March 21, 2022.

Bausani, Alessandro. *Il Corano.* Translated by Alessandro Bausani. Milano: Rizzoli, 2010.

Bayat, Asef. *Life as Politics: How Ordinary People Change the Middle East.* Stanford, CA: Stanford Univ. Press, 2013.

Beckett, Larry. *Beat Poetry.* London: Beatdom, 2012.

Behdad, Ali. *Belated Travelers: Orientalism in the Age of Colonial Dissolution.* Durham, NC: Duke Univ. Press, 1994.

Ben-Ghiat, Ruth, and Mia Fuller. "Introduction." In *Italian Colonialism*, edited by Ruth Ben-Ghiat and Mia Fuller, 1–12. New York: Palgrave Macmillan, 2005.

Bennett, Jane. *The Enchantment of Modern Life: Attachments, Crossings, and Ethics.* Princeton, NJ: Princeton Univ. Press, 2001.

———. "The Force of Things. Steps towards an Ecology of Matter." *Political Theory* 32, no. 3 (June 2004): 347–72.

———. *Vibrant Matter: A Political Ecology of Things.* Durham, NC: Duke Univ. Press, 2010.

Bensaad, Ali. "The Mediterranean Divide and Its Echo in the Sahara: New Migratory Routes and New Barriers on the Path to the Mediterranean." In *Between Europe and the Mediterranean: The Challenges and the Fears*, edited by Thierry Fabre and Paul Sant-Cassia, 59–61. New York: Palgrave Macmillan, 2007.

Berlant, Lauren, and Lee Edelman. *Sex, or the Unbearable.* Durham, NC: Duke Univ. Press, 2014.

Bhattacharya, Baidik. *Postcolonial Writing in the Era of World Literature: Texts, Territories, Globalizations.* London: Routledge, 2018.

Blanchard, Pascal, Nicolas Bancel, Gilles Boetsch, Dominic Thomas, Corinne Taraud, eds. *Sexe race & colonies: La domination des corps comme instrument de pouvoir.* Paris: Edition La Découverte, 2018.

Blunt, Anne. *A Pilgrimage to Nejd, the Cradle of the Arab Race.* Piscataway, NJ: Gorgias, 2002.

Bonazzi, Robert. "Touching Tender Spots." In *Tender Spot: Selected Poems,* by Naomi Shihab Nye, 14–20. Highgreen: Bloodaxe, 2008.

Booth, Marilyn. *Harem Histories: Envisioning Places and Living Spaces.* Durham, NC: Duke Univ. Press, 2011.

Borradori, Giovanna, ed. *Philosophy in a Time of Terror: Dialogues with Jurgen Habermas and Jacques Derrida.* Chicago: Univ. of Chicago Press, 2003.

Bordeleau, Francine. "Andrée Chedid: Le premier visage." *Nuit Blanche, Magazine Littéraire* 28 (1987): 56–58.

Boudin, Stephanie Lynn. *The Myth of Sacred Prostitution in Antiquity.* Cambridge: Cambridge Univ. Press, 2008.

Bouhdiba, Abdelwahab. *Sexuality in Islam.* Translated by Alan Sheridan. London: Saqi, 2004.

Boullata, Kamal. *Palestinian Art: 1850–2005.* London: Saqi, 2009.

Bowen, Dore. "This Bridge Called Imagination: On Reading the Arab Image Foundation and Its Collection." *Invisible Culture: An Electronic Journal for Visual Culture* 12 (May 2008): 1–13.

Boyd, Monica. "Family and Personal Networks in International Migration: Recent Developments and New Agendas." *International Migration Review* 23, no. 3 (Autumn 1989): 638–70.

———. "Immigrant Women in Canada." In *International Migration: The Female Experience,* edited by Rita J. Simon and Caroline B. Brettell, 45–61. Towota, NJ: Rowman & Allanheld, 1986.

Boyd, Monica, and Deanna Pikkov. "Gendering Migration, Livelihood, and Entitlements: Migrant Women in Canada and the United States." UNRISD, Geneva, 2005. https://www.unrisd.org/publications/opgp6 (accessed October 15, 2020).

Bracey, John H., Jr., Sonia Sanchez, and James Smethurst. *SOS/Calling All Black People: A Black Arts Movement Reader.* Amherst, MA: Univ. of Massachusetts Press, 2014.

Brah, Avtar. *Cartographies of Diaspora: Contesting Identities.* London: Routledge, 1996.

Braidotti, Rosi. *Nomadic Theory: The Portable Rosi Braidotti.* New York: Columbia Univ. Press, 2012.

Breeze, Jean "Binta." "The Wife of Bath in Brixton Market." iPoems. Accessed March 25, 2022. https://www.youtube.com/watch?v=MiyKat1QzbQ.

Brioni, Simone, dir. *Aulò: Roma postcoloniale.* REDigital, 2012.

Brooks, Daphne A. *Bodies in Dissent: Spectacular Perfromances of Race and Freedom, 1850–1910.* Durham, NC: Duke Univ. Press, 2006.

Brossard, Nicole. "Au fil de la narration et des générations." In *Regenerations/Régénerations: Canadian Women's Writing/Écritures des femmes au Canada,* edited by Marie Carrière and Patricia Demers, 3–20. Edmonton: Alberta Univ. Press, 2014.

Brown, Wendy. *Walled States, Waining Sovereignty.* Cambridge, MA: MIT Press, 2010.

———. *Undoing the Demos: Neoliberalism's Stealth Revolution.* Cambridge, MA: MIT, 2015.

Bucknor, Michael A. "Dub Poetry as a Postmodern Art Form: Self-Conscious of Critical Reception." In *The Routledge Companion to Anglophone Caribbean Literature,* edited by Michael A. Bucknor and Alison Donnell, 255–64. London: Routledge, 2011.

Bucknor, Michacl A. and Alison Donnell, eds. *The Routledge Companion to Anglophone Caribbean Literature.* London: Routledge, 2011.

Bunce, Mel, Suzanne Franks, and Chris Paterson, eds. *Africa's Media Image in the Twenty-First Century: From the "Heart of Darkness" to "Africa Rising."* London: Routledge, 2016.

Burns, Lorna. *Postcolonialism after World Literature: Relation, Equality, Dissent.* London: Bloomsbury, 2019.

Butler, Judith. *Frames of War: When Is Life Grievable?* London: Verso, 2009.

———. *Precarious Life: The Powers of Mourning and Violence.* London: Verso, 2004.

———."'What Shall We Do without Exile?' Said and Darwish Address the Future." *Alif: Journal of Comparative Poetics* 32 (2012): 30–54.

Calderwood, Eric. "Franco's Hajj: Moroccan Pilgrims, Spanish Fascism, and the Unexpected Journeys of Modern Arabic Literature." *PMLA* 132, no. 5 (October 2017): 1097–116.

———. "The Invention of al-Andalus: Discovering the Past and Creating the Present in Granada's Islamic Tourism Sites." *Journal of North African Studies* 19, no. 1 (2014): 27–55.

Campanini, Massimo. *Averroè*. Bologna: Il Mulino, 2010.

Caputo, John D., ed. *Deconstruction in a Nutshell: A Conversation with Jacques Derrida*. Fordham: Fordham Univ. Press, 1997.

Carrière, Marie. "Des méprises identitaires: Migrance et écriture au Québec et au Canada anglais." In *Migrance Comparée/Comparing Migration: Les Littératures du Canada et du Québec/The Literatures of Canada and Québec*, edited by Marie Carrière and Catherine Khordoc, 57–71. Bern: Peter Lang, 2008.

Carrière, Marie and Caterine Khordoc, eds. *Migrance Comparée/Comparing Migration: Les Littératures du Canada et du Québec/The Literatures of Canada and Québec*. Bern: Peter Lang, 2008.

Carrière, Marie and Patricia Demers, eds. *Regenerations/Régénerations: Canadian Women's Writing/Écritures des femmes au Canada*. Edmonton: Alberta Univ. Press, 2014.

Cartwright, Mark. "Tyrian Purple." In *World History Encyclopedia*. July 21, 2016. https://www.worldhistry.org/Tyrian_Purple/.

Casanova, Pascale. *The World Republic of Letters*. Translated by Malcolm De Bevoise. Cambridge, MA: Harvard Univ. Press, 2007.

Cassano, Franco. *Southern Thought and Other Essays on the Mediterranean*. Edited and translated by Norma Bouchard and Valerio Ferme. New York: Fordham Univ. Press, 2012.

Cavarero, Adriana. *For More Than One Voice: Toward a Philosophy of Vocal Expression*. Translated by Paul A. Kottman. Stanford, CA: Stanford Univ. Press, 2005.

———. *Inclinations: A Critique of Rectitude*. Stanford, CA: Stanford Univ. Press, 2016.

Ceola, Patrizia, ed. *Migrazioni narranti. L'Africa degli scrittori italiani e l'Italia degli scrittori africani: Un chiasmo culturale e linguistico*. Padova: Libreria Universitaria, 2011.

Chafer, Tony, and Emmanuel Godin. *The End of the French Exception? Decline of Revival of the "French Model."* London: Palgrave Macmillan, 2010.

Chakravorty, Mrinalini. "The Dead That Haunt *Anil's Ghost*: Subaltern Difference and Postcolonial Melancholia." *PMLA* 128, no. 3 (May 2013): 542–58.

Charara, Hayan. *Inclined to Speak: An Anthology of Contemporary Arab American Poetry*. Fayetteville: Univ. of Arkansas Press, 2008.

Cheah, Pheng. *What Is a World? On Postcolonial Literature as World Literature*. Durham, NC: Duke Univ. Press, 2016.

Cobham, Catherine. "Sex and Society in *Qa'al Madina*." In *Critical Perspectives on Yusuf Idris*, edited by Roger Allen, 77–84. Colorado Springs: Three Continents, 1994.

Cohen, Robin. *Global Diasporas*. New York: Routledge, 2008.

Collectif Cases Rebelles. "Les corps épuisés du spectacle colonial." *Cases Rebelles PanAfroRévolutionnaire*, September 2018. http://www.cases-rebelles.org/les-corps-epuises-du-spectacle-colonial/ (accessed November 10, 2018).

Contreras, Narciso. *Libya: A Human Marketplace*. Milano: Palazzo Reale, 2017.

Cooke, Miriam. *War's Other Voices: Women Writers on the Lebanese Civil War*. Syracuse, NY: Syracuse Univ. Press, 1996.

———. *Women and the War Story*. Berkeley: Univ. of California Press, 1997.

———. *Women Claim Islam: Creating Islamic Feminism through Literature*. London: Taylor & Francis, 2000.

Cooke, Miriam, and Bruce B. Lawrence, eds. *Muslim Networks from Hajj to Hip Hop*. Chapel Hill: Univ. of North Carolina Press, 2005.

Cooke, Miriam, Erdag Göknar, and Grant Parker. *Mediterranean Passages: Reading from Dido to Derrida*. Chapel Hill: Univ. of North Carolina Press, 2008.

Coope, Jessica A. *The Most Noble of People: Religious, Ethnic, and Gender Identity in Muslim Spain*. Ann Arbor: Univ. of Michigan Press, 2017.

Cooppan, Vilashini. "The Ethics of World Literature: Reading Others, Reading Otherwise." In *Teaching World Literature*, edited by David Damrosch, 34–43. New York: MLA, 2009.

Corrao, Francesca Maria. *Poeti arabi di Sicilia*. Messina: Mesogea, 2002.

Covi, Giovanna. "Creolizing Cultures and Kinship: Then and There, Now and Here." *Synthsis: An Anglophone Journal of Comparative Literary Studies* 7 (2015): 106–32.

Creswell, Robyn. *City of Beginnings: Poetic Modernism in Beirut*. Princeton, NJ: Princeton Univ. Press, 2018.

Crypt Gallery London. *Radical Love—Female Lust*. Exhibition. http://cryptgallery.org/event/radical-love-female-lust/ (accessed January 16, 2017).

Curti, Lidia. "Voices of a Minor Empire: Migrant Women Writers in Contemporary Italy." In *The Cultures of Italian Migration: Diverse Trajectories and*

Discrete Perspectives, edited by Anthony Tamburri and Graziella Parati, 45–55. Madison, WI: Fairleigh Dickinson Univ. Press, 2011.

D'Andrea, Anthony. "Neo-Nomadism: A Theory of Post-Identitarian Mobility in the Global Age." *Mobilities* 1, no. 1 (2006): 95–119.

Dahab, Elizabeth F., ed. *Voices of Exile in Contemporary Canadian Francophone Literature.* Lanham, MD: Lexington, 2009.

Dal Lago, Alessandro. *Non-persone: L'esclusione dei migranti in una società globale.* Milano: Feltrinelli, 1999.

Damrosch, David. *What Is World Literature?* Princeton, NJ: Princeton Univ. Press, 2003.

Damrosch, David, ed. *Teaching World Literature.* New York: MLA, 2009.

Darwish, Mahmoud. "Edward Said: A Contrapuntual Reading." Translated by Mona Anis. *Cultural Critique* 67 (Autumn 2007): 175–82.

———. "'Tibāq / Antithesis'—Homage to Edward Said." YouTube video, 14:36, July 24, 2016. https://youtu.be/G-Cxxg-D2T.

De Certeau, Michel. *The Practice of Everyday Life.* Translated by Steven Rendall. Berkeley: Univ. of California Press, 1988.

Deheuvels, Luc-Willy, Barbara Michalak-Pikulska, Paul Starkey, and Mike Thompson, eds. *Intertextuality in Modern Arabic Literature since 1967.* Durham, NC: Duke Univ. Press, 2006.

Del Boca, Angelo. *Italiani, brava gente?* Milano: Beat Edizioni, 2014.

Dematteis, Giuseppe. *Geografia come immaginazione: Tra piacere della scoperta e ricerca di futuri possibili.* Roma: Donzelli Editore, 2021.

Derrida, Jacques. "Passages—From Traumatism to Promise." In *Points . . . Interviews, 1974-1994*, edited by Elisabeth Weber, 372–95. Translated by Peggy Kamuf & others. Stanford, CA: Stanford Univ. Press, 1995.

———. "Shibboleth: For Paul Celan" In *Sovereignties in Question: The Poetics of Paul Celan*, edited by Thomas Dutoit and Outi Pasanen, 1–64. Fordham: Fordham Univ. Press, 2005.

———. *Specters of Marx: The State of Debt, the Work of Mourning, and the New International.* Translated by Peggy Kamuf. New York: Routledge, 1994.

Derrida, Jacques, and Gianni Vattimo, eds. *Religion.* Cambridge, MA: Polity, 1998.

Devet, Annelys, Kurt van Belleghem, and Hugo Herrera Tobón. *Subjective Atlases.* Accessed December 7, 2020. www.subjectiveatlas.info.

Devi, Gayatri. *A Princess Remembers: The Memoirs of the Maharani of Jaipur.* Columbia, MO: South Asia, 1995.

Dewey, Anne Day. *Beyond Maximus: The Construction of Public Voice in Black Mountain Poetry*. Stanford, CA: Stanford Univ. Press, 2007.

Dimock, Wai Chee. "Literature for the Planet." *PMLA* 116, no. 1 (January 2001): 173-88.

Diprose, Rosalyn. *Corporeal Generosity: On Giving with Nietzsche, Merleau-Ponty, and Levinas*. Albany: State Univ. of New York Press, 2002.

Djebar, Assia. *Far from Medina*. London: Quartet, 1994.

Dohra, Ahmad. *Rotten English: A Literary Anthology*. New York: W. W. Norton, 2007.

Donadey, Anne. "In Memoria: Assia Djebar, 1936-2015." *PMLA* 131, no. 1 (2016): 147–52.

Dorigo Ceccato, Rosella. "The Figure of the Lover in Popular Arabic Drama of the Early Twentieth Century." In *Love and Sexuality in Modern Arabic Literature*, edited by Roger Allen, Hilary Kilpatrick, and Ed de Moor, 24–32. London: Saqi, 1995.

Droste, Magdalena. *Bauhaus, 1919–1933*. Bern: Taschen, 2006.

Dupré, Louise. "Women's Writing in Quebec: From Rhetoric to New Social Propositions." In *The Rhetoric of Canadian Writing*, edited by Conny Steenman-Marcusse, 21–36. Amsterdam: Rodopi, 2002.

Edwards, Brian T. *After the American Century: The Ends of U.S. Culture in the Middle East*. New York: Columbia Univ. Press, 2017.

El-Ariss, Tarek. *The Arab Renaissance: A Bilingual Anthology of the Nahda*. New York: MLA, 2018.

————. *Trials of Arab Modernity: Literary Affects and the New Political*. New York: Fordham Univ. Press, 2013.

El-Enany, Rasheed, ed. "Preface." In *The Unmaking of the Arab Intellectual: Prophecy, Exile and the Nation*, vii–iii. Edinburgh: Edinburgh Univ. Press, 2017.

Elevald, Mark. *The Spoken Word Revolution: Slam, Hip Hop, and the Poetry of a New Generation*. Naperville, IL: Sourcebooks, 2003.

El Feki, Shereen. *Sex and the Citadel: Intimate Life in a Changing Arab World*. London: Chatto & Windus, 2013.

El Gendi, Yosra A. "Coptic Commemorative Protests and Discourses of Egyptian Nationalism: A Visual Analysis." *Middle East–Topics and Arguments* 8 (May 2017): 45–56.

El Houssi, Leila. *L'Africa ci sta di fronte. Una storia italiana dal colonialismo al terzomondismo*. Roma: Carocci, 2021.

Eliot, T. S. "The Waste Land." Poetry Foundation. Accessed June 7, 2018. https://www.poetryfoundation.org/poems/47311/the-waste-land.

Elkholy, Sharin N. *The Philosophy of the Beats.* Lexington: Univ. of Kentucky Press, 2012.

Elkhoury, Fouad. "Le plus beau jour." Accessed January 27, 2019. www.fouad elkhoury.com.

Elmusa, Sharif S. "Vital Attitude of the Poet: Interview with Naomi Shihab Nye." *Alif: Journal of Comparative Poetics* 27 (2007): 107–13.

Elsadda, Hoda. *Gender, Nation, and the Arabic Novel: Egypt, 1892–2008.* Edinburgh: Edinburgh Univ. Press, 2012.

El-Shakry, Omnia. "AHR Roundtable 'History without Documents': The Vexed Archives of Decolonization in the Middle East." *American Historical Review* 120, no. 3 (June 2015): 920–34.

Encyclopedia Britannica. "Tyre." *Encyclopedia Britannica.* Accessed May 15, 2021. https://www.britannica.com/place/Tyre.

———. "Sevilla." *Encyclopedia Britannica.* Accessed June 6, 2021. https://www.britannica.come/place/Sevilla.

Euben, Roxanne Leslie. *Journeys to the Other Shore: Muslim and Western Travelers in Search of Knowledge.* Princeton, NJ: Princeton Univ. Press, 2008.

Fabre, Thierry and Paul Sant-Cassia, eds. *Between Europe and the Mediterranean: The Challenges and the Fears.* New York: Palgrave Macmillan, 2007.

Fadda-Conrey, Carol. *Contemporary Arab-American Literature: Transnational Reconfigurations of Citizenship and Belonging.* New York: New York Univ. Press, 2014.

Fakhreddine, Huda. "The Prose Poems and the Arabic Literary Tradition." *Middle Eastern Literature* 19, no. 3 (2016): 243–59.

Fanjul, Serafín. *Al-Andalus, l'invention d'un mythe.* Paris: Toucan, 2017.

Faraone, Christopher A., and Laura K. McClure. *Prostitutes and Courtesans in the Ancient World.* Madison: Univ. of Wisconsin Press, 2006.

Faradj, Hisseine. "The 'Guernica' Connection: The Crimes of Assad and the Ghost of Franco." *Al Jadid* 22, no. 74 (2018): 10–11.

Farhoud, Abla. *Le bonheur a la queue glissante.* Montréal: L'Exagone, 1998.

———. *Le fou d'Omar.* Montréal: vlb éditeur, 2005.

Felski, Rita. "Introduction." *New Literary History* 33 (2002): 607–22.

Fox, Kevin Anthony, Jr. "The Ring of the Dove: Race, Sex, and Slavery in al-Andalus and the Poetry of Ibn Hazm." *Journal of South Asian and Middle Eastern Studies* 42, no. 3 (Spring 2019): 54–68.

Fricke, Adrienne. "Forever Nearing the Finish Line: Heritage Policy and the Problem of Memory in Postwar Beirut." *International Journal of Cultural Property* 12, no. 2 (May 2005): 163–81.

Frishkopf, Mark, ed. *Music and Media in the Arab World.* Cairo: American Univ. of Cairo Press, 2010.

———. "Tarab in the Mystic Sufi Chant of Egypt." In *Colors of Enchantment: Visual and Performing Arts of the Middle East,* edited by Sherifa Zuhur, 233–69. Cairo: American Univ. of Cairo Press, 2001.

Gallien, Claire. "A Decolonial Turn in the Humanities." *Alif: Journal of Comparative Poetics* 40 (2020): 28–58.

Gana, Nouri. *The Edinburgh Companion to the Arab Novel in English: The Politics of Anglo Arab and Arab American Literature and Culture.* Edinburgh: Edinburgh Univ. Press, 2013.

Gannit, Ankori, *Palestinian Art.* London: Reaktion, 2006.

García-Arenal Rodriguez, Mercedes, and Gerard A. Wiegers, eds. *The Expulsion of the Moriscos from Spain: A Mediterranean Diaspora.* Leiden: Brill, 2014.

Gardiner, Michael E. *Critiques of Everyday Life.* London: Routledge, 2000.

Gauvin, Lise. *L'écrivain francophone à la croisée des langues.* Paris: Éditions Karthala, 1997.

———. "Introduction." In *L'écrivain francophone à la croisée des langues,* 5–15. Paris: Éditions Karthala, 1997.

Generale, Alessandra. "When Migrants Do Not Arrive in Europe: The Memorandum of Understanding." EULOGOS ATHENA: Décryptons ensemble l'actualité européenne, March 4, 2020. https://www.eu-logos.org/2020/03/04/when-migrants-do-not-arrive-in-europe-the-memorandum-of-understanding/.

Gerosa, Emanuele, dir. *One More Jump.* Torino: GraffitiDoc, 2019.

Ghermandi, Gabriella. *Regina di fiori e di perle.* Roma: Donzelli Editore, 2011.

Ginsburg, Faye, Lila Abu-Lughod, and Brian Larkin, eds. *Media Worlds: Anthropology on New Terrain.* Berkeley: Univ. of California Press, 2002.

Gioni, Massimiliano, Gary Carrion-Murayari, Natalie Bell, Negar Azimi, Kaelen Wilson-Goldie, and Sarah Stephenson, eds. *Here and Elsewhere.* New York: New Museum, 2014.

Gnisci, Armando, ed. *Nuovo Planetario Italiano: Geografia e antologia della letteratura della migrazione in Italia e in Europa.* Troia: Città Aperta Edizioni, 2006.

Gomez-Vega, Ibis. "Extreme Realities: Naomi Shihab Nye's Essays and Poems." *Alif: Journal of Comparative Poetics* 30 (2010): 109–33.

Gordon, Alastair. *Naked Airport: A Cultural History of the World's Most Revolutionary Structure*. Chicago: Univ. of Chicago Press, 2004.

Gröndhal, Mia. *Tahrir Square: The Square of the Egyptian Revolution*. Cairo: American Univ. of Cairo Press, 2011.

Grosz, Elizabeth, and Elspeth Probyn, eds. *Sexy Bodies: The Strange Carnalities of Feminism*. London: Routledge, 1995.

Gualtieri, Sarah M. A. *Between Arab and White: Race and Ethnicity in the Early Syrian American Diaspora*. Berkeley: Univ. of California Press, 2009.

Gunaratne, Anjuli I., and Jill M. Jarvis. "Introduction: Inheriting Assia Djebar." *PMLA* 131, no. 1 (2016): 116–27.

Gunn, Giles. "Introduction: Globalizing Literary Studies." *PMLA* 116, no. 1 (2001): 16–31.

Habekost, Christian. *Verbal Riddim: The Politics and Aesthetics of African-Caribbean Dub Poetry*. Amsterdam: Rodopi, 1993.

Hage, Rawi. *Cockroach*. London: Penguin, 2008.

Hajdari, Gëzim. *Ombra di cane / Hije qeni*. Frosinone: Dismisuratesti, 1993.

Halabi, Zeina G. *The Unmaking of the Arab Intellectual: Prophecy, Exile, and the Nation*. Edinburgh: Edinburgh Univ. Press, 2017.

Halberstam, Judith. *The Queer Art of Failure*. Durham, NC: Duke Univ. Press, 2011.

Hammad, Hanan. "The Other Extremists: Marxist Feminism in Egypt 1980-2000." *Journal of International Women's Studies* (March 2011): 217–33.

Hammad, Suheir. *breaking poems*. New York: Cypher, 2008.

———. *Drops of This Story*. Danbury, CT: Writers & Readers, 1996.

———. *ZaatarDiva*. New York: Cypher, 2005.

Handal, Nathalie. "Drops of Suheir Hammad: A Talk with a Palestinian Poet Born Black." *Al Jadid: A Review and Record of Arab Culture and Art* 3, no. 20 (Summer 1997). https://www.aljadid.com/content/drops-suheir-hammad-talk-palestinian-poet-born-black.

Handal, Nathalie, ed. *The Poetry of Arab Women: A Contemporary Anthology*. New York: Interlink, 2000.

Hanru, Hou, and Giulia Ferracci, eds. *Home Beirut: Sounding the Neighbors*. Roma: Fondazione MAXXI, 2018.

Hanssen, Jens-Peter, and Daniel Genberg. "Beirut in Memoriam—A Kaleidoscopic Space Out of Focus." In *Crisis and Memory in Islamic Societies: Proceedings of the Third Summer Academy of the Working Group Modernity and Islam Held at the Orient Institute of the German Oriental Society in Beirut,* edited by Andreas Pflitsch and Angelika Neuwirth, 231–62. Würzburg: Ergon, 2001.

Harb, Lara. *Arab Poetics: Aesthetic Experience in Classical Arabic Literature.* Cambridge: Cambridge Univ. Press, 2020.

Harb, Sirène. *Articulations of Resistance: Transformative Politics in Arab-American Poetry.* London: Routledge, 2019.

Hartman, Michelle. *Breaking Broken English: Black-Arab Literary Solidarities and the Politics of Language.* Syracuse, NY: Syracuse Univ. Press, 2019.

———. "Dreams Deferred, Translated: Radwa Ashour and Langston Hughes." CLINA 2, no. 1 (June 2016): 61–76.

———. "'This Sweet / Sweet Music': Jazz, Sam Cooke, and Reading Arab American Literary Identities." MELUS 31, no. 4 (Winter 2006): 145–65.

Hass, Amira. "How Israel Prevents Palestinian Farmers from Working their Lands." *Haaretz,* May 28, 2017. https://www.haaretz.com/middle-east-news /palestinians/.premium-how-israel-keeps-palestinian-farmers-off-their-lands -1.5477256.

Hassan, Wail S. *Immigrant Narratives: Orientalism and Cultural Translation in Arab American and Arab British Literature.* Oxford: Oxford Univ. Press, 2011.

———. *The Oxford Handbook of Arab Novelistic Traditions.* Oxford: Oxford Univ. Press, 2017.

Haugbolle, Sune. *War and Memory in Lebanon.* Cambridge: Cambridge Univ. Press, 2010.

Hazm, Ibn. *The Ring of the Dove, Or the Dove's Neck-Ring.* Translated by A. R. Nykl. Eastford, CT: Martino Fine Books, 2014.

Heller Levi, Jan, and Christoph Keller, eds. *The Essential June Jordan.* Port Townsend, WA: Copper Canyon, 2021.

Heng, Geraldine. *The Invention of Race in the European Middle Ages.* Cambridge: Cambridge Univ. Press, 2018.

Hickman, Daniel Nathan. "Ibn Hazm: An Islamic Source of Courtly Love." PhD diss., Univ. of Tennessee, 2014.

Hiddleston, Jane. *Writing after Postcolonialism: Francophone North African Literature in Transition.* London: Bloomsbury, 2017.

———. "Writing World Literature: Approaches from the Maghreb." PMLA 124, no. 5 (2009): 1768–77.

Highmore, Ben, ed. *The Everyday Life Reader.* London: Routledge, 2002.

Hirsch, Marianne. "'What We Need Right Now Is to Imagine the Real': Grace Paley Writing against War." PMLA 124, no. 5 (October 2009): 1768–77.

Hoffman-Ladd, Valerie J. "Mysticism and Sexuality in Sufi Thought and Life." *Mystic Quarterly* 18, no. 3 (September 1992): 82–93.

Holzhey, Christoph F. E., ed. *Tension/Spannung*. Wien: Verlag Turia und Kant, 2010.

Homsi Vinson, Pauline. "Ghada Samman: A Writer of Many Layers." *Al Jadid* 8, no. 39 (Spring 2002). https://www.aljadid.com/content/ghada-samman-writer -many-layers (accessed June 24, 2017).

hooks, bell. "Eating the Other: Desire and Resistance." In *Black Looks: Race and Representation*, 366–80. Boston: South End, 1992.

Hornung, Alfred, and Martina Kohl, eds. *Arab American Literature and Culture*. Heidelberg: Winter Verlag, 2012.

Hout, Syrine. *Post-War Anglophone Lebanese Fiction: Home Matters in the Diaspora*. Edinburgh: Edinburgh Univ. Press, 2012.

Huggins, Nathan Irvin. *Voices from the Harlem Renaissance*. Oxford: Oxford Univ. Press, 1976.

Hurt, Byron, dir. *Hip-Hop: Beyond Beats and Rhymes*. Produced by God Bless the Child Productions. 2006.

Ireland, Susan, and Patrice J. Proulx, eds. *Textualizing the Immigrant Experience in Contemporary Québec*. Westport, CT: Praeger, 2004.

Irving, Washington. *Tales of the Alhambra*. Berkeley: Mint Editions, 2021.

Izzo, Donatella. "American Studies in Europe / European American Studies: Local and Global Challenges." *RSA Journal* 29 (2018): 184–94.

Jacobi, Renate. "Theme and Variations in Umayyad Ghazal Poetry." *Journal of Arabic Literature* 23, no. 2 (July 1992): 109–19.

Jad, Islah. "Islamist Women of Hamas: Between Feminism and Nationalism." *Inter-Asia Cultural Studies* 12, no. 2 (2011): 176–201.

Jankowiak, William R., ed. *Intimacies: Love and Sex across Cultures*. New York: Columbia Univ. Press, 2008.

Jayyusi, Salma Khadra. "Introduction." In *On Entering the Sea: The Erotic and Other Poetry of Nizar Qabbani*, v–xviii. Translated by Lena Jayyusi and Sharif Elmusa. New York: Interlink, 1996.

———. *Trends and Movements in Modern Arabic Poetry*. Amsterdam: Brill, 1977.

Johnson, Barbara. *The Feminist Difference: Literature, Psychoanalysis, Race, and Gender*. Cambridge, MA: Harvard Univ. Press, 2000.

Johnson, Joyce. *The Voice Is All: The Lonely Victory of Jack Kerouac*. New York: Viking, 2012.

Johnson, Peter. "About This Journal." *The Prose Poem: An International Journal.* Accessed December 15, 2020. https://digitalcommons.providence.edu/prose poem/about.html.

Johnston, David. "At Least 31 Are Dead, Scores Are Missing after Car Bomb Attach in Oklahoma City Wrecks 9-Story Federal Office Building." *New York Times*, April 20, 1995. https://archive.nytimes.com/www.nytimes.com /learning/gen.

Jónsson, Már. "The Expulsion of the Moriscos from Spain in 1609–1614: The Destruction of an Islamic Periphery." *Journal of Global History* 2, no. 2 (2007): 195–212.

Jordan, June. "Moving towards Home." In *The Essential June Jordan*, edited by Jan Heller Levi and Christoph Keller, 91–93. Port Townsend, WA: Copper Canyon Press, 2021.

Juvonen, Tuula, and Marjo Kolehmainen, eds. *Affective Inequalities in Intimate Relationships.* London: Routledge, 2020.

Kadi, Joanna, ed. *Food for Our Grandmothers: Writings by Arab-American and Arab-Canadian Feminists.* Boston, MA: South End, 1994.

Kadir, Djelal. "What Does the Comparative Do for Literary History?" *PMLA* 128, no. 3 (May 2013): 644–51.

———. *Memos from the Besieged City: Lifelines for Cultural Sustainability.* Stanford, CA: Stanford Univ. Press, 2011.

Kaltner, John, and Younous Mirza. *The Bible and the Qur'an: Biblical Figures in the Islamic Tradition.* London: Bloomsbury, 2018.

Kamboureli, Smaro. *Making a Difference: An Anthology of Ethnic Canadian Writing.* Oxford: Oxford Univ. Press, 1996.

Kaplan, Caren, and Kristin Ross. "Introduction." *Yale French Studies* 73 (1987): 1–4.

Kamen, Henry. "The Mediterranean and the Expulsion of Spanish Jews in 1492." *Past & Present* 119 (May 1988): 30–55.

Kaur, Herpreet Grewal. "Rebel Queen—A Thorn in the Crown." *Guardian*, December 31, 2010. https://www.theguardian.com/lifeandstyle/2010/dec/31 /rebel-queen-thorn-crown.

Kerouac, Jack. *On the Road.* New York: Penguin, 1997.

Khairallah, As'ad E. "Love and the Body in Modern Arabic Poetry." In *Love and Sexuality in Modern Arabic Literature*, edited by Roger Allen, Hilary Kilpatrick, and Ed de Moor, 210–23. London: Saqi, 1995.

Khalaf, Samir. *Heart of Beirut: Reclaiming the Burj.* London: Saqi, 2006.

Khater, Akram Fouad. *Inventing Home: Emigration, Gender, and the Middle Class in Lebanon, 1870–1920.* Berkeley: Univ. of California Press, 2001.

Khorasani, Noushin Ahmadi. *Iranian Women's One Million Signatures: Campaign for Equality, the Inside Story.* Syracuse, NY: Syracuse Univ. Press, 2010.

Kilpatrick, Hilary. "Introduction: On Love and Sexuality in Modern Arabic Literature." In *Love and Sexuality in Modern Arabic Literature,* edited by in Roger Allen, Hilary Kilpatrick, and Ed de Moor, 9–15. London: Saqi, 1995.

Kilito, Abdelfattah. *Arabs and the Art of Storytelling: A Strange Familiarity.* Translated by Mbarek Sryfi and Eric Sellin. Syracuse, NY: Syracuse Univ. Press, 2014.

———. *Je parle toutes les langues mais en arabe.* Paris: Actes Sud, 2015.

Knight, Brenda, ed. *Women of the Beat Generation: The Writers, Artists and Muses at the Heart of the Revolution.* Berkeley, CA: Conari, 1996.

Komla-Ebri, Kossi. *Imbarazzismi: Quotidiani imbarazzi in bianco e nero.* Eorle, BG: Marna, 2002.

———. *Nuovi imbarazzismi: Quotidiani imbarazzi in bianco e nero . . . e a colori.* Eorle, BG: Marna 2004.

Kosic, Anika, and Anna Triandafyllidou. "Italy." In *European Immigration: A Sourcebook,* edited by in Anna Triandafyllidou and Ruby Gropas, 185–94. Aldershot: Ashgate, 2007.

Koshy, Susan. "Minority Cosmopolitanism." *PMLA* 126, no. 3 (May 2011): 592–609.

Kuhn, Thomas S. *The Essential Tension: Selected Studies in Scientific Tradition and Change.* Chicago: Univ. of Chicago Press, 1977.

Kuortti, Joel, Kaisa Ilmonen, Elina Valovirta, and Janne Korkka, eds. *Thinking with the Familiar in Contemporary Culture "Out of the Ordinary."* Leiden: Brill, 2019.

Kurson, Ken. "Poet Naomi Shihab Nye Grew Up in Ferguson and the West Bank." *Observer/Culture,* January 1, 2014. http://observer.com/2014/09/palestinian-american-poet-naomi-shihab-nye-grew-up-in-ferguson-and-the-west-bank.

Laachir, Karima. "Saudi Women Novelists and the Quest for Freedom: Raja Alem's *The Doves' Necklace.*" In *Resistance in Contemporary Middle Eastern Cultures: Literature, Cinema, and Music,* edited by Karima Laachir and Saeed Talajooy, 32–48. New York: Routledge, 2013.

Laachir, Karima, and Saeed Talajooy, eds. *Resistance in Contemporary Middle Eastern Cultures: Literature, Cinema and Music.* New York: Routledge, 2013.

Labanca, Nicola. *La Guerra d'Etiopia: 1935–1941.* Bologna: Il Mulino, 2015.

——. *La guerra italiana per la Libia: 1911–1931*. Bologna: Il Mulino, 2012.

——.*Oltremare: storia dell'espansione coloniale italiana*. Milano: Mondadori, 2013.

Lakhous, Amara. "Maghreb." In *Nuovo Planetario Italiano: Geografia e antologia della letteratura della migrazione in Italia e in Europa*, edited by Armando Gnisci, 185–194. Troina: Città Aperta Edizioni, 2006.

Lalonde, Michèle. "Speak White." *Littérature Québécoise*. Accessed January 26, 2019. www.littquebecoise.weebly.com.

Lamm, Kimberly. "Seeing Feminism in Exile: The Imaginary Maps of Mona Hatoum." *Michigan Feminist Studies* 18 (2004). https://quod.lib.umich.edu /cgi/t/text/text-idx?cc=mfsfront;c=mfs;c=mfsfront;idno=ark5583.0018.001;g =mfsg;rgn=main;view=text;xc=1 (accessed July 15, 2018).

Lamrabet, Asma. *Femmes et hommes dans le Coran: Quelle egalité?* Paris: Al-bouraq, 2012.

——. *Women in the Qur'an: An Emancipatory Reading*. Translated by Myriam Francois-Cerrah. London: Square View, 2016.

Landau, Paul S., and Deborah D. Kaspin. *Images and Empires: Visuality in Colonial and Postcolonial Africa*. Berkeley: Univ. of California Press, 2002.

Larkin, Craig. "Reconstructing and Deconstructing Beirut: Space, Memory, and Lebanese Youth." In *Divided Cities/Contested States*, Working Paper No. 8, 2009. Accessed June 27, 2018. http://www.conflict incities.org/PDFs/WorkingPaper8_21.5.09.pdf.

Lee, Robert D. "Foreword." In *Rethinking Islam: Common Questions, Uncommon Answers*, vii–xiii. Edited and translated by Robert D. Lee. Boulder, CO: Westview, 1994.

Lefebvre, Henry. "The Everyday and Everydayness." *Yale French Studies* 73 (1987): 7–11.

——. "Reflections on the Politics of Space." Translated by Michael J. Enders. *Antipode* 8, no. 2 (1976): 30–37.

Leiris, Michel. *Phantom Africa*. Translated by Brent Hayes Edwards. Kolkata: Seagull, 2017.

Lemieux-Couture, Marie-Christine. "Speak Rich en Tabarnaque." Speak White Evolution, March 16, 2016. https://speakwhiteevolution.wordpress.com/2016 /03/16/speak-rich-en-tabarnaque-de-marie-christine-lemieux-lesage/.

Lewis, Robert. "Jama Masjid of Delhi." *Encyclopedia Britannica*. Accessed October 30, 2020. https://www.britannica.com/place/Jami-Masjid-mosque-Delhi -India.

Lombardi-Diop, Cristina, and Gaia Giuliani. *Bianco e nero: storia dell'identità razziale degli italiani*. Milano: Mondadori, 2013.

———. "Postracial/Postcolonial Italy." In *Postcolonial Italy: Challenging National Homogeneity*, edited by Cristina Lombardi-Diop and Caterina Romeo, 175–90. New York: Palgrave Macmillan, 2012.

Lombardi-Diop, Cristina, and Caterina Romeo, eds. *Postcolonial Italy: Challenging National Homogeneity*. New York: Palgrave Macmillan, 2012.

Lorde, Audre. *Sister Outsider: Essays and Speeches*. Berkeley, CA: Crossing, 1984.

———. "Uses of the Erotic: The Erotic as Power." In *Sister Outsider: Essays and Speeches*, 87–91. Berkeley, CA: Crossing, 1984.

Love, Heather. *Feeling Backward: Loss and the Politics of Queer History*. Cambridge, MA: Harvard Univ. Press, 2007.

Ltaif, Nadine. *Ce que vous ne lirez pas*. Montréal: Éditions du Noroît, 2010.

———. *Changing Shores*. Translated by Christine Tipper. Toronto: Guernica, 2008.

———. "Écrire pour vivre l'échange entre les langues." In *Literary Pluralities*, edited by Christl Verduyn, 81–83. Petersborough, ON: Broadview, 1998.

———. *Élégies du Levant*. Montréal: Éditions du Noroît, 1995.

———. *Entre les fleuves*. Montréal: Guernica, 1991.

———. *Journeys*. Translated by Christine Tipper. Toronto: Guernica, 2020.

———. *Les Métamorphoses d'Ishhtar*. Montréal: Guernica, 1991.

———. *The Metamorphoses of Ishtar*. Translated by John Mikhail Asfour. Toronto: Guernica, 2011.

———. *Vestige d'un jardin*. Montréal: Ateliers Graff, 1993.

Lubin, Alex. *Geographies of Liberation: The Making of an Afro-Arab Political Imaginary*. Chapel Hill: Univ. of North Carolina Press, 2014.

Makar, Farida. "'Let Them Have Some Fun': Political and Artistic Forms of Expression in the Egyptian Revolution." *Mediterranean Politics* 16, no. 2 (2011): 307–12.

Makdisi, Saree. "Laying Claim to Beirut: Urban Narrative and Spatial Identity in the Age of Solidere." *Critical Inquiry* 23, no. 3 (1997): 664–705.

Mailhot, Laurent, and Pierre Nepveu. *La poésie québécoise: Des origines à nos jours*. Montréal: Éditions TYPO, 2003.

Majaj, Lisa Suhair. "Arab-American Literature: Origins and Developments." In *Arab American Literature and Culture*, edited by Alfred Hornung and Martina Kohl, 61–86. Heidelberg: Winter Verlag, 2012.

Bibliography

Malik, Kenan. "How We All Colluded in Fortress Europe." *Guardian*, June 10, 2018. https://www.theguardian.com/commentisfree/2018/jun/10/sunday-essay-how-we-colluded-in-fortress-europe-immigration.

Mallette, Karla. *European Modernity and the Arab Mediterranean: Toward a New Philology and a Counter-Orientalism*. Philadelphia: Univ. of Pennsylvania Press, 2010.

———. *The Kingdom of Sicily, 1100–1500: A Literary History*. Philadelphia: Univ. of Pennsylvania Press, 2005.

Malti-Douglas, Fadwa. "Blindness and Sexuality: Traditional Mentalities in Yusuf Idris." In *Critical Perspectives on Yusuf Idris*, edited by Roger Allen, 89–96. Colorado Springs: Three Continents, 1994.

———. *Woman's Body, Woman's Word: Gender and Discourse in Arabo-Islamic Writing*. Princeton, NJ: Princeton Univ. Press, 1991.

Maraini, Toni. *Ballando con Averroè: Racconti di viaggio in un mondo musulmano che non fa paura*. Alberobello, BA: Poiesis, 2015.

Marchi, Lisa. "The Alchemy of Rawi Hage's Fiction." In *Beirut to Carnival City: Reading Rawi Hage*, edited by Krzysztof Majer, 191–208. Leiden: Brill, 2020.

———. "Engaging with Otherness in Everyday Life: Naomi Shihab Nye's Defamiliarizing Poems." In *Thinking with the Familiar in Contemporary Culture "Out of the Ordinary,"* edited by Joel Kuortti, Kaisa Ilmonen, Elina Valovirta, and Janne Korkka, 119–33. Leiden: Brill, 2019.

———. *In filigrana: Poesia arabo-americana scritta da donne*. Napoli: La scuola di Pitagora, 2020.

Mattawa, Khaled. *How Long Have You Been With Us? Essays on Poetry*. Ann Arbor: Univ. of Michigan Press, 2016.

———. *Fugitive Atlas*. Minneapolis, MN: Graywolf, 2020.

———. "Introduction." In *These Are Not Oranges, My Love: Selected Poems*, translated by Khaled Mattawa, vii–xv. Riverdale, NY: Sheep Meadow, 2008.

———. *Mahmoud Darwish: The Poet's Art and His Nation*. Syracuse, NY: Syracuse Univ. Press, 2014.

———. *Mare Nostrum*. Louisville, KY: Sarabande, 2019.

———. "Resisting the Lapse into Monologue: On the Poetics of Bilingualism in American Poetry." In *How Long Have You Been With Us? Essays on Poetry*, 61–73. Ann Arbor: Univ. of Michigan Press, 2016.

Mattawa, Khaled, and Munir Akash. *Post Gibran: Anthology of New Arab American Writing*. Syracuse, NY: Syracuse Univ. Press, 2000.

Mattawa, Khaled, and Pauline Kaldas. *Dinazard's Children: An Anthology of Contemporary Arab American Fiction.* Fayetteville: Univ. of Arkansas Press, 2004.

Mehrez, Samia. "Experimentation and the Institution: The Case of Ida'a 77 and Aswat." In *The View from Within: Writing and Critics on Contemporary Arabic Literature,* edited by Ferial J. Ghazoul and Barbara Harlow, 177–96. Cairo: American Univ. of Cairo Press, 1994.

———. *Translating Egypt's Revolution: The Language of Tahrir.* Cairo: American Univ. of Cairo Press, 2012.

Mehrez, Samia, and Mona Abaza, eds. *Arts and the Uprising in Egypt: The Making of a Culture of Dissent.* Cairo: American Univ. of Cairo Press, 2019.

Menocal, María Rosa. *The Ornament of the World: How Muslims, Jews, and Christians Created a Culture of Tolerance in Medieval Spain.* New York: Back Bay, 2002.

Mercer, Lorraine, and Linda Strom. "Counter Narratives: Cooking Up Stories of Love and Loss in Naomi Shihab Nye's Poetry and Diana Abu-Jaber's *Crescent.*" MELUS 32, no. 4 (Winter 2007): 33-46.

Mernissi, Fatima. *Dreams of Trespass: Tales of a Harem Girlhood.* New York: Perseus, 1995.

———. *Islam and Democracy: Fear of the Modern World.* Translated by Mary Jo Lakeland. Cambridge, MA: Basic Books, 2002.

Merolla, Daniela, and Sandra Ponzanesi. *Migrant Cartographies: New Cultural and Literary Spaces in Post-Colonial Europe.* Lanham, MD: Lexington, 2005.

Mersal, Iman. *Jughrāfiyā badīla.* Al-Qāhira: Dār Sharqiyāt, 2006.

———. "Eliminating Diasporic Identities." *PMLA* 123, no. 5 (October 2008): 1581–89.

———. *Mamarr mu'tim yaṣluh lita'llum al-raqs.* Al-Qāhira: Dār Sharqiyāt, 1995.

———. "Revolutionary Humor." *Globalization* 8, no. 5 (October 2011): 669–74.

———. "S. J. Fowler Interviews Iman Mersal for Poetry Parnassus." July 6, 2012. http://imanmersal.blogspot.com/2012/07/sj-fowler-interviews-iman-mersal-for.html.

———. *These Are Not Oranges, My Love: Selected Poems.* Translated by Khaled Mattawa. Riverdale, NY: Sheep Meadow, 2008.

———. "The Tragedy of Being Mahmoud Darwish." March 30, 2012. http://imanmersal.blogspot.com/2012/03/tragedy-of-being-mahmoud-darwish.html.

———. "Writing on the Threshold: poètes migrants ou poètes errants." Poetry reading. Univ. of Trento, May 22, 2014.

Metwalli, Mohamed. *Angry Voices: An Anthology of the Off-beat Egyptian Poets.* Fayetteville: Univ. of Arkansas Press, 2009.

Micone, Marco. "Speak What." *Le théâtre dans la cité* 50 (1989): 83–85.

Mohammed Aden, Kaha. *Fra-intendimenti.* Milano: Nottetempo, 2018.

Mojab, Shahrzad and Afiya S. Zia. "Race, Class, and Agency: A Return to Marxist Feminism." *Journal of Labor and Society* 22, no. 3 (June 25, 2019): 259–73.

Moore, Lindsay. *Arab, Muslim, Woman: Voice and Vision in Postcolonial Literature and Film.* London: Routledge, 2008.

Moretti, Franco. "Conjectures on World Literature." *New Left Review* 1 (January–February 2000): 54–68.

———. *Distant Reading.* London: Verso, 2013.

Morrison, Toni. *Playing in the Dark: Whiteness and the Literary Imagination.* New York: Vintage, 1992.

Mouawad, Wajdi. *Anima.* Paris: Acte Sud, 2012.

Mufti, Aamir R. *Forget English! Orientalism and World Literature.* Cambridge, MA: Harvard Univ. Press, 2016.

Naber, Nadine. *Arab America: Gender, Cultural Politics, and Activism.* New York: New York Univ. Press, 2012.

Najmi, Samina. "Naomi Shihab Nye's Aesthetic of Smallness and the Military Sublime." MELUS 35, no. 2 (Summer 2010): 151–71.

Nakas, Kassandra, Britta Schmitz, and Walid Raad. *The Atlas Group (1989–2004): A Project by Walid Raad.* Köln: Walter Koenig, 2007.

"Naomi Shihab Nye." Poetry Foundation. Accessed June 18, 2018. https://www.poetryfoundation.org/poets/naomi-shihab-nye.

Nawyn, Stephanie J. "Gender and Migration: Integrating Feminist Theory into Migration Studies." *Sociology Compass* 4, no. 9 (2010): 749–65.

Nepveu, Pierre. *L'Ecologie du réel. Mort et naissance de la littérature québécoise contemporaine.* Montréal: Boréal, 1999.

New Museum. *Here and Elsewhere.* Exhibition. Accessed March 26, 2022. https://www.newmuseum.org/exhibitions/view/here-and-elsewhere.

Newman, Janet. "Spaces of Power: Feminism, Neoliberalism, and Gendered Labor." *Social Politics* 20, no. 2 (2013): 200221.

Ngai, Sianne. *Ugly Feelings.* Cambridge, MA: Harvard Univ. Press, 2007.

Nien-Ming Ch'ien, Evelyn. *Weird English.* Cambridge, MA: Harvard Univ. Press, 2005.

Nischik, Reingard M., ed. *History of Literature in Canada: English-Canadian and French Canadian*. Rochester: Camden House, 2008.

Nye, Naomi Shihab. *Tender Spot: Selected Poems*. Highgreen: Bloodaxe, 2008.

———. *Words under the Words: Selected Poems*. Portland, OR: Far Corner, 1995.

Nye, Naomi Shihab, and Joy Castro. "Nomad, Switchboard, Poet: Naomi Shihab Nye's Multicultural Literature for Young Readers: An Interview." MELUS 27, no. 2 (Summer 2002): 225–36.

Obbink, Dirk. "Chapter 2. Sappho Fragments 58-59: Text, Apparatus, and Translation." Accessed December 8, 2020. https://chs.harvard.edu/CHS/article/display /6045.2-dirk-obbink-sappho-fragments-58%E2%80%9359-text-apparatus -criticus-and-translation.

Olson, Alix. *Word Warriors: 35 Women Leaders in the Spoken Word Revolution*. Emeryville, CA: Seal, 2007.

Olson, Charles. "Projective Verse." Poetry Foundation. Accessed July 27, 2015. https://www.poetryfoundation.org/articles/69406/projective-verse.

Orfalea, Gregory, and Sharif Elmusa. *Grape Leaves: A Century of Arab American Poetry*. New York: Interlink, 1999.

Ostle, Robin. "The Romantic Imagination and the Female Ideal." In *Love and Sexuality in Modern Arabic Literature*, edited by Roger Allen, Hilary Kilpatrick, and Ed de Moor, 33–45. London: Saqi, 1995.

Overton, Bill. *The Novel of Female Adultery: Love and Gender in Continental European Fiction, 1830–1900*. London: Palgrave Macmillan, 1996.

Parati, Graziella. *Migration Italy: The Art of Talking Back in a Destination Culture*. Toronto: Univ. of Toronto Press, 2005.

———. *New Perspectives in Italian Cultural Studies: Definition, Theory, and Accented Practices*. Madison, NJ: Fairleigh Dickinson Univ. Press, 2012.

Parati, Graziella, and Marie Orton, eds. *Multicultural Literature in Contemporary Italy*. Lanham, MD: Rowman & Littlefield, 2007.

Pepicelli, Renata. "Rethinking Gender in Arab Nationalism: Women and the Politics of Modernity in the Making of Nation-States. Cases from Egypt, Tunisia and Algeria." *Oriente moderno* 97, no. 1 (March 2017): 201–19.

Pessoa, Ferdinand. *The Book of Disquiet*. Translated by Richard Zenith. London: Penguin, 2002.

Petit, Philippe. *Trattato di funambulismo*. Prefazione di Paul Auster e traduzione di Danilo Bramati. Milano: Ponte alle Grazie, 1999.

Pflitsch, Andreas, and Angelika Neuwirth, eds. *Crisis and Memory in Islamic Societies: Proceedings of the Third Summer Academy of the Working Group*

Modernity and Islam Held at the Orient Institute of the German Oriental Society in Beirut. Würzburg: Ergon Verlag, 2001.

Pflitsch Andreas, and Angelika Neuwirth. "Crisis and Memory. Dimensions of their Relationship: An Introduction." In *Crisis and Memory in Islamic Societies: Proceedings of the Third Summer Academy of the Working Group Modernity and Islam Held at the Orient Institute of the German Oriental Society in Beirut,* edited by Andreas Pflitsch and Angelika Neuwirth, 1–40. Würzburg: Ergon Verlag, 2001.

Phillips, Amanda. *Sea Change: Ottoman Textiles between the Mediterranean and the Indian Ocean.* Berkeley: Univ. of California Press, 2021.

Pickens, Therí A. *Arab American Aesthetics: Literature, Material Culture, Film, and Theatre.* New York: Routledge, 2018.

———. *New Body Politics: Narrating Arab and Black Identity in the Contemporary United States.* New York: Routledge, 2014.

Pollman, Lisa. "Lust for Life: Contemporary Women Artists on 'Radical Love: Female Lust' at The Crypt Gallery." *Art Radar: Contemporary Art Trends and News from Asia and Beyond,* February 20, 2017. http://artradarjournal .com/2017/02/20/radical-love-female-lust-at-the-crypt-gallery.

Poncian, Japhace. "The Persistence of Western Negative Perceptions About Africa: Factoring in the Role of Africans." *Journal of African Studies and Development* 7, no. 3 (March 2015): 72–80.

Poochigian, Aaron. "A Note on the Text and Translation." In *Stung With Love: Poems and Fragments,* by Sappho. Translated and with an introduction and notes by Aaron Poochigian, with a preface by Carol Ann Duffy, n.p. London: Penguin, 2009.

Pratt, Geraldine, and Victoria Rosner, eds. *The Global and the Intimate: Feminism in Our Time.* New York: Columbia Univ. Press, 2012.

Qabbani, Nizar. *On Entering the Sea: The Erotic and Other Poetry of Nizar Qabbani.* Translated by Lena Jayyusi and Sharif Elmusa. New York: Interlink, 1996.

Qualey, Marcia L. "Laila al-Othman: Too Much Sex in New Saudi (Women's) Literature." ArabLit Arabic Literature and Translation, February 27, 2010. http:// arablit.wordpress.com/2010/02/27/kuwaiti-novelist-says-too-much-sex-in -new-saudi-women-literature.

Quaquarelli, Lucia. *Certi confini: Sulla lettura italiana dell'immigrazione.* Morellini, 2010.

Raad, Walid. *The Atlas Group.* Accessed December 2, 2020. www.theatlasgroup .org.

Racy, A. C. *Making Music in the Arab World*. Cambridge: Cambridge Univ. Press, 2003.

Radhakrishnan, Rajagopalan. *A Said Dictionary*. Hoboken, NJ: Wiley-Blackwell, 2012.

———. "World Literature, by Any Other Name?" *PMLA* 131, no. 5 (2016): 1396–404.

Rahman, Najat. *In the Wake of the Poetic: Palestinian Artists after Darwish*. Syracuse, NY: Syracuse Univ. Press, 2015.

Rakha, Youssef. Review of *This Is Not Literature, My Love*. *Al Ahram* no. 985 (February 11–17, 2010). http://weekly.ahram.org.eg/Archive/2010/985/cu1.htm.

Ramazani, Jahan. *A Transnational Poetics*. Chicago: Univ. of Chicago Press, 2009.

Rancière, Jacques. *Disagreement: Politics and Philosophy*. Translated by Julie Rose. Minneapolis: Univ. of Minnesota Press, 2004.

Reich, Wilhelm. *The Mass Psychology of Fascism*. Translated by Theodore Wolfe. New York: Oregon Institute, 1946.

Reid, Donald Malcolm. *Whose Pharaohs? Archeology, Museums, and Egyptian National Identity from Napoleon to World War I*. Berkeley: Univ. of California Press, 2003.

Reyes, Barbara Jane. "Suheir Hammad, *breaking poems* (Cypher Books, 2008)." Poetry Foundation. Accessed May 17, 2017. http://www.poetryfoundation.org /harriet/2009/08/suheir-hammad-breakingpoems-cypher-books-2008/.

Rich, Adrienne. *Arts of the Possible: Essays and Conversations*. New York: W. W. Norton, 2001.

Romeo, Caterina. "Racial Evaporations: Representing Blackness in African Italian Postcolonial Literature." In *Postcolonial Italy: Challenging National Homogeneity*, edited by Cristina Lombard-Diop and Caterina Romeo, 221–36. London: Palgrave Macmillan, 2012.

Rosemont, Franklin, and Robin D. G. Kelley. *Black, Brown, and Beige: Surrealist Writings from Africa and the Diaspora*. Austin: Univ. of Texas Press, 2010.

Rosi, Gianfranco, dir. *Fuocoammare*. Roma: Rai Cinema, 2016.

Rottenberg, Catherine. *The Rise of Neoliberal Feminism*. Oxford: Oxford Univ. Press, 2018.

Ruba, Salih. *Gender in Transnationalism: Home, Longing, and Belonging Among Moroccan Migrant Women*. London: Routledge, 2013.

Rubiera, Maria Jesús, and Mikel de Epalza. "Al-Andalus: Between Myth and History." *History and Anthropology* 18, no. 3 (2007): 269–73.

Said, Edward W. *Beginnings: Intentions and Methods.* New York: Columbia Univ. Press, 1985.

———. *Covering Islam: How the Media and the Experts Determine How We See the Rest of the World.* London: Vintage, 1997.

———. *Culture and Imperialism.* London: Vintage, 1993.

———. "Globalizing Literary Studies." *PMLA* 116, no. 1 (January 2001): 64–68.

———. *Humanism and Democratic Criticism.* New York: Columbia Univ. Press, 2004.

———. *Orientalism.* London: Pantheon, 1978.

———. *Reflections on Exile and Other Essays.* Cambridge, MA: Harvard Univ. Press, 2002.

Salaita, Steven. *Arab American Literary Fictions, Cultures, and Politics.* New York: Palgrave Macmillan, 2007.

———. *Modern Arab American Fiction: A Reader's Guide.* Syracuse, NY: Syracuse Univ. Press, 2011.

Salhi, Zahia Smail, and Ian Richard Netton. *The Arab Diaspora: Voices of an Anguished Scream.* London: Routledge, 2006.

Saliba, Georges. *A History of Arabic Astronomy: Planetary Theories during the Golden Age of Islam.* New York: New York Univ. Press, 1995.

———. *Islamic Science and the Making of the European Renaissance.* Cambridge, MA: MIT Press, 2007.

Samekh, S. "The Neo-Classical Arabic Poets." In *Modern Arabic Literature,* edited by M. M. Badawi, 36–81. Cambridge: Cambridge Univ. Press, 1993.

"Sappho." Poetry Foundation. Accessed December 5, 2020. https://www.poetry foundation.org/poets/sappho.

Sappho. *Stung with Love: Poems and Fragments of Sappho.* Translated and with an introduction and notes by Aaron Poochigian, with a preface by Carol Ann Duffy. London: Penguin, 2009.

Sardar, Ziauddin, and Robin Yassin-Kassab, eds. *Reclaiming Al-Andalus.* London: Hurst, 2013.

Sawalha, Aseel. *Reconstructing Beirut: Memory and Space in a Postwar Arab City.* Austin: Univ. of Texas Press, 2010.

Sayad, Abdelmalek. "El Ghorba: From Original Sin to Collective Lie." *Ethnography* 2, no. 1 (2000): 147–71.

Saylor, Elizabeth Claire, and Marjorie Stevens. "Mapping Women Writers in the Mahjar." ArcGIS Online. Accessed November 27, 2020. https://www.arcgis

.com/apps/MapJournal/index.html?appid=1e09d680f93144dc8cb10e42abf
fbf79.

Scego, Igiaba. *Adua*. Milano: Giunti, 2016.

———. *La linea del colore*. Roma: Bompiani, 2020.

———. *La mia casa è dove sono*. Milano: Rizzoli, 2010.

Scego, Igiana, and Rino Bianchi, eds. *Roma negata: Percorsi postcoloniali nella città*. Roma: Ediesse, 2014.

Schneidermann, Daniel. "Un beau livre de viols coloniaux." *Libération*, October 7, 2018. https://www.liberation.fr/debats/2018/10/07/un-beau-livre-de-viols -coloniaux_1683813.

Scott, James C. *Domination and the Arts of Resistance: Hidden Transcripts*. New Haven, CT: Yale Univ. Press, 1990.

Seigneurie, Ken. *Standing in the Ruins: Elegiac Humanism in Wartime and Post-war Lebanon*. New York: Fordham Univ. Press, 2011.

Selim, Samah. "The New Pharaonism: Nationalist Thought and the Egyptian Village Novel, 1967–1977." *Arab Studies Journal* 8, no. 2 and 9, no. 1 (Fall 2000–Spring 2001): 10-24.

Shackleton, Mark, ed. *Diasporic Literature and Theory—Where Now?* Newcastle: Cambridge Scholars, 2008.

Shahid Ali, Agha, ed. *Ravishing DisUnities: Real Ghazals in English*. Middle-town, CT: Wesleyan Univ. Press, 2000.

Sharabi, Hisham. *Neopatriarchy: A Theory of Distorted Change in Arab Society*. Oxford: Oxford Univ. Press, 1992.

Shohat, Ella, ed. *Talking Visions: Multicultural Feminism in a Transnational Age*. Cambridge, MA: MIT Press, 2001.

Sibhatu, Ribka. *Aulò. Canto poesia dall'Eritrea*. Roma: Sinnos, 2004.

———. *L'esatto numero delle stelle*. Roma: Sinnos, 2012.

Simon, Rita J., and Caroline Brettell, eds. *International Migration: The Female Experience*. Totowa, NJ: Rowman & Allanheld, 1986.

Simon, Sherry. *Cities in Translation*. London: Routledge, 2012.

Smethurst, James Edward. *The Black Arts Movement: Literary Nationalism in the 1960s and 1970s*. Chapel Hill: Univ. of North Carolina Press, 2005.

Smith, Marc Kelly, and Joy Kraynak. *Take the Mic: The Art of Performance Poetry, Slam, and Spoken Word*. Naperville, IL: Sourcebooks, 2009.

Smith, Roberta. "Giorgio Morandi Creates a Universe on a Tabletop." *New York Times*, November 19, 2015. https://www.nytimes.com/2015/11/20/arts/design /giorgio-morandi-creates-a-universe-on-a-tabletop.html.

Sollors, Werner. *Multilingual America*. New York: New York Univ. Press, 1998.

Sonneborn, Liz. *Averroes (Ibn Rushd): Muslim Scholar, Philosopher, and Physician of the Twelfth Century*. New York: Rosen, 2006.

Sorbera, Lucia. "An Invisible and Enduring Presence: Women in Egyptian Politics." In *Informal Power in the Greater Middle East: Hidden Geographies*, edited by Luca Anceschi, Gennaro Gervasio, and Andrea Teti, 159–74. London: Routledge, 2014.

Spinelli, Altiero, and Ernesto Rossi. *Le Manifeste de Ventotene*. Accessed March 26, 2022. https://www.senato.it/application/xmanager/projects/leg18/file/repository/relazioni/libreria/novita/XVII/Per_unEuropa_libera_e_unita_Ventotene6.763_KB.pdf.

Stanford Friedman, Susan. "Why Not Compare?" *PMLA* 126, no. 3 (May 2011): 753–62.

Stefani, Giulietta. *Colonia per maschi: italiani in Africa orientale, una storia di genere*. Verona: Ombre Corte, 2007.

Steenman-Marcusse, Conny, ed. *The Rhetoric of Canadian Writing*. Amsterdam: Rodopi, 2002.

Stevens, Simone. "Nazik al-Mala'ika (1923-2007) Iraqi Woman's Journey Changes Map of Arabic Poetry." *Al Jadid: Review & Record of Arab Culture and Arts* 13–14, nos. 58–59 (2007–8). https://www.aljadid.com/content/nazik-al-malaika-1923-2007-iraqi-woman-%E2%80%99s-journey-changes-map-arabic-poetry (accessed September 26, 2018).

Stewart, Kathleen. *Ordinary Affects*. Durham, NC: Duke Univ. Press, 2007.

Stoler, Ann Laura. *Along the Archival Grain: Epistemic Anxieties and Colonial Common Sense*. Princeton, NJ: Princeton Univ. Press, 2010.

———. *Duress: Imperial Durabilities in Our Times*. Durham, NC: Duke Univ. Press, 2016.

Tamburri, Anthony, and Graziella Parati. *The Cultures of Italian Migration: Diverse Trajectories and Discrete Perspectives*. Madison, NJ: Fairleigh Dickinson Univ. Press, 2011.

Thiong'o, Ngugi wa. *Globalectics: Theory and the Politics of Knowing*. New York: Columbia Univ. Press, 2014.

Tijani, Ishaq. *Male Domination, Female Revolt: Race, Class, and Gender in Kuwaiti Women's Fiction*. Leiden: Brill, 2009.

Towsend Warner, Sylvia. *Summer Will Show*. London: Penguin, 2009.

Triandafyllidou, Anna, and Ruby Gropas, eds. *European Migration: A Sourcebook*. Aldershot: Ashgate, 2007.

Trías, Eugenio. "Thinking Religion: The Symbol and the Sacred." In *Religion*, edited by Jacques Derrida and Gianni Vattimo, 95–110. Cambridge, MA: Polity, 1998.

Trilling, Daniel. "The Irrational Fear of Migrants Carries a Deadly Price for Europe." *Guardian*, June 28, 2018. https://www.theguardian.com/commentisfree /2018/jun/28/migrants-europe-eu-italy-matteo-salvini.

Tsikata, Prosper Yao. "The Historical and Contemporary Representation of Africa in Global Media Flows: Can the Continent Speak Back for Itself on Its Own Terms?" *South African Journal for Communication Theory and Research* 40, no. 1 (2014): 34–48.

Tuéni, Nadia. "Beyrouth." In *Liban: Poèmes d'amour et de guerre. A Bilingual Anthology*, edited by Christophe Ippolito and translated from the French by Samuel Hazo and Paul B. Kelley, 10. Syracuse, NY: Syracuse Univ. Press, 2006.

Tuqan, Fadwa. *A Mountainous Journey: An Autobiography*. Edited by Salma Khadra Jayyusi. Translated by Olive Kenny and Naomi Shihab Nye. St. Paul, MN: Graywolf, 1990.

Tytell, John. *Naked Angels: The Lives and Literature of the Beat Generation*. Chicago: Grove, 1976.

UNACTAD. *The Besieged Palestinian Agricultural Sector*. Geneva: UNACTAD, 2015.

Vallières, Pierre. *Nègres blancs d'Amérique*. Montreal: Parti pris, 1968.

Verduyn, Christl. *Literary Pluralities*. Petersborough, ON: Broadview, 1998.

———. "Perspectives critiques dans des productions littéraires migrantes au féminin, au Québec et au Canada." *Journal of Canadian Studies* 3, no. 3 (Fall 1996): 78–96.

Vijaisri, Priyadarshini. *Recasting the Devadasi: Patterns of Sacred Prostitution in Colonial South India*. Delhi: Kanishka, 2004.

Vince, Natalya. "France, Islam, and Laïcité: Colonial Exceptions, Contemporary Reinventions and European Convergences." In *The End of French Exception? Decline and Revival of the "French Model,"* edited by Tony Chafer and Emmanuel Godin, 153–70. London: Palgrave Macmillan, 2010.

Vinson, Pauline Homsi. "Ghada Samman: A Writer of Many Layers." *AlJadid Magazine* 8, no. 39 (Spring 2002). https://www.aljadid.com/content/ghada -samman-writer-many-layers (accessed November 20, 2020).

Wadud, Amina. *Inside the Gender Jihad: Women's Reform in Islam*. London: Oneworld, 2002.

Warner, Marina. *Stranger Magic: Charmed States and the Arabian Nights.* London: Vintage, 2012.

———. "At Tate Liverpool." *London Review of Books,* March 8, 2018, 28–29.

Weber, Charlotte. "Between Nationalism and Feminism: The Eastern Women's Congresses of 1930 and 1932." *Journal of Middle East Women's Studies* 4, no. 1 (Winter 2008): 83–106.

Weber, Elisabeth, ed. *Points . . . Interviews, 1974–1994.* Translated by Peggy Kamuf and others. Stanford, CA: Stanford Univ. Press, 1995.

Westmoreland, Mark. "Catastrophic Subjectivity: Representing Lebanon's Undead." *Alif: Journal of Comparative Poetics* 30 (2010): 176–210.

Wild, Stefan. "Nizār Qabbāni's Autobiography: Images of Sexuality, Death and Poetry." In *Love and Sexuality in Modern Arabic Literature,* edited by Roger Allen, Hilary Kilpatrick, and Ed de Moor, 200–209. London: Saqi, 1995.

Willis, Deborah, Ellyn Toscano, and Kalia Brooks Nelson, eds. *Women and Migration: Responses in Art and History.* Cambridge: OpenBook, 2019.

Woolf, Virginia. *A Room of One's Own.* London: Hogarth, 1929.

Yimer, Dagmawi, dir. *Va' Pensiero-Storie Ambulanti.* 2013.

Zuhur, Sherifa, ed. *Colors of Enchantment: Visual and Performing Arts in the Middle East.* Cairo: American Univ. of Cairo Press, 2001.

Index

LISA MARCHI has worked for many years as a language facilitator for undocumented minors, refugees, and asylum seekers, an intercultural teaching practice that has deeply influenced her scholarly work. As a Researcher at the University of Trento in Italy, she specializes in contemporary US poetry, with a specific emphasis on global interconnections, particularly between North America, Europe, and the Arab region. Her research interests span across many disciplines, including Arabic and Islamic studies, women's writing and gender studies, and migration and diaspora studies.

Lisa's essays have appeared in international journals, such as *Comparative Literature Studies* and *Canadian Literature*, as well as in collective volumes. She is the author of *In filigrana: Poesia arabo-americana scritta da donne* (2020), the first monograph written in Italian and entirely dedicated to contemporary Arab American poetry written by women.

Lightning Source UK Ltd.
Milton Keynes UK
UKHW011954310722
406641UK00002B/111

9 780815 637554